DISTRIBUTED BY
CHALFANT PRESS, INC.
BISHOP, CALIFORNIA 93514

Binding and Cover — Chalfant Press
Cover photo — Dept. of Water and Power, Los Angeles

The Water Seekers

Remi A. Nadeau

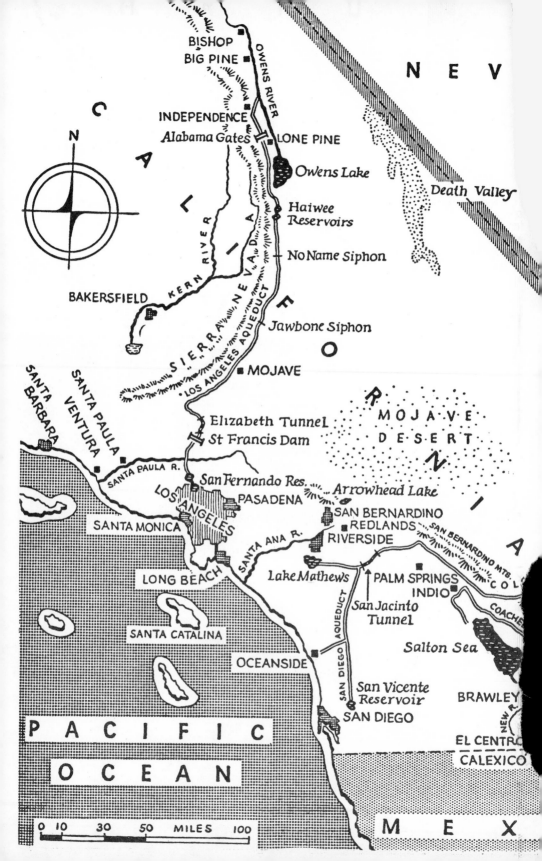

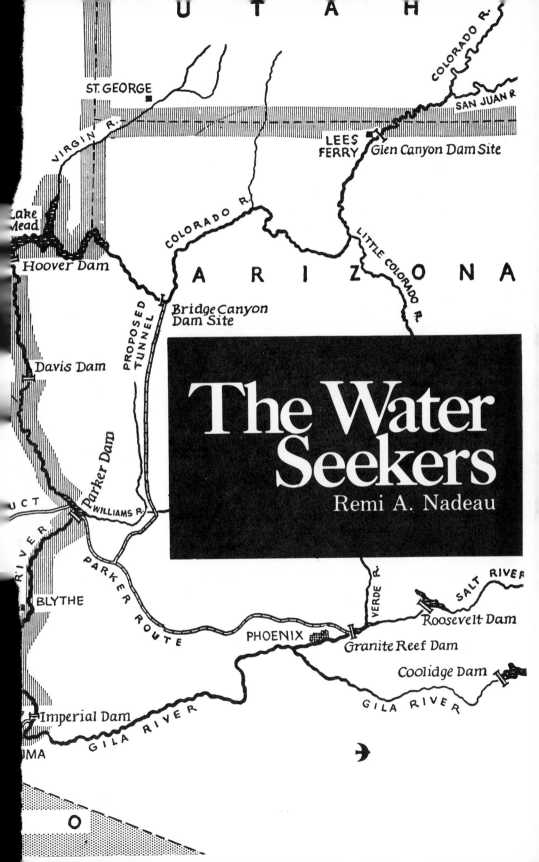

The Water Seekers

Remi A. Nadeau

Photograph sources:

courtesy the Los Angeles Department of Water and Power (LADWP), photographs appearing on pages 116, 117, 118, 119, 120, 121, 122, 123, 125, 126, 127, 128 top, 129;

courtesy the Metropolitan Water District of Southern California (MWD), photographs appearing on pages 130, 131, 132, 133;

courtesy the State of California Department of Water Resources (DWR), photographs appearing on pages 134, 135;

courtesy the Los Angeles *Times*, photograph appearing on page 124 bottom.

Nadeau, Remi A
    The water seekers.

    Bibliography: p.
    1. Water-supply—California, Southern—History.
I. Title.
TC424.C2N3   363.6'1'097949   73-85418
ISBN 0-87905-016-0

Revised Edition

Manufactured in the United States of America

To my loving wife, Margaret

Part 1

1: "WHOEVER BRINGS THE WATER..."

In January 1877 a lanky young man with a careless slouch shuffled off a boat at San Pedro, the primitive harbor serving what was then the equally primitive city of Los Angeles, California.

He asked directions with an Irish brogue. He had the air, if not the attire, of a sailor. He had spent four years at sea after leaving his Dublin home at age eighteen. His name was William Mulholland, and he had ten dollars in his pocket. He had little education, but he could read and he had an unabating appetite for the printed word. And he had the ability to size up a big problem and come up with an equally big answer.

Southern California's immediate problem was obvious, as young Mulholland rode the twenty-three miles from San Pedro to Los Angeles. Out the train window he could see the cracked soil, the empty irrigation ditches, the withered crops. It was Southern California's Great Drought of 1877, and the grass which should have been green in January was brown and stunted. Within weeks cattle and sheep by the thousands would be dying of starvation.

In Los Angeles the talk of the townsfolk was of water, of rain, and of the clouds that kept passing overhead without shedding a drop.

Yet Mulholland could also see the land's potential. The air was dry and balmy. His Irishman's eye told him the soil was rich. The orange groves and the resort hotels that had sprung to life in the years just before his arrival told him that this backwater corner of California held promise.

The city of Los Angeles then had some 15,000 people—the county of Los Angeles perhaps 30,000. There was room for ten

3

times, maybe 100 times, that number. But one ingredient was missing.

"Whoever brings the water," Mulholland is said to have remarked, "will bring the people."

Over the next half-century it was William Mulholland who brought the water. Starting as a ditch tender, he rose to head the Los Angeles waterworks; he planned and built a 240-mile aqueduct—then the longest municipal water conduit in the world—to tap the snows of California's Sierra Nevada. He planned another and still longer aqueduct that tapped the snows of the Rockies and brought water not just to Los Angeles but to a constellation of cities across Southern California.

To a land that had previously depended on sparse rainfall averaging 15 inches a year, Mulholland caused enough water to flow each year to cover two million acres a foot deep.

And did the man who brought the water also bring the people?

By the time Bill Mulholland died the Los Angeles population was nearly a million and a half and the county some three million. He used to joke about the publicity people who flooded the East with ballyhoo about the wonders of Los Angeles. The only way to stop the growth of Los Angeles, he chuckled, was to kill the secretary of the Chamber of Commerce. But he might equally have referred to himself. The truth was that if the water wouldn't have come most of the people wouldn't have come, and those who did come wouldn't have stayed.

All his life Mulholland felt responsible for going out and finding all the water Los Angeles needed. While he was head of the waterworks, no Angeleno was ever going to go thirsty.

And Mulholland instilled this principle in those around him and those who followed him. They went on to bring water to Southern California from a third and still longer aqueduct tapping the snows of Northern California—both the Sierra Nevada and the Cascade Range.

Today the population of Los Angeles approaches three million, the county seven million. Now the water seekers of Southern California plan to tap other sources still farther north with aqueduct systems that challenge the mind.

Why? Is it just Mulholland's ethic—let no man come to Los Angeles to find a dry faucet? This is the rallying cry for the water battle, but it is not the cause.

The root cause was the booster spirit that infected all Angelenos—native and adopted. In the latter nineteenth century they realized that, as one of them put it, "climate has a cash value." The cash was realized at the counters of the resorts and hotels, the ticket cages of the sightseeing fraternity, and the tills of every shopkeeper who gloried in the coming of new customers. But basically the cash was realized in the sale of land to new settlers—the region's main occupation, if not religion. And about the time Mulholland first arrived in Los Angeles it was realized that the value of land was determined absolutely by the sureness of the water supply. It made the difference between ground that was useless and ground with unlimited potential—whether for crops, homes, or factories.

"Sell the water and throw the land in free" became the credo of real estate men subdividing the rolling hills of Southern California. When Mulholland's first aqueduct was being promoted, one observer put the issue clearly, "the [property] values based on an adequate water supply are too enormous to be neglected."

With such motivation, Los Angeles and its sister cities took on some of the world's most experienced water fighters. They found truth in the old Western saying, "Steal my horse, run off with my wife, but damn you, don't touch my water."

Up in Owens Valley, on the east side of California's Sierra Nevada, the embattled farmers seized the Los Angeles Aqueduct and made a sport of blasting it with dynamite.

Arizona and its sister states in the upper Colorado basin fought California all the way from the banks of the river to the halls of Congress.

The upper counties of California blocked the massive Feather River project till they got their price, and the states of the far Northwest have more than once rattled their political sabers at the mention of the Columbia River.

Like Britain, Southern California may not have won many of its battles but so far it has won its war. And the result is that it has been able to import people as fast as it imported water. It did so, that is, until the influx began to destroy the very values that had been so widely advertised.

Today Southern California has lost its booster spirit. It has vanished along with the clear skies, the uncrowded beaches, the unjammed streets, and the delightful countryside that made Los Angeles the mecca of tourist and settler. Its place has been taken by a new Los Angeles attitude—grudging tolerance of the tourist, who might become a settler, and a nostalgic desire to escape Los Angeles and somehow find a haven away from the choking smog and the dehumanizing congestion.

The new truth came out in the analysis of statistics following the 1970 census. An official report acknowledged that Los Angeles County was losing about 35,000 people per year. A bank research study showed that approximately 25,000 more people left California than arrived to settle in the year 1970. And the California Poll reported that nearly one of three Californians would leave the state if they could.

This was heresy, not to say sacrilege, according to the old religion. But it was the gasp of a culture that had turned its original objective—to settle the vacant land—into a blind dogma that persisted long after its reason had disappeared. In achieving its old values it had succeeded far too well for its own good. And it was time now not only to reject the old values but to search for the new.

Mulholland's original creed was that Los Angeles should always gather to itself enough extra water to grow on. For if it once reached the limits of its water supply, without planning for more, it would have to mark time for years while it captured the next source and built the next canal.

The frightful thought of turning people back for lack of water haunted Angelenos for decades, but today the idea has lost its terror. It now suggests a sensible way to halt the growth that has become a liability. To a city whose very air is corrupted by too many machines brought by too many people, the drive to get more water to get more people seems incredible—like some self-destructive instinct of human lemmings.

More than this, the plight of Los Angeles suggests a flaw in the morality that transferred water from remote farmlands to the "higher uses" of a big city.

At the time, the "greatest good for the greatest number" was an effective slogan to convince Presidents and senators. But the definition of "good" runs into trouble when it is reduced from values to numbers. And mere men can often be so sure of what is good that they can injure others in its name.

In retrospect it is difficult to discern the supreme good in the process of encouraging people from all parts of the country to come and settle in one corner of the country. And even considering only Los Angeles itself, the "good" was only temporary and now turns out to be—in the eyes of many—"bad."

The need to rethink such values in the use of water was never more urgent. New water conquests—vaster than any Mulholland ever dreamed—are on the drawing boards. Inevitably these conquests will generate new water conflicts in which the "right" and the "good" will be hoisted by both sides.

The following pages tell how two such conflicts rose, how they climaxed, and how they ended. They help to tell us what we may expect and how we may decide.

2: THE TEAM OF MULHOLLAND AND EATON

When Bill Mulholland first reached Southern California, he was caught in the mining fever of the day and spent an unsuccessful year prospecting in Arizona. After returning to Los Angeles, he got a job drilling a water well near the harbor and was so impressed with the thrill of developing nature's resources that he resolved then and there to become an engineer.

Of necessity Mulholland started at the bottom as a *zanjero*, or ditch tender, with the privately owned Los Angeles City Water Company. He lived in a one-room wooden shack at the present location of the Mulholland memorial fountain at Los Feliz and Riverside Drive; his job was to keep the main *zanja madre*, which flowed by his house, clear of weeds and debris.

Mulholland's energetic shovel-wielding was noticed one day by the water company's president, who stopped his carriage and abruptly demanded who the *zanjero* was and what he was doing. Mulholland, never a man to suffer imposition, looked over the side of the ditch and shouted that it was none of the intruder's damned business. The president drove on; and when Mulholland's fellow workmen told him whom he had rebuffed, he dropped his shovel, donned his coat, and went to the company office to "get my time" before being fired. But the president, who evidently appreciated both industry and spirit in his subordinates, started Mulholland on his ascendancy by making him foreman of the company's ditch gang.

Through the early 1880s Mulholland worked by day in the Water Department and schooled himself at night. Thomas Brooks, who roomed with him in modest quarters near the Plaza, later recalled that in the evenings Mulholland used to lull him to sleep with his endless fund of humorous stories and would then stay up as late as 3 a.m. reading geometry and engineering books.

It was the beginning of an amazing self-imposed education which helped to make Mulholland one of the most paradoxical characters in a city which has never been known for conformity. On the one hand he displayed a refined taste for literature and classical music, a profound appreciation for the beauties of nature, and a deep Christian faith founded on simple confidence in the basic good of man. On the other, he was a fellow of rough temperament and even rougher speech, whose repertoire of swearwords and ribald jokes would shame a mule skinner. When a citizen once wrote to the Los Angeles water commissioners and admiringly referred to the superintendent as a "water witch," Mulholland offered the relatively mild comment that, while he had never been called that before, he had often been called "something that rhymes with it."

7

When Mulholland became superintendent of the water system in 1886, he brought to the organization a spirit of practical orderliness. As a manager he maintained efficiency among his subordinates by a gruff and commanding exterior. Yet the understanding heart which they detected underneath, and the ready defense he gave them whenever criticism came from an outsider, earned "the Chief" an intense loyalty from his men. Mulholland did not exclude himself from his exacting discipline; rising in the early hours, he worked on a punctual schedule and set an energetic pace which his employees were scarcely able to follow.

Having few outside interests, Mulholland's contentment was founded on two rocks: his large and congenial family, and a keen pride in his task as official water seeker to a great city. While at times drawing the largest salary of any Los Angeles employee, he cared little for money or material possessions. It is said that a clerk who was once cleaning out Mulholland's desk unearthed a check for $6000 which had been set aside and forgotten.

The Chief, in fact, never felt at home behind a desk. Leaving paperwork to others, he spent most of his daylight hours in the field. Years of constructing and inspecting the city's waterworks were revealed in his suntanned face and rugged features. Such firsthand experience, together with his own natural confidence, yielded Mulholland the complete trust of Los Angeles citizens. The most important decisions and policies were made by the City Council members on his simple recommendation. "They have always been," he once said, "in the habit of taking my word."

This was the man who, Moses-like, was to lead the Angelenos out of the desert. It was a task for a prophet of demigod proportions. For the same climate that made Southern California one of the world's most desirable spots to live, and hence generated its massive tide of immigration, has also produced its crucial water limitation.

Like the ancient races of the arid eastern Mediterranean, Southern Californians must root all growth on a hard-won water foundation. Their long campaign for this precious element has extended beyond California's own borders, has involved the ambitions of the entire West and the politics of the nation. To a large extent the story of Southern California's economic development is the story of water quests and its water fights. Among its most revered heroes is the William Mulholland who went to far-off rivers and, like Hezekiah, "made a pool, and a conduit, and brought water into the city. . . ."

Southern California's sparse water supply—less than two per cent of the state's total—might be less a troublemaker if it were delivered evenly. The land suffers from recurring droughts. The Los Angeles region may get as little as six inches of annual rainfall, and in the wet years much of the water volume has run to waste in floods, inflicting harsh damage and even loss of lives on the Southland community.

Its greatest recorded deluge struck in the winter of 1861-62. For a solid month following Christmas Eve the rain fell steadily; whole vineyards were washed away or buried in sand; water ran four feet deep through the newly founded town of Anaheim; adobe stores in Los Angeles crumbled under the onslaught, while merchants worked frantically in water up to their waists to save their goods.

Alternating with the wet years have been cycles of extreme drought, leaving Southland farmers without a constant source of water for the confident planting of crops. The drought rather than the flood years have shaped Southern California development. A year after the flood of 1861-62 a drought began which hastened the last days of California's colorful rancho era. For two years the rains failed. Hills, ordinarily covered with green native grasses in winter and spring, were parched and sterile. California's great herds of longhorn cattle, economic basis of its languid Spanish period, were rudely decimated. From the San Joaquin Valley to San Diego County, thousands of carcasses littered the countryside. The calamity wiped out the Southland's cattle and brought the storied "Days of the Dons" to a wretched and inglorious end.

Out of the ashes of Southern California's stock industry rose a virile agricultural economy. With their herds gone and their vast landholdings burdened with delinquent mortages, the cattle barons of the southern ranges had no course but to sell out. They or their creditors subdivided the ranchos through the late sixties and early seventies, and the near vacuum of Southern California began to fill with droves of eager farm families.

Since its founding in the late eighteenth century, Los Angeles has had to fight for water. Holding rights to the Los Angeles River through an ancient Spanish ordinance, it soon encountered competition for its use from nearby San Fernando Mission. Around the present North Hollywood the padres dammed the river for irrigation purposes, and Los Angeles rose in anger at its own diminished supply. Only after a bitter legal battle did the pueblo secure the dam's removal in 1810.

By the 1860s Los Angeles was moving toward another and more desperate water wrangle. Driven by the need for a better distributing system than open ditches and water carts, the City Council offered inducements to enterprisers who would lay an underground pipe system through the town. The first stalwart to take the job installed wooden pipes that leaked abundantly and formed great mud holes in the streets. He then started a new system of iron pipes, fed by a reservoir in the Los Angeles River and a giant waterwheel which lifted the flow up from the city's main water ditch, the *zanja madre*. When the flood of 1867-68 washed out his dam, the contractor relinquished all connection with the exasperating Los Angeles waterworks.

His interest was taken over by three local enterprisers, including Prudent Beaudry, one of the first merchants and developers in Los Angeles. They promptly offered to complete the new system and pay the city a modest yearly rental in return for a thirty-year lease on the Los Angeles waterworks and rights. A furious public opposition greeted the move. Two other factions offered competing proposals, both of which substantially underbid the Beaudry offer. But when the City Council came to pass the measure on July 20, 1868, the president silenced protests with the admonition, "We don't care to hear any speeches." The city's precious water rights were then turned over to private hands in one of the first skirmishes of the long contest between public and private ownership of Los Angeles utilities.

For an annual rental of four hundred dollars and a modest amount of construction, Beaudry's company exercised control of the city's water for a length of time which spanned all the events of her tumultuous early growth—the coming of the railroads, the great boom of 1887, the fight for the modern harbor at San Pedro, the development of the huge citrus industry, and the discovery of oil. From a population of about 4500 when the company acquired its works in 1868, Los Angeles had sprouted to nearly 100,000 by the time the lease expired in 1898. Thus when the city officials chose to take back the water system, the company fought to retain such a valuable asset. But after long negotiations and a hotly contested bond election, it turned over the sprawling establishment to the city for $2,000,000 in February 1902.

Beaudry and his original associates had not lived to benefit by the transactions, but their places had been taken by others who had found themselves caught in an unwelcome struggle to keep the mushrooming city supplied with water. To them fell the responsibility and the credit for a desperate development of local sources at a time when the city's population was zooming and the river's water volume was fading from drought. One of their employees, the company superintendent, William Mulholland, lived to become the water hero of Los Angeles and one of the most noted engineers in the world.

Mulholland faced his first big crisis when the drought of the 1890s hit Los Angeles. The danger was not at first apparent, for while the region was gripped by almost rainless seasons the slow percolation process in the basin of the Los Angeles River allowed several years to pass before the flow faded. Mulholland believed that the local development of springs and other sources would meet the emergency.

But a warning that the local supply would never suffice came from Fred Eaton, a native Angeleno, son of a forty-niner who had helped to found Pasadena. Eaton's vigorous public career had made him a leading figure in the city's water problems; his rise in Los Angeles politics had been spectacular. Like Mulholland, he was a self-educated engineer and, as Mulholland's predecessor in the post of Los Angeles water superintendent, had encouraged Mulholland to study hydraulics and fit himself for promotion. Exactly a day apart in age, Eaton and Mulholland became hearty companions, each appreciating the other's ability and ready humor.

Thus after Eaton's election as city engineer in 1886, he never lost contact with Mulholland and the city's water situation. During the drought of the nineties he launched a personal quest for an outside water source for Los Angeles. By the time Eaton swept into the mayor's office in 1899, he had reconnoitered as far as the Kings River in the Sierra and even to the distant Colorado. The first he dismissed as yielding too little water by any gravity aqueduct; the second was altogether too costly a possibility for a city of less than 100,000 people.

As early as 1892, however, Eaton had visited another source over two hundred miles northward in Inyo County—the bountiful Owens River which drained much of the eastern Sierra slope. Here in the serene and mountainbound Owens Valley, first won from warring Paiutes in the 1860s, a pioneer community had been abiding for a generation. Originally supported by flourishing cattle and mining industries, the valley had subsisted on a rising agricultural economy since the first big irrigation ditches were built in the late 1870s. On this foundation a series of farm communities sprang up, from Lone Pine and Independence in the lower valley to Big Pine and Bishop in the more developed northern end. By the time Eaton saw the valley so much water was being diverted by the resourceful farmers that the level was already beginning to sink in Owens Lake, the expanse of briny water at the river's lower end.

Eaton returned to Los Angeles and described the region as a magnificent source to his friend Mulholland. In 1892, however, the drought had scarcely begun, and the Chief laughed at the need for any water beside the Los Angeles River, which had served the community during his fifteen years in California.

"We have enough water here in the river," Mulholland chided, "to supply the city for the next fifty years."

"You are wrong," Eaton replied. "I was born here and have seen dry years—years that you know nothing about. Wait and see."

During the decade of drought that followed, as Mulholland himself described it, "our population climbed to the top and the bottom appeared to drop out of the river." In an attempt to develop its last drop of moisture, Mulholland had already launched a plan to catch the underground flow by a system of infiltration galleries. But the strategic spot for the headworks, situated in the narrows between the Cahuenga and Verdugo hills, was owned by two private enterprisers who asked an extreme price for their land and water rights.

Los Angeles moved to condemn the property, claiming rights to the entire river and the underground basin by virtue of its original Spanish pueblo grant. After a six-year legal battle the celebrated case of Los Angeles vs. Pomeroy and Hooker was settled by the state Supreme Court in 1899. The city won the last and most far-reaching suit in a legal defense of the Los Angeles River which had lasted nearly a century. Henceforth it held rights to all water in the basin needed for its municipal supply and could even prevent farmers upstream from pumping water from wells. The San Fernando Valley, then witnessing the beginnings of irrigation, found its development abruptly cut off and its future condemned.

Already, however, the fruits of the city's victory were fading in relentless drought. Nature herself had attacked the Los Angeles River, and she was, as Mulholland commented, "beyond the reach of mundane law and exempt from suit."

At first his frantic pursuit of improvements was hindered by the water company's unwillingness to spend money while negotiations were pending for sale to the city. But in February 1902 the transaction was complete; Mulholland and his staff were retained in charge and immediately mended their water defenses. The infiltration galleries were built to catch all the underground flow of the Los Angeles River, while meters were introduced for factories and other heavy users to reduce consumption.

Yet the continued drought drove the Los Angeles River down to a new low by the summer of 1903. In mid-July the city's consumption began to exceed the inflow into its reservoirs, which were able to hold little more than a two-day supply. Mulholland immediately ordered drinking water pumped from the *zanja madre*, the community's main irrigation ditch.

Still the rate of use outran the supply. Actual water famine was only averted by periodic letups in the hot spell, when temporary drops in consumption allowed the reservoirs to fill again. Mulholland reported that but for the metering of the most wasteful users the reservoirs would have gone dry.

Already, in fact, the Chief was turning in desperation to underground sources with a large pumping plant below the city. But, as in the case of numerous other wells in the area, this only aided the ten-year drought in lowering the water table.

It soon became clear that at the current rate of growth Los Angeles was not only approaching its own limit but was entering into a contest for water with outlying agricultural districts. Already San Fernando Valley—rendered barren by city lawsuits to prevent the pumping of water—stood as an example of sacrifice before the prior necessity of Los Angeles.

By 1904 the sprouting city was close to actual thirst. During the heat of the summer there was no water available for park ponds, and as Mulholland reported, "It might as well be made known that it is not probable there ever will be in the future."

Beginning on July 20, a severe hot spell brought a ten per cent rise in consumption over supply. The reservoirs were half emptied in ten days. Mulholland sent out warnings against lawn sprinkling and other excessive use. Public reaction and a timely relief in the heat wave lowered consumption enough to allow the reservoirs to be replenished. Once more Los Angeles had escaped actual thirst.

While the Chief took on heroic stature among Los Angeles citizens as a water magician, they were more impressed by another realization. Their city's spectacular growth, and its exuberant plans for future greatness, had now been cut off for lack of water. The hopes for increased expansion that had been raised by development of Henry Huntington's new Pacific Electric transit system, the Los Angeles harbor, the latest Eastern rail connection via Salt Lake would never be fulfilled. The belief by Huntington and other enthusiasts that Los Angeles was destined to be "the most important city in the country, if not in the world" was now exploded like a promoter's dream.

If Los Angeles apparently stood at the end of her resources, Mulholland did not. In desperation he remembered Fred Eaton's mention of a water source in the Sierra. While Los Angeles reeled from the water famine of July 1904, Mulholland went to Eaton and asked him to "show me this water supply." It was the beginning of a monumental adventure which would set Los

Angeles' course of water imperialism, precipitate the West's most tumultuous water war, and incidentally catch up and determine the lives of the two engineers.

3: WINNING OF OWENS RIVER

By the time Mulholland turned to Eaton's suggestion the water potentialities of Owens Valley had been discovered by no less a force than the United State Government. Engineers of the young Reclamation Service, turning with gusto to the initial task of surveying the West's potential irrigation projects, had entered the valley in June 1903. They found not only an ideal reservoir site at Long Valley, just north of Owens Valley, but also a farming community thriving on a newfound market in the booming Tonopah gold mines of Nevada.

As soon as Owens Valley's alert citizens realized the purpose of the government surveying party, they virtually exploded with enthusiasm. After languishing for decades because of its isolated position between the Sierra and the great Southwestern desert, Owens Valley seemed ready—in the conviction of its people—to blossom as a large-scale agricultural empire.

In Fred Eaton's view, the situation called for strategy. To get a closer view of the government's plans, he turned to one of his many friends, Joseph B. Lippincott, chief of Reclamation Service operations in the Southwest. A noted builder of irrigation systems throughout California, Lippincott had long been an adviser on water matters for cities from Denver to Los Angeles. He was one of those gaunt but tireless workers whose energy seems to come from nowhere. A careful technician, Lippincott was essentially a serious-minded engineer, one of the best known in Southern California. It was not surprising that, when he headed for the Owens River in August 1904 to inspect the federal investigations, Fred Eaton was one of several friends accompanying him for an "outing" in the Sierra.

Journeying to Yosemite, they crossed the Sierra by pack train over Tioga Pass; at Mono Lake they met J. C. Clausen, the young California engineer who had charge of the government surveys. Riding southward with them into the Owens River country, Clausen gave Lippincott an enthusiastic report on the yearlong investigation.

His words did not fall unheeded by Fred Eaton. By the time the group reached Long Valley, which Clausen had recognized as the natural reservoir site for an Owens Valley reclamation project, Eaton knew the government had a feasible irrigation project

14

which would obstruct any outside use of the water once it was approved in Washington and dam construction was begun. If Los Angeles were to gain this vast watershed for its own, he must act—and quickly.

But if Eaton's mind was racing ahead during the party's laborious recrossing the Sierra, Lippincott and his other companions are said to have been ignorant of his monumental scheme. Back in Los Angeles, Eaton confided to William Mulholland that the city must move immediately if it intended to stake a claim in Owens River. Within a week after his return Eaton was on his way north again to show the water supply to Mulholland.

Driving a two-horse buckboard, the two friends "roughed it" across the Mojave Desert, camping in the open and living on simple rations of bacon and beans. On September 24 they stood in the shadow of the massive Sierra, two hundred and fifty miles from Los Angeles, while Eaton showed Mulholland a placid valley of green fields and abundant water. In the meandering Owens River and its tributaries flowed at least 400 cubic feet of water per second—enough to provide a city of 2,000,000 people.

The main obstacle in the scheme was easily apparent. For days Eaton went over the ground with Mulholland, proving by barometer and rough calculations that the water could be diverted around briny Owens Lake and carried southward by gravity. Convinced at last, Mulholland jubilantly returned to Los Angeles. He had glimpsed the key that would free his city from stagnation.

Ahead of him, Mulholland knew, lay more than engineering obstacles. There were the questions of water rights, of federal authorization, of financial backing, and countless smaller issues that must be overcome before construction could begin. But to Mulholland they were a challenge, the thing on which he thrived.

The first problem was Eaton himself. Instead of returning with Mulholland he had hurried to New York City to interest Eastern investors in his part of the venture. For Fred Eaton had conceived it as joint private and municipal enterprise.

Mulholland, however, had no such intention. Quickly he sought out William B. Mathews, smooth and able Los Angeles city attorney. Finding him already in New York on business, Mulholland wired him of Eaton's movements. Mathews hurriedly got in touch with Eaton and intercepted his plans with the argument that "the city ought to be given a chance, at least, to act on the matter. . . ." The enterpriser agreed to return and open negotiations directly with Los Angeles.

It was not the first contribution that Mathews had made to the city's water foundations. An energetic Los Angeles attorney since the early nineties, he had been a leading spirit in the city's legal fight for title to the entire Los Angeles River watershed and in the campaign for municipal ownership of the waterworks. Soft-spoken and deliberate, Mathews was at his best in the hard strategy of a courtroom trial or as an irresistible advocate of the city's cause before congressional committees in Washington. In his dealings with opponents of Los Angeles he exemplified the velvet glove on the iron fist—a man of inordinate patience, of scrupulous fair play, of moderate approach, but absolutely unswerving in purpose. Nor did Mathews allow his practicality to dilute a basic quality of idealism. Behind his suave exterior, an imaginative mind nurtured the dream of a vast city-owned water and power system to bring unlimited industrial and residential growth. Elected city attorney in 1901, Mathews left the office a few years later to become the Water Department's chief counsel and to share Mulholland's place as creator of the city's modern water foundations.

Through the winter of 1904-5 the two men were negotiating with Eaton for an agreement on the Owens Valley scheme. They soon found, however, that Eaton had already realized he must offer Los Angeles more than an idea. In mid-March 1905 he traveled to Carson City, Nevada, and asked cattleman Thomas B. Rickey if he would sell his Owens Valley ranch. To Rickey the property was merely several thousand acres of grazing land. But to Eaton it was the Long Valley dam site, the aqueduct diversion point north of Independence, and the necessary water rights southward to Owens Lake.

On March 22, after a week of discouraging negotiation, Eaton snatched his hat and headed in despair for the railroad station. Rickey followed and settled for a two-month option of $450,000. To bind the deal Eaton handed him $100—a paltry consideration for an option on the cornerstone of any Owens River project.

His bargaining position bolstered, Eaton took his proposal to the Los Angeles Board of Water Commissioners. Within a month a party of seven city officials was in Owens Valley to see the water source at firsthand—posing as "cattle buyers" while Eaton signed hotel registers "Fred Eaton and friends." They could not afford to reveal their true purpose, for fear of sending an army of speculators flocking to Owens Valley.

On their return, however, the officials found that Los Angeles newspaper editors had not overlooked their absence. To insure press silence they explained the whole scheme with the understanding that the secret would be kept until notification from the water board that the deal had been closed. In this way the

16

Los Angeles taxpayers would be protected from the land sharks who would be expected to descend on such a public project.

As for the details of Eaton's plan, the city authorities were exultant. Mulholland had told them, on the basis of his rough field surveys and calculations, that the 250-mile aqueduct would cost just about $23,000,000. From a report by Mulholland and J. B. Lippincott, who thus made himself vulnerable to conflict-of-interest charges, they had final confirmation of the distressing lack of water sources in Southern California. The abundance of the sparkling liquid in Owens Valley they had seen with their own eyes.

One more obstacle remained before Los Angeles could commit itself to Eaton's proposal. The Reclamation Service had placed its stake in the Owens River and was busy investigating the valley's possibilities as an irrigation project. Los Angeles faced formidable odds as long as the federal government held an interest in the headwaters of the river.

But J. B. Lippincott, head Southwestern engineer for the Reclamation Service, had known of Eaton's scheme for months—at least since the fall of 1904. Though an enthusiastic reclamationist, he was first of all a citizen of the ambitious city of Los Angeles. Rightly or wrongly, he told Water Department officials that the government might step aside in favor of the municipal project. It must be, however, "public owned from one end to the other." Late in May 1905 the chief engineer of the Reclamation Service was in Los Angeles, backing up Lippincott's stand.

Here was the first big crisis in the city's enormous water program. Eaton was notified that there would be no room for a private enterpriser with the Owens Valley scheme. It was a soul-searching decision for Eaton, bringing into conflict his fundamental training as a public servant and his equally strong financial ambition. But the man was big enough to relinquish his interest.

"God bless him," Mulholland later commented. "I would like to see a monument to him a mile high when the city gets the aqueduct through."

The sacrifice left Eaton determined to make no more concessions. He insisted on keeping those parts of the Rickey ranch not needed for the aqueduct, including some 4000 head of cattle. As it was conceded that the Long Valley reservoir would not be needed in the initial aqueduct plans, Eaton withheld it too. The day after a verbal agreement was reached, however, Mulholland and Mathews approached Eaton for an easement in Long Valley to be used when the city grew big enough to need a year-to-year storage reservoir.

17

This was too much for Fred Eaton. He told them he was giving them "enough for the money" and would not let them flood his valley. Bargaining became so heated that Mulholland and Mathews left him with the threat that they would close negotiations and "stop all proceedings." Next day they came back and secured Eaton's reluctant consent to a reservoir easement permitting a dam one hundred feet high.

For the first time, they had dealt with Eaton, as Mulholland described it, "at swords' points and arms' lengths." The important compromise which resulted allowed only a small fraction of Long Valley's capacity as a reservoir and made it certain that there would be insufficient water for both Los Angeles and Owens Valley in any future drought. Though none of the parties could foresee it at the time, here was born the bitter Los Angeles Aqueduct controversy and the basis for the eventual sacrifice of Owens Valley.

Before the end of May, Eaton took up Rickey's option and turned it over to the city, causing the cattleman to howl indignantly that the two of them had missed an opportunity to reap a fortune. Eaton and his son Harold then began buying the remaining water rights in lower Owens Valley and conveying them to Los Angeles. But at this point the water secret commenced to burst at the seams. More than one Los Angeles promoter appeared in Owens Valley to option land for resale to the city at exorbitant prices. Eaton not only found himself hurrying to complete the buying but found land values rising as Inyo farmers saw a sudden and mysterious interest in their remote agricultural land.

One of the first to realize the city's connection in the Eaton dealings was Wilfred W. Watterson, president of the Inyo County Bank of Bishop. Born in San Joaquin Valley, Watterson had arrived in the Owens River country with his parents in 1885. A general merchandising business in Bishop had brought them the means to found the Inyo County Bank, of which Wilfred was now president and his brother, Mark Q. Watterson, treasurer.

A man of high affability and universal popularity, Wilfred had recently brought the first automobile into the valley—a fifteen-horsepower White Steamer. On Sundays he would drive it, loaded with rollicking Inyo citizens, over every dusty road in upper Owens Valley. But though equally cordial in his business dealings, he was a man highly conscious of his own financial interests and jealous of his position of leadership in valley affairs.

Watterson's fears of invasion by Los Angeles were confirmed when City Clerk Harry J. Lelande arrived to complete the transactions which Eaton had placed in escrow at the Inyo County Bank. Though young in years, Lelande was experienced enough as a public official to guard his steps carefully in a town where his movements were the object of well-based suspicion. After completing the transfer of one important ranch property, he immediately walked to the Bishop Post Office and mailed the deed to the courthouse at Independence. But Wilfred Watterson, discovering his identity, called him back to his office at the bank and made an abrupt demand.

"We want that deed back."

"What deed?" inquired Lelande innocently.

When Watterson named the transaction, Lelande explained that he did not have the document.

"You're not telling the truth," Watterson charged. Stepping to his feet, he locked the office door.

Lelande made no move to oppose him but declared steadily, "I can't give you something I haven't got—and wouldn't be obliged to if I did."

Watterson opened a drawer and laid a revolver on his desk. Calmly he ordered the astounded city clerk to shed his coat and trousers and allow his pockets to be searched. When the deed was not produced, Watterson pocketed the revolver, called to an employee outside his office, and told Lelande, "We're going over to your hotel room and see if we can find that deed."

Gathering himself together, the outraged Lelande accompanied the two men across the street while Watterson berated him for "buying land in an underhanded way for the city of Los Angeles." In Lelande's room in the Bishop Hotel, his satchel was ransacked in vain, and Watterson abruptly left him without an apology.

Declaring that the banker would "not hear the last of this," Lelande lost little time in telephoning to W. B. Mathews; although the city attorney was sympathetic, he advised Lelande not to "make any fuss over it." To the city officials as well as to the Owens Valley banker, the incident of the missing deed was insignificant enough, but it symbolized the greater struggle only then beginning for possession of Owens River.

By this time Lippincott and the Reclamation Service realized that the abandonment of their operations in Owens Valley would require a public explanation. A three-man board of engineers was appointed to examine the proposed government project and, as the head of the Reclamation Service described it, "bring the matter to an early close."

When the group met in San Francisco late in July, the decisive report was made by J. C. Clausen, the young engineer who had conducted the surveys in Owens Valley. Though cautioned by Lippincott to keep his remarks "general," Clausen gave a glowing account of prospects for reclamation in Owens Valley. Lippincott then told the board that, regardless of its feasibility, the government project should be abandoned in favor of Los Angeles. In their report of July 28, 1905, the engineers favored the project—unless the men who had bought key property for Los Angeles had made it impractical.

This, of course, is precisely what they had done. On the same day that the government board rendered its report Bill Mulholland arrived in Los Angeles after a final land-buying trip in Owens Valley with Fred Eaton.

"The last spike is driven," Mulholland jubilantly told city officials; "the options are all secured."

Also on that last Owens Valley trip had been a Los Angeles *Times* reporter. On the same day, with or without Mulholland's knowledge, a dispatch reached the *Times* from Independence. Next morning the paper appeared with the banner headline, "Titanic Project to Give City a River." Over the whole front page was spread the sensational Owens River story. Many amazed readers had never heard of the place before.

But all at once Los Angeles saw its destiny unfolding again. Fed by this new water source, it could reach a population of 2,000,000. With the one obstacle to development suddenly removed, Angelenos greeted the news, as one observer described it, "with acclamations of joy."

Most especially the *Times* hailed the prospects for San Fernando Valley, whose agriculture had previously been choked off by the city's prior need of the Los Angeles River.

"To put it mildly," declared the paper, "the values of all San Fernando Valley lands will be doubled by the acquisition of this new supply."

Copies of the *Times* were no sooner dumped on the depot platform at Burbank than valley property began to soar. Within ten days Burbank city lots had jumped five hundred per cent, new buildings were going up, and real estate firms had optioned thousands of dollars' worth of ranch land in San Fernando Valley. Other property in much of Los Angeles County doubled in price. Angelenos were moving fast to make good on the cash value of water.

Less enthusiastic, however, were the other Los Angeles newspaper editors, who had agreed to hold the Owens River story until the water board gave a signal. Most indignant of all was William Randolph Hearst's new Los Angeles *Examiner*; as the only other morning paper in town, it had suffered a

20

twenty-four-hour scoop by the *Times*. When the *Examiner* promptly charged the *Times* with breaking faith, the latter retorted that it had simply "got the anxiously-awaited news of the consummation of the deal before anyone else, and printed it."

While the two newspapers squabbled, the worst effect of the *Times* story was felt in Owens Valley. Its settlers, maddened enough by the abandonment of their reclamation project in favor of Los Angeles, were doubly confounded to hear the first word of it from a Los Angeles newspaper. Their rage was complete at the *Times* observation that "it probably means the wiping out of the town of Independence" and a quotation from Mulholland that Owens Valley land "in most cases is so poor that it doesn't pay to irrigate it." Telegraph wires had scarcely relayed the news story to Owens Valley when its outraged citizens turned to find an object for their wrath.

It was soon learned that Fred Eaton and his son were still in Bishop, closing some last-minute affairs. While the streets of the town buzzed with threats, a friend found the two men at the old Clark Hotel and warned that a mob was forming to seize them.

With remarkable calm the Eatons packed their bags, left the hotel, and walked down a block to the livery stable. When the hostlers refused to hitch Eaton's team to his buckboard, the two did their own harnessing while a menacing crowd watched from across the street. Eaton refused to be flustered but made the concession of taking off a red sweater in response to his son's warning that it would "make too good a target." Climbing into the wagon, the two swung the team into the street and drove out of town at a deliberate pace. Bishop watched them go in anger, unable to bring itself to the point of violence.

Fred Eaton left the valley by train the night of July 31, after writing a letter to the Independence newspaper denying any wrongdoing. He intended to spend his fortune and his life in Inyo County, he announced, and hoped that "in being a good neighbor I shall have an opportunity to retrieve myself and clear away all unhappy recollections." Then he stormed into Los Angeles and roared his fury at the position in which the *Times* story had caught him.

"Up there in the Owens River country," he declared, "they say I sold them out, sold them out and the government too; that I shall never take the water out of the valley; that when I go back for my cattle they will drown me in the river."

Owens Valley, in fact, was only beginning to bare its rage. It moved now to strike back at the most vulnerable link in the city's careful plan—Lippincott's arbitrary rejection of the

21

proposed federal reclamation scheme. First spokesman for the valley was the land registrar at Independence, who immediately took its cause to the highest authority in letters to the Secretary of the Interior and even to the White House. Because of Eaton's friendship with Lippincott, he told Theodore Roosevelt, farmers had optioned land to him believing he was a government agent.

"In justice, therefore," he concluded, "to the people here, in the interest of fairness and of the honor of the Reclamation Service, I appeal to you not to abandon the Owens River project. . . ."

At the same time the whole valley was joining him in outraged protest. In a rousing mass meeting at Bishop on August 2 the settlers vented their rage in fervent speeches against the deeds of Eaton and Lippincott and chose a citizens' committee to take action. A demand was then sent to the Interior Secretary for an investigation of Reclamation Service men who were using their positions to turn the valley's water over to Los Angeles.

Furious journalistic support was provided by editor Willie A. Chalfant, whose newspapers had recorded valley history since his father had arrived with its first press thirty-five years before. Under the startling headline, "Los Angeles Plots Destruction," his Inyo *Register* had already trumpeted the news of what he called "the greatest water steal on record." But the paper's main attack fell on "Judas" B. Lippincott, as Chalfant called him, who was charged with having used the government machinery "with a view to despoiling the very lands it was supposed to reclaim. . . ."

Inflamed by such outcries, feeling against Lippincott ran so high that when he passed through Bishop in August on an inspection trip to Long Valley a group of stalwarts conspired to waylay him on his return and "ride him out of the valley." But cooler heads prevailed at a mass meeting on the day of his expected arrival, and Lippincott was allowed to pass out of Inyo County on his own accord.

By this time the barrage of valley protests was taking effect in Washington. Engineer A. P. Davis was bearing the brunt of it as acting director of the Reclamation Service in the absence of his chief and wrote him hurriedly that "we cannot clear the skirts of the Reclamation Service too quickly nor completely." An investigation of Lippincott's operations was ordered, during which some of the charges were disproved and others supported.

One damaging fact could scarcely be overlooked: while serving as an officer in the Reclamation Service, Lippincott had also been employed as a consulting engineer by the Los Angeles Water Department. And despite his original acceptance of the reclamation job on the understanding that he could maintain his private practice, such a dual interest was specifically forbidden by federal law.

Although Lippincott was never formally charged with these complaints, Arthur Davis had decided by the last of August that "the only safe way for the Reclamation Service is to encourage him to devote his time to private practice. . . ." The following May, Lippincott resigned his Reclamation Service post—and promptly took a $6,000-a-year job on the Los Angeles Aqueduct. It was regarded in Owens Valley as a final installment in his "reward for past services."

Lippincott had been a leading instrument in the city's plans, but he had also succeeded in burdening them with the uncompromising antagonism of some four thousand Owens Valley citizens. As for Eaton and the other Los Angeles men, they realized too late that their determined secrecy had struck in the wrong quarter. They had been so absorbed in protecting the city against speculators that they had been blind to the ambitions of Owens Valley settlers.

By late August 1905 the harrassed Los Angeles water seekers were fighting the cry of scandal from another direction. Possibly still chagrined at the *Times* scoop, the editor of the *Examiner* had been doing some shrewd research in local records. On August 24, in the midst of a bond campaign for an initial $1,500,000 to launch the project, his paper scored its own scoop with a charge aimed at both the *Times* and the Owens River scheme.

Early in 1905, as the *Examiner* explained, the 16,200-acre Porter Ranch had been purchased by a group of investors which included Harrison Gray Otis of the *Times* and Edwin T. Earl of the *Express*, two political enemies who had united to support the Owens River project. General Otis, a man of extraordinary achievements as a soldier and newspaperman, had even then gained nationwide notice as a fiery exponent of the open shop. Earl had made a fortune in the fruit shipping business and since 1899, as publisher of the Los Angeles *Express*, had offered political opposition to Otis. The *Examiner's* implication was that through inside knowledge before the aqueduct scheme was made public these men were able to buy up San Fernando lands which stood to be transformed from desert to garden by the application of Owens River water. To leave no mistake, the *Examiner* next day followed with a caustic editorial.

"Why should Mr. Eaton and his confreres have given the profitable tip to Messrs. Otis, Earl & Co.?" asked the editor. "Was this a consideration for newspaper support?"

The effect of the accusations was instantaneous. Earl sent for the *Examiner* editor, told him that he was misinformed, and concluded that he was too suspicious. Fred Eaton later came around to the *Examiner* office and in a fit of anger threatened to assault its editor. Otis' *Times* called the charge "the very essence of absurdity" and pointed out that the first payments on the property had been made in 1903, when the Owens River project was unheard of. The *Examiner* promptly replied that, while an option had been taken in 1903, "the real money" had not been laid down until the spring of 1905, when the aqueduct scheme took definite shape.

The explanation was not far wrong on details, but it had taken a tremendous jump at conclusions. In October 1903, George K. Porter, son of a founder of San Fernando, had given a three-year option on his ranch at a price of more than a half million dollars. The prospective buyer was L. C. Brand, president of the Title Guarantee and Trust Company, who planned to extend an electric railway to the valley town and subdivide the land for sale to incoming settlers. It was a formula which both Brand and his associate, Henry E. Huntington, were then using with success throughout Los Angeles County. Sharing the venture with him were Huntington, Otis, Earl, and several others noted for their heavy investments in Southern California real estate. Not long afterward they were joined by General Moses H. Sherman, pioneer street-railway magnate and a member of the Los Angeles water board.

At the outset they could not possibly have known of the Owens River project, or of its benefit to San Fernando Valley as a source of irrigation water, for it had not even taken definite form in Fred Eaton's mind. But after the fall of 1904, when Mulholland returned from Owens Valley and outlined the scheme to a handful of city officials, they could well have caught the news. While General Sherman was not one of those whom Mulholland originally notified, his position on the water board gave him a valuable ear to the ground during the first whisperings of Owens River.

At any rate, on November 28, Otis and his associates incorporated the San Fernando Mission Land Company and took up the option on the Porter Ranch in March 1905. Although they had originally sought the three-year option for one of their familiar subdivision developments, they probably exercised it within a year in the belief that the city was bringing in a new water source to be shared by San Fernando Valley.

The early charge, however, that "Otis, Earl & Co." were given inside information in return for newspaper support is warranted more by hearsay than by fact. Certainly the later exaggerations of the affair, which picture Otis and his fellows conceiving the Owens River project as a way to irrigate their San Fernando lands at public expense, have no foundation in the record. Eventually they made millions in valley real estate, but their main offense consisted in doing what any other investors would have done when they got wind of an unexpected benefit to land they had optioned.

Most Angelenos, in fact, were too aware of their city's desperate water needs to be swayed by the *Examiner's* San Fernando story. Mulholland had already announced that defeat of the initial Owens River bond issue would mean "utter ruin for Los Angeles." Around August 26 the annual hot spell struck the city and water consumption began to soar. Reservoir levels dropped at the rate of 3,000,000 gallons a day. By the first of September Mulholland warned that at current consumption rates Los Angeles would probably be out of water within three weeks.

Later on the enemies of the aqueduct charged that this water famine, as well as those of 1903 and 1904, was artificially created by city officials to get a favorable vote on the aqueduct bonds. It was alleged by some that water was turned into the sewers to lower the levels in the reservoirs; yet since those reservoirs were never connected with the sewer system, this would have been impossible.

Others have claimed that, in contradiction to Mulholland's warnings, the reservoirs always held plenty of water. But the Chief knew better than the skeptics the absolute need for maintaining a safe margin against actual thirst. As Thomas Brooks, who was then in charge of city water distribution, has wryly commented, "A reservoir's no good if it's dry!" The plain fact then confronting the Los Angeles water officials was a ten-year drought which by 1905 brought a forty per cent deficiency in the flow of the Los Angeles River.

The hot spell subsided a few days before the first bond election, leaving Los Angeles citizens with another pointed reminder that no San Fernando bugaboo could hide their basic water dilemma. Even the *Examiner* was won over when the water board agreed to engage an impartial board of nationally known engineers to pass on the project.

At the same time William Randolph Hearst arrived from San Francisco and, possibly at the request of city officials, told his Los Angeles editor to "help them along on the bond issue." On September 3, in a front-page editorial said to have been written by Hearst himself, the *Examiner* wheeled about and supported the Owens River project. Four days later the people voted in the initial bonds by a 14-1 majority.

25

"Owens River is ours," crowed the Los Angeles *Times*, "and our business now is to hustle and bring it here, and make Los Angeles the garden spot of the earth and the home of a million contented people."

City officers W. B. Mathews and William Mulholland, steering their Owens River aqueduct over a rough course of accusations, had placed it a step further toward the day when dirt would fly. Ahead of them lay a more formidable task that carried them from local affairs to the national scene. Since most of the aqueduct route and reservoir sites lay along public lands, the blessing of the federal government was needed. And this time they would have to go beyond the Reclamation Service to the halls of Congress. By mid-September the water board was enlisting the aid of Senator Frank P. Flint, veteran lawmaker from Los Angeles, whose prominence in the national Republican party made him a valuable ally in the city's descent on Washington.

But Owens Valley, having lost the first battle for its reclamation project, now threw itself into the path of this new Los Angeles effort. On hand to defend its cause was Congressman Sylvester C. Smith, whose district included Inyo County. A man of energy and nerve, Smith had given up his private career as a Bakersfield newspaper editor a few years previously to devote himself entirely to public affairs. He now leaped to the side of Owens Valley, charging that it was to be desolated for the benefit of irrigation in San Fernando Valley.

By January 1906, Smith had proposed a compromise for the Los Angeles plan. Let the Reclamation Service, he said, proceed with its reservoir project and distribute the water first to Owens River farmers, then to the city of Los Angeles for domestic purposes only. If any were left it should go to additional irrigation in Inyo County.

To Mulholland and Mathews the suggestion was unthinkable. Their whole project was based on the belief that most of the Owens River flow would eventually be needed by the booming city of Los Angeles. In order to hold title to all the water rights they had acquired in Owens Valley, it would be necessary to show a fairly constant use of them. At first there would be a surplus, but the water men planned to use this on agricultural lands in San Fernando Valley, into which the city's residential area would eventually expand. They could not allow their water source to be restricted against irrigation by Smith's proposal.

In Owens Valley, however, the people took up the plan with the battle cry, "Not one drop for irrigation!" Inyo County newspapers swung behind it, while W. W. Watterson and other valley

26

leaders wrote articles for Los Angeles consumption favoring not more than 300 cubic feet per second for municipal use only. The valley was perfectly willing, said W. A. Chalfant, "to accommodate need, but not greed."

First skirmish in the "no irrigation" fight came in mid-June 1906 when Senator Flint introduced the city's bill to get a right of way for its aqueduct across public lands. It passed the Senate with little opposition, but Sylvester Smith was waiting for it in the House. There the Public Lands Committee promptly sidetracked the bill by referring it to the Interior Department for approval. Smith then offered his amendment prohibiting irrigation.

With the bill thus in jeopardy, Mulholland, Mathews, and two other Los Angeles delegates boarded the eastbound train for the scene of conflict. On June 21 they met with Smith in Senator Flint's Washington office. There they agreed to accept his amendment forbidding irrigation if he would support the right-of-way bill itself. With his point apparently won, Smith went with them next day to urge approval from Secretary Ethan A. Hitchcock, head of the Interior Department. The amended bill, providing for municipal use only, was then sent back to the House committee freed of opposition.

But all this was merely a Los Angeles holding action. If Congressman Smith believed he had won his "no irrigation" crusade for Owens Valley, he was reckoned without the cunning of the Los Angeles delegation. As long as a higher authority remained above the Secretary of the Interior, its members were not reluctant to make a final stand. Late on the night of June 23, just before action was due in the House, Senator Flint called at the White House.

Theodore Roosevelt listened while he outlined the issue and explained that Los Angeles was now providing water for the next half century of growth. A continuous consumption of the whole supply, even if partly for irrigation, would be necessary to protect its water rights under existing law. It was, Flint said, "a hundred- or a thousandfold more important to the state and more valuable to the people as a whole if used by the city than if used by the people of Owens Valley."

The President was convinced. When he proposed to Secretary Hitchcock that the irrigation limit be withdrawn, however, he was told that this would permit a few individuals to benefit by an irrigation scheme—an idea obviously planted by Congressman Smith's statements on the Otis-Brand syndicate in San Fernando Valley. Yet at the same time other government officials, having already been visited by the Los Angeles delegation,

27

backed up the city's stand. Chief Forester Gifford Pinchot, Roosevelt's personal friend, assured him that "there is no objection to permitting Los Angeles to use the water for irrigation purposes."

It was a puzzling decision for Roosevelt. But in the end he was probably swayed by the added fact that a power company which had located in the Owens River gorge was also fighting the Los Angeles bill. To the veteran trust buster this was enough to warrant automatic support for the city's plans. While Senator Flint and the Interior officials sat in his office, Roosevelt dictated a letter asking that the irrigation restriction be removed. As for the opposition of the "few settlers in Owens Valley," he declared that "their interest must unfortunately be disregarded in view of the infinitely greater interest to be secured by putting the water in Los Angeles. . . ."

The House Public Lands Committee was considering the Los Angeles bill, together with Smith's "no irrigation" amendment, when the President's letter arrived. Its effect on the committee members was immediate. Realizing that it was impossible to fight Roosevelt's decree against water limitation, Smith announced bitterly that he submitted "to the orders of the schoolmaster." He secured several minor amendments, but the main issue had been won by Los Angeles.

On June 27, 1906, the city's delegates were able to send home a jubilant message: "Owens River right-of-way bill has passed." Early in July they arrived by train in Los Angeles to receive a victors' welcome. "We got what we went after," beamed Mulholland.

But when Owens Valley heard the outcome in a telegram from Smith, its settlers angrily called it another relentless step in what seemed now to be a conspiracy against them. More than ever the isolated community had the desperate feeling of loneliness. In the absence of protection by even the federal government, it must look to its own resources for defense. It was plain that the Los Angeles water seekers, made desperate by their city's thirst, were pushing their project with every political weapon.

Nor was this the end to the government's contribution. Now committed wholeheartedly to the Los Angeles cause, the Interior Department moved next to proclaim the formal abandonment of its Owens River reclamation project in July 1907. But thousands of acres of public land, withheld from entry while the scheme was pending, were not restored. Los Angeles was being protected from private water and power filings which might impede its plans.

To gain the same defense throughout the whole length of Owens Valley, city authorities asked the government in September 1907 to "extend the eastern boundary of the Sierra Forest Reserve." Such a request fell within the province of Chief Forester Gifford Pinchot, apostle of the conservation movement then capturing the country. The fact that the Forest Service Law had specifically exempted from reservation any land more valuable "for agricultural purposes than for forest purposes" did not deter Pinchot from including the plans of Los Angeles in his conservation program.

Three separate investigators were sent into the valley before a report was returned favoring forest extension over an area where the only trees in sight for miles in any direction were those planted by farmers. On April 20, 1908, the proclamation extending the Sierra Reserve came to President Roosevelt's desk with Pinchot's approval.

When Congressman Smith heard of it, he hurried to Roosevelt's office and found there his old water foe, Senator Flint. Smith promptly charged that the Forest Service was being used "to confiscate property for the benefit of Los Angeles," which "intends to make use of part of the water from Owens River to irrigate lands at San Fernando." Flint denied the accusation and declared that Smith was "misrepresenting Los Angeles." The irate congressman then turned to Theodore Roosevelt, who was about to sign the proclamation before him.

"I hope, Mr. President," Smith cautioned, "that you will not be found on the side of Los Angeles in this fight."

Roosevelt answered with distracting calm, "That's exactly what I am doing right now."

"Well, I should like to talk with you further before you act," pleaded Smith.

"You don't need to talk," snapped the President. "I am doing the talking."

With that he signed the proclamation and extended the National Forest Reserve over treeless Owens Valley. Nearly four years later the restriction was removed by President Taft after it had protected the Los Angeles water rights from harassment by speculators during most of the aqueduct construction.

Yet Los Angeles could have been accommodated without such wholesale juggling of the public domain. Individual applications in specified areas could have been made subject to the city's approval without making it, as one Inyo spokesman stated, "the suzerain of Owens Valley." To the extent that this purpose was aided by federal officials, from Lippincott to Roosevelt, they have hailed in Los Angeles and vilified in Owens Valley.

Reaction of Inyo's citizens, in fact, ranged from bitterness to defiance when they received Smith's telegram announcing the forest extension. Chalfant of the *Register* looked ahead with the weary hope that "there may be a new deal some other day." The Inyo *Independent*, agreeing that "Los Angeles has been given all that she asked for," added ominously, "except the water."

But the city's water men were too engrossed in the swift progress of their plans to hear the warning. Since the fall of 1906, when the promised board of consulting engineers had pronounced the aqueduct "admirable in conception and outline," they had been hurrying with the final details. One last step separated them from actual construction—voting of bonds for the $23,000,000 which Mulholland had said the big ditch would cost. With the election set for June 12, 1907, Los Angeles launched another of its familiar water campaigns. The foes already assembling gave promise that this would be the most tumultuous of all.

In January the president of the Pacific Light and Power Company interviewed Mulholland and asked about "the possibility of making some arrangement with the city" about the project. But with some choice sites for power generation waiting along the aqueduct, the Los Angeles water men were not inclined to relinquish the opportunity to private hands. They were, in fact, as determined to enter the field of public power as the electric companies were to keep them out. And here began the first clash in the public-private power battle that would rock Los Angeles for a generation.

Opening shots had already been fired by the Los Angeles *Evening News*, which according to common gossip had received financial support from the power companies since its inception in 1905. The paper's editor was Samuel T. Clover, a capable but hot-tempered newspaperman who had been an editorial writer for the *Express* until he locked horns with publisher Earl and found himself out of a job. When Clover, not a man of means, promptly turned up with his own newspaper and soon began attacking the Los Angeles Aqueduct, conclusion-jumping was in order. Any connection with the power companies, however, was denied by Clover, who in fact seemed to conduct his fight with the sincere conviction that the water project was against the city's interest.

The gist of his objections was that the scheme had been hatched to benefit Otis and the San Fernando land syndicate, and that to pay for it the people were being heaped with "financial burdens so excessive that they may ruin the city's credit. . . ." To bolster his cause he also claimed that the waters of the Owens River were too strongly impregnated with alkali and that an ample 200 second-feet of water was available from the Los Angeles, San Gabriel, and other Southland rivers. But, said Clover, "what good would that do the Porter Ranch syndicate?"

By mid-May 1907 the bond contest was mounting in fury, with the rest of the city's six newspapers all clamoring for Owens River water. Heading the drive was the *Times*, which showed by statistics that other Southern California water sources were far too slim and that the added taxes for the aqueduct were small enough to make it a remarkable bargain. As for the alkalinity of Owens River, the *Times* took the *News's* own figures to prove that it was purer than the current supply from the Los Angeles River. With editor Samuel Clover persistently calling the $23,000,000 issue the "Alkali Bonds," the *Times* in turn labeled him "Alkali Sammy." Otis' paper remained silent on the San Fernando land accusation, however, until Mayor A. C. Harper came to see him and explained that it was undermining his support of the aqueduct bonds.

"If you are willing to come out with a denial," he told Otis, "it will be a good campaign argument for Owens River."

Otis agreed and, when asked whether he could back up the refutation "in case of a comeback," said that he could. In a prompt letter to Mayor Harper, published in the *Times* on May 24, the general avowed that he had sold his stock in the San Fernando Land Company in February 1905. "As a matter of fact, I have no private property interests whatsoever in the San Fernando Valley." It looked as though the black smudge of "special interest" had been wiped from the aqueduct at last.

But that evening Clover's paper nailed the denial by pointing out that the *Times* had admitted Otis' interest in the San Fernando company as late as August 1906. The *Times* could only answer that it had been mistaken in August 1906. It is a matter of record, however, that Otis still held his interest at least a month after he claimed it had been sold. His denial could hardly be accepted by the public at face value, and on this one issue, at least, Clover came off the victor. Yet while a personal stake in the bond election might have tended to minimize Otis' campaign arguments, the general public did not believe that the Owens River project had been initiated for his benefit or that his interest made it any less imperative to bring in the new water supply.

Clover's frenzied opposition, however, had the effect of rallying the aqueduct's supporters for a heroic fight. When campaign headquarters for the water bonds opened in the Chamber of Commerce offices, they were backed by every type of Los Angeles organization from the Business Men's Bible Class of the Magnolia Christian Church to the Women's Goldfield Mining Exchange.

No medium of expression was overlooked in publicizing the aqueduct. An informative pamphlet, the *Owens River Primer*, was circulated by the thousands. Store windows carried placards for the water bonds, while two business houses displayed detailed replicas of Owens Valley and the proposed aqueduct. Legitimate theaters showed photographic slides of scenes in Owens Valley. Newspapers carried large advertisements exhorting the people to "Work and Vote for the Owens River Water Bonds June 12." Pedestrians' coat lapels blossomed with buttons bearing the slogan "I'm for Owens River Water," to which were attached tiny vials of the liquid. Automobiles were decked with huge pennants displaying the words "Owens River—Vote for it June 12." For once Angelenos were taking the same talent for publicity with which they had belabored the East for years and turning it on each other.

Even the city's high school children studied the problem, held auditorium debates, and on the evening of June 8 staged a street parade for the aqueduct. Added support came from the Los Angeles Ministerial Union, which voted to set Sunday, June 9, as "Aqueduct Day" in the city's churches. Throughout town, churchgoers heard sermons based on such texts as "He showed me a river" and "Everything shall live whithersoever the river cometh." Comedy was provided by members of a Los Angeles men's club, who drank toasts to the success of the project with Owens River water that had been bottled and sealed before a notary public. At a ladies' afternoon card party the hostess made a point of using Owens River water in the tea. The aqueduct's enthusiasts were obviously determined to explode the alkali myth.

Equal zeal was shown by the project's opponents, who passed out handbills bearing the message "Help defeat the greatest swindle ever organized west of New York." Chief speaker in the anti-bond campaign was the fiery Job Harriman, Socialist nominee for governor of California in 1898 and for U. S. Vice-President in 1900. Curiously uniting with private power interests against a pioneer public enterprise, he argued that the Los Angeles River could supply all the city's needs without bringing in outside water that would benefit the San Fernando landowners.

But the rallying point of opposition was Sam Clover and his *Evening News*, which was soon charging vehemently that Mulholland, Lippincott, and other water officials had initiated the project for the rather pointless purpose of being "continued in office" at their regular high salaries. Lippincott finally became so incensed at these jibes that when an *Evening News* reporter went to interview him at his office he slammed the door with the exclamation that he had "nothing to say!"

This personal attack on the city's water men helped to lose Clover the sympathy of most Angelenos. Outraged merchants began withdrawing their advertising, while the paper's circulation dropped almost ten per cent during the spring of 1907. Facing financial ruin, Clover still continued his uphill fight. By June 8 he was devoting almost the whole newspaper to the campaign, startling his readers with a two-page headline: "Taxpayers: The Bonds Will Swamp You. Vote No If You Would Save Your Property."

The assault also served to stir Mulholland from his campaign silence, despite his own oft-spoken words that "politics and water don't mix." Armed with maps, charts, and a glib Irish tongue, the engineer took his crusade before men's organizations in every precinct of the city.

"Our population has doubled since 1904," he warned his listeners, "while our water supply has diminished." Because the Owens River was the only adequate source, "the defeat of these bonds would be absolutely fatal to the prosperity of this city."

The Chief's entry into the campaign marked its final, spirited climax. For ten days before the election Mulholland, Lippincott, and Mayor Harper spoke at campaign meetings almost every night—sometimes several during the same evening. The main crisis, however, came in a rousing rally in Simpson's Auditorium on Hope Street, held two nights before the balloting. Aided by lantern slides, Lippincott earnestly was describing the abundance and purity of Owens River water when a fly blundered into the machine and was projected onto the screen. For an embarrassing moment it seemed that the intruder was fulfilling Sam Clover's claims on the contamination of Owens Valley water. But the rally chairman was equal to the emergency.

"That is a picture," he announced, "of the only microbe in Owens River."

Over on Spring Street that same night the aqueduct foes gathered in their last big rally. Job Harriman and other speakers argued that the city did not need such a water supply, that the aqueduct could never be built for $23,000,000, and that it would be demolished with the next earthquake. It was a last, futile effort to stem a tide of enthusiasm for Mulholland's aqueduct.

On the morning of June 12, after one of the most turbulent campaigns Los Angeles had ever seen, the aqueduct forces began harvesting their votes. Some eighty-four autos and twenty carriages, donated for the cause, shuttled through the precincts all day long to bring supporters to the polls. That night the results showed a 10-1 victory for the Owens River project. There was no doubt that Los Angeles had voiced a mighty cry for water.

Undaunted, the plucky Sam Clover put out an extra and made an editorial bow to the will of the people. "The *Evening News*," he said, ". . . has been beaten to a standstill. We will take our medicine without a protest."

More than anything else the Owens River campaign was the cause of his paper's demise the following spring. "Our love for Los Angeles," he declared in a final editorial, "impels us to hope we were wrong." Clover had, in fact, performed the invaluable service of forcing Angelenos to fight for their aqueduct, had left them with a militant spirit of unity where water was concerned.

4:   THE BIG DITCH

With the technicalities past, Mulholland now took his battle to the rugged mountains and forbidding desert that lay in the aqueduct's route. From the beginning there seemed no question that the Chief himself, who had ample experience in building water storage projects throughout Southern California, would superintend the digging of the great ditch.

"I wanted one big job before I died," he once remarked. "I'll be glad to know that I did it."

His first assistant was tall, methodical J. B. Lippincott, with whom Angelenos were already acquainted from his part in the acquisition of the Owens River. Though Mulholland was sometimes exasperated at Lippincott's painful paper work, more than once it came to his rescue when city officials demanded figures and records. Handling the complicated legal matters of rights of way and financing was W. B. Mathews, who left his job as city attorney to become legal counsel for the aqueduct and afterward for the Water Department.

"I did the work," Mulholland used to say, "but Mathews kept me out of jail."

At the outset the Chief cautioned that construction of the big ditch would be less of a problem than supplying Los Angeles with water from local sources in the meantime. Already, in the high-level sections of the city, faucets were dry early in the evenings during the summer. But by this time almost half of the water services were metered and seven new municipal pumps were drawing underground water from the surrounding territory. Mulholland was able to make water resources meet water consumption as he embarked on the strenuous task of building the largest aqueduct in the Western Hemisphere.

From its head gate on Owens River north of Independence, a great open ditch was surveyed along the foothills of the massive Sierra to take the water out of Owens Valley and into the first reservoir site at Haiwee. South of this main storage point the flow was to be carried by closed conduit—first through a series of tunnels and steel siphons along the jagged mountains that form the west rim of the Mojave Desert and then in a covered concrete trough across a corner of that desert to the Coast Range north of Los Angeles. Here, with a catchment reservoir at each end, the giant five-mile Elizabeth Tunnel would take the stream through the mountains and afford the generation of electric power in San Francisquito Canyon. After another series of tunnels and siphons across the rugged canyon country below, the water would splash into the final reservoirs at San Fernando Valley, 223 miles south of the Owens River intake.

By the end of 1907 Mulholland's crews were in the midst of a gigantic preparatory operation that rivaled the actual excavation itself. A 240-mile telephone line, more than 500 miles of roads and trails, and some 2300 buildings and tent houses were constructed to facilitate work along the route. To provide another needed item of 1,000,000 barrels of cement, Los Angeles constructed its own cement plant at Monolith on the Tehachapi plateau.

The scarcity of water in this desert region almost eliminated the use of steam power. So the city built two hydroelectric plants on Owens Valley creeks and 169 miles of transmission lines, making the aqueduct the first major engineering project in America constructed primarily by electric power.

Throughout this early period Mulholland's great concern was whether civic officials would leave him alone enough to get the preliminary work done. Actual excavation was scarcely under way by December 1908 when the Los Angeles Chamber of Commerce invited Mulholland to attend a meeting. Its members, knowing little of the engineering preliminaries involved, intended to know why so much time had been consumed and so little dirt removed. In the midst of the meeting the chairman asked Mulholland for an informal report on aqueduct progress.

35

"Well, we have spent about $3,000,000 all told, I guess," Mulholland answered solemnly, "and there is perhaps nine hundred feet of aqueduct built. Figuring all our expenses, it has cost us about $3300 per foot."

He paused while the startled Chamber members digested his words.

"But by this time next year," he concluded, "I'll have fifty miles completed and at a cost of under $30 per foot, if you'll let me alone."

The tension in his audience resolved into cordiality.

"All right, Bill," laughed the chairman. "Go ahead; we're not mad about it."

By the middle of 1908 word of the Los Angeles undertaking had traveled through the construction camps of the West, and an army of transient labor began converging on Los Angeles. "Blanket stiffs," they were called—a roistering, hard-drinking lot but experienced in the drill and shovel work of great engineering achievements. Fresh from Western colleges came a different breed—hardy young engineers who gained their first field experience in the rigorous desert life on Mulholland's ditch and who proved their mettle as the backbone of aqueduct construction.

The American public as a whole did not fail to notice the spectacle of the Southwest's largest city reaching more than two hundred miles across arid desert for life-giving water. Throughout the Eastern states people watched the project unfold with the realization that Los Angeles had now taken first rank among the great cities of the country. Correspondents from *Scribner's*, the *Literary Digest*, and other national magazines kept America informed on the progress of Mulholland's ditch. Los Angeles found the aqueduct as valuable a publicity item as any project of its famed Chamber of Commerce. Many an Eastern family headed for Los Angeles with the conviction that its bold water pioneering had made it a city of opportunity.

Actual excavation had begun as early as September 1907, when a crew of forty men pitched camp in San Francisquito Canyon and broke ground at the south portal of Elizabeth Tunnel. Built to carry Owens River water through the Coast Range into Southern California, the five-mile bore would determine the length of time for construction of the entire aqueduct. By early October another hard-bitten crew was opening the north face, determined to reach the center mark before the rival gang beyond the crest.

At first the men at the tunnel headings drilled the powder holes with hand tools; but early in 1908 heavier equipment arrived, and the work was ordered pushed ahead "with all possible speed." Henceforth electric motors hummed at the tunnel mouths, driving the air compressors which sent power to the drillers deep inside the mountain. At each face of the bore two grimy stalwarts attacked the granite with their vibrating air hammers, making such a dreadful clatter that orders could be given only in signs. After every blast a fresh crew would take over and shovel the "muck" into electrically operated cars. When the face was cleared, the new gang started up the air hammers for another bite into the granite mountain.

By July 1908 a system of bonus payments was begun to carry the work forward at even greater speed. A base rate of advance was fixed at eight feet per day; beyond this each underground workman received forty cents a foot in addition to his regular pay. As a result the air drills and explosions shattered the mountain at a faster pace than before. In some months the advance was doubled over the ordinary base progress. While many miners earned a majority of their pay in bonuses, Mulholland was able to drive the tunnel through at a saving of $500,000 and 450 days out of the original estimates.

At the south portal the crews soon captured the American hard-rock tunnel record, repeatedly breaking their own mark to reach the furious pace of 604 feet in a single month during April 1910.

In the north end the treacherous rock made the advance less spectacular. To superintend this back-breaking job, Mulholland picked John Gray, a stocky, round-faced tunnel expert with long experience in the mines of Colorado, Wyoming, and Mexico. Working in water-soaked granite, broken and fissured by the nearby San Andreas Fault, Gray drove his crews forward in a race to beat the south-portal crews to the center in spite of obstacles.

The advance went well until mid-August 1908, when the miners struck a body of saturated sand and gravel that brought dangerous caving and flooding. Work was stopped for a month and a half while an auxiliary shaft was sunk from the surface three thousand feet south of the north portal. Gray then began driving back from the bottom of the shaft, to approach the caved section from both ends.

Several times Gray and his men struck whole pockets of water and were forced to flee for their lives through the tunnel. But by timbering the sides as fast as they were formed and finally by driving overlapping steel rails in advance of the heading to hold back cave-ins, the obstacle was conquered.

Early in April 1909, Gray connected with the auxiliary shaft. Despite continued floods of water, in which his tunnelers sometimes waded to the hips, they were soon driving ahead faster than the rival crews beyond the crest. When the two headings finally met on February 28, 1911, the south-portal men had covered the longer distance, but monumental handicaps had given John Gray a lasting reputation as the best tunnel man on the aqueduct.

Along the Sierra foothills north of Mojave, full-scale operations could not be launched until a standard-gauge railway had been built to haul an estimated 320,000 tons of materials. Contracting for delivery of this freight, the Southern Pacific Railroad began grading the road northward from Mojave early in May 1908. The tracks connected with the narrow-gauge near Lone Pine by October 1910, bringing Owens Valley its long-sought rail outlet to the south.

Construction on the ditch itself was opened as fast as the tracks advanced, starting with the formidable Jawbone Division just north of Mojave. At the sight of this rugged series of jutting crags and gaping canyons, the original board of inspecting engineers had shown some alarm. "That is very rough and difficult country for canal digging," one of them told Mulholland as the group surveyed the badlands from a nearby ridge.

"It is rough on top," agreed the quick-witted Mulholland, "but we are not going to dig on top." The conduit would be burrowed underground, he assured them, clinching the argument with the sober observation, "When you buy a piece of pork you don't have to eat the bristles."

Headquarters for the Jawbone was Cinco, a railroad supply station fairly roaring with construction activity. In and out of spur tracks freight cars were shunted day and night. It was a canvas town of innumerable tents—barracks, mess halls, stores, blacksmith shops—whose flimsy sides flapped wildly in the frequent desert winds. From this bustling center long lines of mule teams hauled machinery and supplies to outlying construction camps along the conduit.

Over precipitous mountain roads the teams were joined by some of the earliest traction engines in existence. In the first few months of operation the clanking "Caterpillars" showed a definite saving in cost over the jerk-line mule teams; but when the desert elements took their toll in repeated breakdowns and repairs, Mulholland was forced to abandon them and fall back on slower but more reliable mule power.

Progress on the Jawbone was in full swing by the fall of 1908. A thousand men were driving more than eleven miles of tunnels while the Sierra foothills shook to the rumble of blasting powder. The brawny crew on the two-mile Red Rock Tunnel, longest in the division, set the world's record for soft-rock tunneling with the feverish advance of 1061 feet in a single month.

Superintending the division was A. C. Hansen, who had come to the aqueduct from flood control work on the lower Colorado. A tall and wiry Scandinavian, Hansen believed in hard work and made himself an example for his crewmen. But though Mulholland respected him as an engineer of the first rank, he could not refrain from taking advantage of Hansen's lack of humor. On one of his inspection trips he was questioning the superintendent on the tunneling progress and learned that a miner had been cut off by a landslide in one of the excavations.

"We have been talking to him," explained Hansen, "through a two-inch pipe driven through the muck."

Mulholland considered that from the miner's point of view this effort was hardly enough.

"How long has he been in there?" he asked.

"Three days."

"Then he must be nearly starved to death."

"No," replied Hansen, "we have been rolling hard-boiled eggs to him through the pipe."

The Chief assessed the man's predicament in the light of this added service.

"Well," he asked abruptly, "have you been charging him board?"

It was Hansen's turn to consider the situation. "No," he answered. "Do you think I ought to?"

But if Hansen took the suggestion seriously, his problem was removed the next day when a rescue party extricated the stranded miner.

As the railroad progressed northward, new divisions were sparked with activity. Where the tracks swung sharply away from the aqueduct around the El Paso Mountains, a spur line was built eight miles up Red Rock Canyon and operated by the aqueduct for almost two years. Farther north on the rugged Grapevine and Little Lake divisions, activity was opening in 1909 as fast as men and equipment could be spared from completed sections of the Jawbone. Here the route of supply for most of the tunnel work was usually straight up the mountainsides. Men and materials were carried up by surface trams or aerial cables, either of which offered a breathtaking ride to the uninitiated visitor.

Along the entire route, over mountains and desert from San Fernando Reservoir to Owens Valley, swarms of men and machines continued to carve the great trough. Either Mulholland or Lippincott was always in the field observing progress, making decisions on changes in plans, and impressing shovel operators and tunnel foremen with comments on their performance records. Through winter storms and summer heat the work went on—in round-the-clock, eight-hour shifts for the tunnel crews and two ten-hour shifts for the "outside" workers.

It was said that the aqueduct was built by "hobo" labor, and statistics showed that the average man did not stay on the job more than two weeks at a time. Most of them drew their pay at the end of a ten-day bonus period and hiked to the next headquarters down the line, stopping at the nearest "rag camp"—the term for the tent saloons that sprang up as close to the conduit as law would permit. One tunnel foreman recalls that he regularly had "one crew drunk, one crew sobering up, and one crew working."

The "boom town" of the aqueduct, and the Mecca of every "tunnel stiff" able to reach it in one or two days' hike, was the rail center of Mojave, roughly halfway between Los Angeles and Owens Valley. It was a town with a single dirt street separating the rail yards from a solid row of false fronts and wooden awnings that housed saloons, gambling joints, and dance halls. On pay days Mojave fairly roared around the clock, while a dozen clanking pianos and wheezing phonographs mingled with the raucous laughter of the revelers. Next day most of them would awaken in a Mojave alley to find their pockets empty and ahead of them a long walk back to their headquarters on "the big ditch."

By contrast the workingmen's lives in these white-tented aqueduct camps were notably austere and peaceful. At mealtimes, announced by the ringing of the cook's triangle, they left their tools on the mountainsides and converged on the barracks in the canyon below. Inside the mess hall there was little time spent in dinner conversation; with scarcely a word the hungry horde passed the serving pans down the length of the long tables and tackled the meal almost as another chore in the day's routine.

Desert heat and lack of refrigeration made the food increasingly bad in proportion to the distance from Los Angeles. Meat spoiled, bread became infested with weevils, and most of the fare was restricted to simple imperishables. Many times the boisterous workmen were infuriated to riot by the "grub" placed before them. Tables were kicked over and the food thrown on the floor and walls. Sometimes the mess tents were torn down and the cooks chased out of camp. More than once the mess contractor was warned by aqueduct officials that the business might be taken from him, but Mulholland believed that the city itself could scarcely do better in feeding several thousand men in desert heat without refrigeration.

Other conditions along the conduit were better calculated to help morale. Pay and promotions were based solely on a man's ability to do his job, and there was a certain fellowship developed among men engaged in a common and inspiring undertaking. In the evenings at every camp the office porch was a social gathering place, where groups of men would sit on the rails and steps to talk of news up and down the big ditch or of what they planned to do "when the damned thing is finished." Inside the office a late-burning light would reveal the division chief at work over maps and blueprints that were being carried out in life-size scale up on the mountainside.

By the spring of 1910 the work was being pushed forward beyond Mulholland's own expectations. The red tape and indifference which could have plagued such a public undertaking was largely eliminated by the pressure of his driving energy. Across the country his aqueduct was respected for its remarkable progress with a minimum of expense and accidents. By persuading the city's New York bond buyers to purchase aqueduct securities at a faster rate than guaranteed in their contract, Los Angeles officials were taking advantage of enlarged funds to make all possible speed on the ditch. With almost two-thirds of the work finished, Lippincott returned from a trip afield to report progress at a record pace and the aqueduct organization "in a high state of efficiency."

In mid-May 1910, however, a flurry in the money market caused the New York bonding firm to curtail investments. It not only quit buying bonds ahead of schedule but refused to take any at all until the schedule had caught up with the number of bonds already bought. As this would be a matter of months, it meant a financial calamity for Mulholland and the aqueduct.

At the current high rate of advance, little more than a month's supply of funds was on hand when the crisis came. Frantic telegrams were sent immediately to New York without avail. With the aqueduct payroll at a record 3900 men, Mulholland ordered a drastic cut on May 20.

Within a few days the force was reduced to 1100 men. Whole divisions were closed down completely, with only the Elizabeth Tunnel kept under full force. North of Mojave eighty per cent of the workers were laid off. Only enough men were retained to prevent the work from falling into disrepair. The town of Mojave, ordinarily booming with the trade of 3000 nearby workers, became a dead camp overnight.

Mulholland, W. B. Mathews, and a Chamber of Commerce official hurriedly boarded an eastbound train to plead with New

York's bond buyers for relief. But if the aqueduct was in dire straits, the New York bankers were more concerned with the shaky money market. His efforts fruitless, Mulholland returned to Los Angeles on May 26 and outlined a plan for slow-time activity until the crisis passed.

"The work will be suspended," he told the press, "on those portions where it is farthest advanced and the efforts continued where it has lagged." To the city authorities he soon reported the most damaging result of the debacle—the scattering of the high-geared, finely knit organization that had been pressing the ditch forward at the rate of seven miles a month.

But on the most northerly Owens Valley Division, where some fifty men were dredging an open canal, Superintendent Harvey A. Van Norman found encouragement from his crewmen. Calling them together when word reached him of the financial crisis, the husky young engineer announced he would have to shut down operations and dismiss them all for lack of funds. The men looked at one another, exchanged a few remarks, and then asked the chief:

"You can keep the cookhouse going, can't you?"

Van Norman assured them that he could guarantee grub for a month or more. To his immense satisfaction the entire crew decided it could stay on without pay until Mulholland got money matters in order once again. Throughout the aqueduct curtailment, dirt continued to fly in the Owens Valley Division.

Meanwhile the effects of the slowdown were promptly felt in another quarter, starting a round of trouble for Mulholland's ditch. On July 19 the mess contractor demanded a raise in meal allowances to compensate for the smaller number of paying boarders. Aqueduct officials accordingly raised the board five cents per meal on condition that he improve the mess.

But when the new rate went into effect in November 1910, it was branded an injustice by union men who were then trying to organize the aqueduct workers. Already the Western Federation of Miners, linked at that time with the radical Industrial Workers of the World, had made considerable headway with the men in the remaining tunnels of the Little Lake, Grapevine, and Elizabeth divisions. The new board schedule had been in effect only two weeks when the union called a strike and more than seven hundred men walked off the work. Elizabeth Tunnel was practically closed down, while most of the tunnel and shovel work farther north was carried on with skeleton crews.

If Mulholland were now twice confounded by the appearance of labor strife, he gave no outward sign. A union deputation met with aqueduct officials on November 15 and demanded either a return to the old board rate or a corresponding wage increase, as well as "the unqualified right to board where we please. . . ." With language that may have been too strong under the circumstances, the aqueduct authorities told the miners' committee that the demands could not be granted. In rapid order the metalworkers and steam-shovel operators on the ditch made their demands for higher wages and shorter hours. In each case they were refused.

As the strike dragged on week after week, it became apparent that the W.F.M. had chosen the wrong time to tie up the aqueduct. The continued weakness in finances made the shutdown of the expensive tunnel work a timely occurrence, and Mulholland was in no hurry to renew activity. By the end of January 1911 the unions sent a final communiqué to the mayor and City Council, warning that "as there seems no possible way to settle this strike with the city officials in order to secure justice the aqueduct employees will have to try by all means in their power to make the taxpayers aware of the facts in the present situation."

Political action at the polls by Los Angeles labor elements was evidently the meaning of the threat. But Mulholland continued to operate without heeding the union organizers. When the New York banking house resumed buying aqueduct bonds in February 1911 and the long money shortage was over, he began to recruit a full complement of aqueduct workers.

Though a labor shortage continued for several weeks, Mulholland began advancing transportation money to prospective crewmen bound for points along the ditch and extended the bonus system to cement and siphon crews where necessary. By May 1911 the entire aqueduct, from the San Fernando dams to the Owens River intake, was under full steam once more. The superior pay opportunities on Mulholland's ditch gave the miners little stomach for a continued strike.

Rebuffed in their wage demands, the labor chiefs turned to fulfill their threat of taking the issue to the Los Angeles voters. In the fall elections of 1911 the unions, through the rising Socialist party, waged a furious campaign to capture the city administration. For mayor they supported Job Harriman, the Los Angeles lawyer who had already fought the aqueduct bonds. Paradoxically, the Socialist leader now renewed his attack on the biggest publicly owned project in Southern California. Every conceivable charge was made against Mulholland's aqueduct—that construction was faulty, that working conditions were intolerable, and that it had been launched to serve a few landowners in San Fernando Valley.

Harriman emerged from the primary leading the field and took his party into the final campaign with every hope of capturing the Los Angeles city government. But among the current political factors was the trial in Los Angeles of two labor leaders, the McNamara brothers, charged with the dynamiting of the *Times* Building the year before; Harriman, engaged as part of their legal counsel, had succeeded in whipping up considerable public sympathy. On December 1, four days before the election, the McNamaras pled guilty to the *Times* dynamiting, shocked the entire country, and blew the Socialist campaign into defeat.

But Harriman's charges against the aqueduct, repeated for two months to an interested public, could not be overlooked by William Mulholland. Early in December he asked the City Council for a public investigation of aqueduct affairs. The Socialists then demanded a majority on the three-man investigating committee. When the City Council appointed only one known "anti-conduit" man, they launched and won an initiative movement to pack the group with two more Socialists.

The "People's Investigating Board" began its probe in the spring of 1912, sending representatives along the aqueduct in search of evidence. For several weeks the board grilled Mulholland, Mathews, and other aqueduct officials on every subject, from the inception of the project to actual construction.

By July the two non-Socialist members of the board resigned in protest against what they termed star chamber methods, giving a minority report which favored the aqueduct on every count. In August the other three members made their report, with heavier criticism than the testimony seemed to justify. Mulholland's ditch received a left-handed exoneration, however, in a remarkable statement that "no evidence of graft has been developed" but that if the board had been given more time "a knowledge of human nature indicates that men would have been found who had succumbed to temptation."

The aqueduct's long trial was over. Having steered his undertaking through hard times and strikes, political attacks and inquisitions, Mulholland realized that a great engineer's job is only partly technical.

Before him there remained the gigantic task of finishing the conduit, and this his crewmen were still accomplishing in spite of opposition. By the middle of 1912 the work was, in point of distance, ninety per cent completed, and Mulholland was able to report that "the end of our task seems fairly in sight." Most of the tunnels had been driven and lined with concrete, while a half dozen earth-fill dams, from Haiwee to San Fernando, were under final construction.

44

Mulholland, almost exhausted from the enormous five-year work, fortified himself with the conviction that, as he had once said, "we are giving the city a magnificent heritage. If it were not for looking ahead to the time of reward, a reward of approbation that will surely come to us, five or six years from now, I could not go on with the work, for I am worn out."

The final task was the installation of inverted siphons—the great airtight pipes by which the water would be made to drop into and out of canyons below the aqueduct grade level. Some of the first of these were laid in the Saugus Division, the mountainous section just north of San Fernando Valley, where two of the siphons were the largest known concrete pipes in the United States. Most of them, however, were made of thick steel sections, rolled and punched at Eastern mills and shipped by rail to be riveted in the field. Varying from eight to ten feet in diameter, they were laid on concrete piers in the canyon bottoms and installed on the hillsides by means of electric tramways. Largest pipe in the whole aqueduct was the four-mile steel and concrete siphon at the west end of Antelope Valley, to which long mule teams hauled steel thirty-five miles from the rail town of Mojave.

The most harrowing siphon work was performed in the rugged Jawbone Division under Superintendent Harvey A. Van Norman, previously chief of Owens Valley dredging operations. Its largest siphon was the 7000-foot monster in Jawbone Canyon, where a drop of 850 feet from the grade of the conduit necessitated steel casing over an inch thick in the bottom section. While neither the stoutest nor the longest siphon on the aqueduct, the Jawbone was described, because of its thickness of steel and extreme pressure head, as "the most noteworthy pipe in the United States."

In January 1912 the work was started in the canyon bottom, where the extra thickness of the steel made it necessary for most of the riveting to be done at the Eastern mill. Several pipes thirty-six feet long, weighing twenty-six tons apiece, were shipped by rail to Cinco station and were pulled the last four miles to the siphon by two specially rigged mule teams. Each outfit had a pair of great flat-decked wagons supported by steel wheels with tires two feet wide. They were drawn by no less than fifty-two mules, using three parallel jerk lines of sixteen mules each, with a lead pair at the head and two wheelers on the tongue. Such a job of mule skinning required highly skilled work from the most experienced drivers on the desert.

The first skinner to take the fifty-two mules up Jawbone Canyon was a burly fellow named Wilson. At the end of his initial round trip he felt so satisfied with himself that he promptly got into a scrap with the corral wrangler at Cinco and beat him over the head with a piece of steel. Division Superintendent Van Norman soon arrived and found that Wilson had been the aggressor. He fired the fifty-two-mule driver on the spot.

"Where you going to get another skinner?" demanded Wilson.

Van Norman told him he was driving into Mojave to recruit one.

"He better come out here shootin'!" boasted the disgruntled teamster. "This is my job."

The engineer knew Wilson was armed and already felt remorseful over the fate of the new driver he would have to hire. Next morning in Mojave he was directed to the hotel room of "Whistling Dick," a leather-skinned teamster, seventy-four years old, who had hauled borax from Death Valley in earlier days.

"Dick," he asked, "how many mules can you drive?"

The old skinner, full of professional pride, threw his head back in wide-eyed disgust.

"Just as far as I can see 'em," he answered solemnly.

Van Norman told him he wanted a fifty-two-mule teamster but warned that Wilson had threatened any man who came to take his place. Apparently unimpressed, Whistling Dick gathered his few belongings and checked out of the hotel.

Just as the two men stepped into the street Wilson himself reeled out of the adjacent saloon and loudly demanded where Dick was going. The grizzled teamster reared back once more and eyed Wilson with contempt.

"None of your damned business," he roared, then added: "And furthermore, I hear you've been braggin' about defendin' that job up on the Jawbone. If you come up there you better come heeled, 'cause I got mine right here." And he patted a significant bulge in his shirt.

Wilson, king of the mule skinners, decided he had no use for that hauling job in Jawbone Canyon. Van Norman, who had been ready to duck for his life, drove peacefully out of town with Whistling Dick, satisfied that he had found the right man.

For several months the gray-bearded mule skinner, perched on the back of his near wheeler, was a familiar sight from Cinco to the Jawbone siphon. While his mules tugged through the heavy sands of the canyon bottom, the mountainsides echoed to Dick's commanding whistles and the crack of his blacksnake.

Transportation of the giant siphon was nearly finished when tragedy one day overtook the plodding mule teams.

46

Unexplainably Whistling Dick fell from his saddle without stopping the mules; the "swamper" on the rear wagon first saw his body lying crushed in the track of the massive wagon wheels. At seventy-four, after a lifetime of mule skinning, Dick had at last fallen victim to his hard-bitten profession.

By March 1913 the great pipe of the Jawbone siphon had inched its way up both sides of the canyon to its points of entry into the adjacent tunnels; the last big project on the Los Angeles Aqueduct was finished.

As early as February 13 a small but jubilant party including Mulholland, Lippincott, and Van Norman arrived at the newly completed intake for the momentous task of turning the Owens River into the big ditch. Mrs. Van Norman christened the canal head gate with a bottle of champagne; and while one of the group took motion pictures of the historic event, Mulholland and his friends turned the wheels that opened the four controlling gates. With a great roaring surge, 200 second-feet of sparkling water poured out of the Owens River bed and into the aqueduct canal.

After Haiwee Reservoir had filled, Mulholland, Van Norman, and other water men released its gates early in May and followed the head of the stream for fifty hours across the Mojave Desert to the reservoir at the upper end of Elizabeth Tunnel, stopping from time to time to observe the flow through manholes in the conduit. Elated with the success of their undertaking, the engineers dispersed to await the filling of this second storage place.

They did not know that ten miles south of Little Lake the Sand Canyon siphon had sprung a huge crack and was spilling water down the north side of the ravine. Built of two underground tunnels down each mountainside and connected by a steel pipe across the canyon, this siphon was the only one of its kind on the aqueduct.

The necessary steel was rushed up from Los Angeles and repairs were begun within forty-eight hours. On May 16 enough water was turned back into the pipe to reveal another small leak on the south slope. Determined to test the siphon to its full capacity, even if it meant destruction, the aqueduct men gradually increased the flow.

As the water burst out of the cracks, the whole south mountainside began to slip. When the flow reached 42 second-feet, the entire covering of the tunnel was lifted upward by the pressure. Water fountained into the air, and the canyon wall burst loose and crashed into the ravine. One side of a corrugated workshop was sheared away by the avalanche; the south end of the steel pipe was bombarded with huge boulders and completely entombed with debris.

Some tiny seams in the otherwise solid granite of the canyon sides had permitted the fatal leaks that brought the destruction of the siphon. Harvey Van Norman, having returned to Mojave from his inspection trip with Mulholland, now received an emergency phone call from Los Angeles.

"Sand Canyon siphon has failed," said the Chief.

Hurrying northward to the wrecked section, the two engineers surveyed the scene. Van Norman, riding a work sled lowered by a rope, went into the pipe and inspected its shattered sides. Above his head as he descended, great chunks of concrete hung from the reinforcing rods, threatening him as long as he remained in the hole. Returning to the surface, Van Norman made his report to Mulholland.

"There's nothing to do with this but put a steel siphon on the surface."

"Go ahead," returned the Chief. In a few days, work on the new pipe began alongside the old, and by early September water was flowing southward without interruption. Except for a short section of power piping in San Francisquito Canyon, the aqueduct was finished at last. Mulholland had built his big ditch in almost exactly the five years and $23,000,000 he had estimated—a remarkable distinction among municipal enterprises.

It had already been announced that the long-heralded ceremony for the aqueduct completion, scheduled for July before the Sand Canyon break, would be held on November 5, 1913. While the reservoirs on either side of Elizabeth Tunnel were allowed to fill, the people of Los Angeles made ready to celebrate the event with typical Southern California enthusiasm. An impressive aqueduct display was built at Exposition Park, formal dedication ceremonies were prepared at the man-made cascade north of the San Fernando reservoirs, and a final grand parade was planned for downtown Los Angeles.

No less exuberantly did Los Angeles—and all of California—turn to William Mulholland in the moment of his greatest triumph. The aqueduct was recognized across the country as the finest in America and second only to the Panama Canal as an engineering feat. The Chief was showered with honors, introduced everywhere as "the Goethals of the West" or "California's Greatest Man." Engineering societies gave him high awards and congratulations, while the University of California conferred on him an honorary doctor's degree.

Early in 1913, as a new mayoralty campaign loomed in Los Angeles, publisher E. T. Earl of the *Express* began campaigning for Mulholland as the city's next mayor. General Otis of the *Times* then wrote to Mulholland that for once Earl had made a suggestion with which he could agree. A committee of determined Angelenos waited on the water chief at his office and one by one recited to him the superlative qualifications which made him exactly suited for the city's highest office. Mulholland was clearly moved by their words. But when they had finished he solemnly put an end to the entire affair with a startling but typical reply:

"Gentlemen, I would rather give birth to a porcupine backwards than be mayor of Los Angeles."

Yet in his hour of success Mulholland was burdened with sorrow over the protracted illness of his wife, Lillian. Her confinement in a Los Angeles hospital during the last few months of aqueduct construction had made his days doubly wearisome. When he awoke each morning, his first move was to call the hospital for word of her status; as soon as he reached Los Angeles after every trip afield, his first steps led to her bedside. As the time for the aqueduct ceremony drew near, Mrs. Mulholland's condition turned suddenly worse, and her recovery was doubtful. When Mulholland left Los Angeles for the San Fernando cascade on November 5, he asked that any change in his wife's condition be reported to him at the dedication ceremony.

But though his wife's health weighed heavily on him, Mulholland's thoughts undoubtedly turned to the significance of the new aqueduct as his staff automobile carried him northward on that historic day. The waters of Owens River, he knew, had not come too soon. Though the city's own water system from the Los Angeles River had been successfully stretched to cover its increased customers, some half-dozen private water companies in the suburbs had been unable to meet demand during the hot days of the previous summer. There were instances where citizens had stayed up till early morning with their faucets wide open to catch enough drippings in pans for domestic needs the next day.

The nightmare of water famine would now be over; Mulholland himself would turn the waters of Owens River into the San Fernando Reservoir. From there water mains were almost completed to carry the vast new source to city water taps, with enough left over to irrigate a valley and provide for a population growth of two million.

At the San Fernando cascade Mulholland found a crowd of some forty thousand exuberant citizens, who had ridden from every point in the Southland by carriage, auto, and train. Climbing to the platform amid a welcoming ovation, he wearily took his seat among the notables of Los Angeles.

49

Immediately the ceremony began. The first speaker, a California congressman, opened with a declaration that captured the entire significance of the event.

"We are gathered here today to celebrate the coming of a king—for water in Southern California is king in fact if not in name."

At length the chairman introduced "the Honorable William Mulholland—the man who built the aqueduct." As though they had been holding themselves in readiness for this moment, the people rose to their feet, clapping and cheering, throwing handkerchiefs and hats in the air. Mulholland trudged forward from his seat, bent and tired, without notes or any idea of what he would say. But after gazing for a moment at the vast assembly, he opened with generous praise for all men who had built the aqueduct, from his top advisers to the humblest laborers.

"This rude platform," he concluded, "is an altar, and on it we are here consecrating this water supply and dedicating this aqueduct to you and your children and your children's children—for all time!"

He shuffled back to his seat in the midst of another ovation. A silver loving cup was presented to him, and another to Lippincott, who made a short speech of his own. Mulholland then stepped to a flagpole on the grandstand and unfurled the Stars and Stripes—an act that was the prearranged signal for the engineers at the top of the cascade to turn the great wheels and release the water. Instantly the crowd sent up its cheers once more, Army cannons boomed, a brass band played furiously.

Mulholland scarcely heard the pandemonium. His eyes were fixed on the gates above, half in wonderment, as though he feared the precious water might not appear. With painful slowness the metal gates rose. A trickle of water emerged and started downward. It grew to a stream, then to a raging torrent, churning and sparkling down the cascade. Just above the grandstand it sprayed over a rise in the incline and roared past toward San Fernando Reservoir.

The Chief took his seat with a sigh that was almost a sob. For a moment he closed his eyes. The tired spirit gave way to a smile. He threw back his head and laughed aloud.

"Well, it's finished!"

Without waiting for the scheduled presentation speeches, by which Mulholland was to turn the aqueduct over to the city, the multitude stampeded to the side of the cascade to watch the seething torrent. Mulholland and Mayor H. H. Rose, who was to receive the water for the city, were left virtually without an audience. With the roar of the water and his own emotion all but stifling his voice, Mulholland turned to the mayor and made the five-word speech that has become famous:

"There it is. Take it."

A few moments later word came to him that his wife had passed her crisis in the hospital and was now out of danger. The Chief went forward joyfully to join the crowd in taking a drink of Owens River water, relieved at last of two burdens that had made this day the climax of his life.

5: THE SEEDS OF CONFLICT

Notably absent from the 1913 dedication ceremonies at San Fernando was the man who conceived the Los Angeles Aqueduct —Fred Eaton. But Mulholland had not failed to mention his old friend as the "father" of the project in his preliminary speech. "He planned it," said the Chief. "We simply put together the bricks and mortar."

Yet even at that time an irreparable breach had begun to separate the two stalwarts who had laid the city's new water foundations. Fred Eaton was convinced that his Long Valley ranch would eventually be needed as a storage reservoir by the sprouting metropolis and was determined that he would not be so generous in its disposition as he had already been in allowing the aqueduct to be a non-profit municipal enterprise.

The city already held an easement to flood the valley with a 100-foot dam. Such a reservoir would contain some 68,000 acre-feet of water—only a fraction of Long Valley's capacity as a year-to-year regulator of supply. A 140-foot dam, according to Mulholland's Water Department report in 1907, would impound 260,000 acre-feet—enough to tide the city over dry years with "the full amount of 400 second-feet for which the aqueduct has been designed." But until Los Angeles had grown enough to need that amount Mulholland believed it was unnecessary to build the Long Valley Dam.

During construction of the aqueduct Fred Eaton talked with Mulholland and offered to sell the city the rest of the 12,000 acres in the Long Valley site. The price he asked was indefinite and based on the land's value to the city as a reservoir; but it was not less than a million dollars. Mulholland, taken aback by Eaton's figures, declined to buy.

On several other occasions Eaton made the same overtures, with growing resentment at Mulholland's repeated refusal to deal. For his part, the Chief was disappointed at Eaton's price demand and believed he was trying to take advantage of his

51

friendship for personal gain. At length the rift became an open break, with the two old friends refusing to meet each other.

"I'll buy Long Valley three years after Eaton is dead," Mulholland is credited with saying. It is a fact, however, that his bitterness on the subject was generally kept to himself. Eaton in turn refused to attend the dedication of the aqueduct in November 1913, with the forlorn excuse that because of autumn rains the first water to come down the cascade would not be true Owens River water.

The impasse caused the city to turn away from any idea of constructing more than a 100-foot dam while Eaton ruled Long Valley. Such a decision would eliminate a guarantee of ample water for irrigators in upper Owens Valley, and its farmers sought a water understanding with Los Angeles. With its aqueduct intake lying below the head gates of most of the irrigating ditches along Owens River, Los Angeles itself stood in need of an agreement with valley water users.

On April 5, 1913, a Los Angeles committee, including Mulholland and W. B. Mathews, met at Bishop with the heads of the valley ditch companies. A list of ten requests was presented by the farmers, and the city men promptly conceded all but one— the abandonment of power development in the Owens River gorge. In general the agreement guaranteed the rights of valley users in storing water and irrigating land without interference and committed the city to recognize the right of each ditch to a certain flow from Owens River.

The conference adjourned with what was hailed as a permanent settlement on Owens Valley water. Mulholland and Mathews left Bishop in an atmosphere of good will and optimism. If this agreement could have been fulfilled by both sides, it almost certainly could have forestalled the worst aspects of the Owens River controversy.

According to the understanding, the valley people brought a friendly suit against Los Angeles on July 2, to give the agreement legal force. But on the same day another suit was filed in Los Angeles to prevent the city from making an agreement on its water rights with the people of Inyo County. The plaintiff was one of the Socialist members of the "People's Board" which had investigated the aqueduct the year before. His backers are said to have been one of the Los Angeles electric companies, which was evidently moved to action by the city's insistence on municipal power development in the Owens River gorge. The injunction suit was thrown out of court the following spring, but it had served a tragic purpose in spiking the only real agreement ever made between Los Angeles and the Owens Valley irrigators.

52

By the end of 1914 the city officials had become wary of guaranteeing a certain flow to valley ditches without first determining the amount of water that would ordinarily be left for the aqueduct. There followed a series of delays, for which both city and valley people were responsible. Los Angeles men at length secured permission to gauge the flow in the irrigation ditches and submitted their figures in 1919. They were not acceptable to valley representatives, who thereupon took two more years to make their own measurements. When the two sides opened negotiations early in 1921, it was apparent that a 100-foot dam could not guarantee enough water for all in time of drought. In one meeting after another the ranchers insisted that only a dam at least 140 feet high could fulfill their needs.

But the growing rupture between valley and city forces did not prevent Water Department officials from opening construction on the 100-foot dam, which the astounding growth of Los Angeles was fast making necessary. Within a year diversion tunnels and other preliminaries had been made for a structure with a base large enough to support a later height of 150 feet, if and when a settlement could be made with Eaton.

Valley irrigators protested that this was no guarantee, and in May 1922 they filed suit to prevent Los Angeles from building its 100-foot dam. They would not allow any interference with the river's flow as long as their irrigation needs were not protected. Later Fred Eaton filed a similar suit on the grounds that no dam should be constructed which could ever create a higher reservoir than the 100-foot easement he had given the city.

If Eaton's purpose was to force Los Angeles to buy Long Valley, he was disappointed. The city stopped work on the dam after spending about $200,000. Neither suit was brought to trial; apparently both sides preferred to avoid a legal battle that might jeopardize their own water claims. Owens River was left uncontrolled, and the storage of ample water for all was tragically forestalled.

By the summer of 1921 it was plain that another drought period had struck California, and the opponents found themselves less concerned with intangible legalities than with an open struggle for the water itself. The seriousness of the shortage became apparent when a party of men invaded Long Valley in July of that year, tearing out some of Fred Eaton's irrigation dams on the mountain streams so that the water could reach Owens River. Part of the group were city men and part valley irrigators, who were supposed to have made this a rather general practice in times of drought.

As late as the spring of 1924, in spite of fiery protests from

Fred Eaton, crews of men were cutting his irrigation ditches. Harold Eaton, then manager of his father's cattle business, was riding along Convict Creek one day and came upon a group of them at work.

"What the hell you doin' here?" he demanded.

"We're going to turn the water back into the river," answered the leader, a Los Angeles representative.

"What'll you do," asked Eaton, "if I go get my shotgun?"

The other replied that he would have to wait and see. Tempers cooled in the conversation that followed and a clash was averted. But in the next few days the men continued to cut the Long Valley ditches. Fred Eaton then placed armed guards along his creeks and restricted the movements of every traveler through his valley.

"They say I am no longer a friend of the city," he told an inquirer. "I deny that. But if they try to take something of mine away from me I'll fight."

To Los Angeles, however, the matter of Eaton's ditches was now only a small part of a larger problem. By the early 1920s the drought cycle, together with the agricultural boom in San Fernando Valley, had placed Los Angeles under threat of another water famine.

Before the aqueduct's completion the city had accepted Mulholland's plan to use excess water only in adjacent farm sections likely to be absorbed in the spreading urban districts. In this way the growing city would never have to deprive the farmers of water, for their lands would gradually be transformed into residential areas as Los Angeles expanded. For such a purpose the San Fernando Valley was by nature the most practical, since over a third of its irrigation water found its way by seepage into the Los Angeles River to be used again by the city.

In May 1915 valley residents voted to join Los Angeles, starting the process of community annexations for water purposes which has given the city the biggest area of any metropolis in the world. Three weeks later the first Owens River water was sold for irrigation. San Fernando Valley, previously a sandy desert that had known only dry wheat farming, began to blossom. Orchards of walnuts and oranges, fields of vegetables and melons sprang up almost as fast as Mulholland's crews laid the city's water pipes. In the southern half of the valley, subdivided in 1911 by a group including General Otis and Harry Chandler of the *Times*, the new towns of Van Nuys and Lankershim (now North Hollywood) were booming with trade. From a total of 3000 crop acres in 1914, the valley's irrigated land spread to an astounding 75,000 acres three years later. Prices leaped from a few dollars per acre to an average of $300 after the coming of Owens River water—giving rise to a classic parody on a Julia Carney poem:

Little drops of water on little grains of sand,
Make a hell of a difference in the price of land.

When the first drought cycle was felt in 1921, San Fernando Valley was using an average of 104 second-feet for irrigation and the city's domestic consumers were taking 125 second-feet, about half of which was supplied by the Los Angeles River. During summer irrigation the valley used as high as 277 second-feet— an amount dangerously near Owens River's mean flow of less than 300 second-feet during the drought.

By the spring of 1923, Haiwee Reservoir was lowered to an alarming level. Mulholland was forced to make several arbitrary shutoffs of irrigation water in San Fernando Valley. Farms were soon suffering from water shortages that threatened the entire alfalfa crop. The aqueduct that had been built for fifty years of growth was already proving inadequate for Los Angeles, whose 576,000 census in 1920 had made it the largest metropolis in the West.

Mulholland's first recourse was to make heavy improvements in Owens Valley's water yield. For several years the city had been pumping water from its rich underground storage. But the water table was already sinking to remote depths, causing more than one farmer in the Independence area to bring injunction suits against municipal pumping. The disputes were almost invariably settled by the city's purchase of the plaintiff's property, but Mulholland knew this exigency could never solve the basic problem of dropping water levels. To get more water for the aqueduct, the department soon renewed the purchase of riparian rights in streams and canals, first in the ranches of the Independence area, and then farther up the river toward the communities of Big Pine and Bishop.

Most of the people in the upper valley saw the city's approach as a disrupting outside force that must be staunchly resisted. Otherwise, they told themselves, the fertile, mountain-bound homeland they had developed would suffer the same fate as the parched and sterile lower valley.

Leading this opposition were the two brothers who dominated the region's economic life, Wilfred and Mark Watterson. Their Inyo County Bank maintained offices in three, and later four, towns in the valley. In 1922 they had bought out the competing First National Bank of Bishop and made themselves the financial kings of eastern California. The role did not detract

55

from their unusual popularity; valley people liked to say of them that they never foreclosed a mortgage or sued a debtor.

Mark, the younger, was the good-natured mixer, inclined to follow the lead of his older and stronger brother. Wilfred, though more dignified and aloof, was nevertheless extremely well liked; when meeting with a group of men he had the ability, according to one observer, to "talk 'em out of their hind legs." His principal weakness was a disposition to invest in risky projects for quick reward—an obviously dangerous trait for a banker.

When his father, William Watterson, had headed the Inyo County Bank, Wilfred had argued in vain for investments in the mining enterprises then abounding in Inyo County. After the elder Watterson's death in 1912, however, Mrs. Eliza Watterson allowed her son to have his way in mining investments. The National Soda Springs Works at Keeler on Owens Lake, the vanadium and tungsten mines on the side of Mount Tom near Bishop, and several other concerns were absorbed by the brothers in the years that followed.

Beginning in 1921, the postwar recession that struck hard at the nation's farmers had forced a large number of Inyo settlers to mortgage their property to the Watterson bank. Thereafter the combination of persuasive ability and financial control gave the Wattersons unusual power in their domain.

When the idea of an irrigation district was brought forward in the spring of 1922 as a means of consolidating the valley's strength against Los Angeles, it was the Watterson brothers who quickly took the leadership in the movement. By turning over the water rights to the district, they urged their neighbors, they would be able to "tie the water to the land." The destiny of the upper valley would then be in the hands of the people as a whole and no longer open to slow conquest by Los Angeles land agents.

Opposition to the district came from another faction led by an uncle of the two bankers, George Watterson. An old and respected citizen of Inyo County, he had headed the valley water negotiations with Los Angeles until he broke with his nephews over the issue of the 140-foot dam, which he insisted would not be worth a costly fight with the city. George Watterson and his friends now argued that the bankers were trying to gain personal control of individual water rights through the proposed irrigation district.

But on December 26, 1922, the citizens of Big Pine and Bishop voted overwhelmingly for the Owens Valley Irrigation District. Wilfred Watterson was installed as president and Mark

Watterson as treasurer. Within a month the owners of all four of the main upper-valley ditches—Owens River Canal, Bishop Creek Ditch, McNally Ditch, and Owens River and Big Pine Canal— had voted to turn their water rights over to the district.

Before the transaction could be completed the Los Angeles Water Department, made desperate by drought, invaded the upper valley in spite of the irrigation district. In March 1923 the Los Angeles officials hired William Symons, president of McNally Ditch, to take options on all the ditch property on a commission basis.

"Leave no one out," he was instructed; "we want them all."

Constructed in 1877, McNally was the oldest large-sized canal on Owens River and hence carried an undeniable right to its 100 second-feet of water. It served most of the rich lands on the east side of the river in the Bishop area, making up an essential part of the new irrigation district. Symons quickly set about his task and retained Leicester C. Hall, a Bishop attorney, to aid him. Both were friends of George Watterson, leader of the anti-district group, who joined them without compensation in securing the options.

Within twenty-four hours the three men covered almost every farmhouse on the river. Offering an average of $7500 per second-foot, they took options on about eighty per cent of the McNally area—a total of more than a million dollars' worth of water.

The news was made known on the streets of Bishop on March 16, and the town fairly roared with indignation. Overnight the Los Angeles Water Department had invaded the upper valley and captured its eastern flank. The men who had taken the options kindled local wrath even higher by taking straightforward pride in their act. Attorney Hall justified it as a needed curb against the ambitions of the Wattersons and is said to have boasted that he had "cut off the left arm of the irrigation district."

But to almost every family in the Bishop area who did not oppose the Wattersons the three option takers became, as one newspaper characterized them, "traitors to this country." The battle lines at last were clearly drawn. From the purchase of McNally Ditch dates the real beginning of the Owens Valley water war.

To agents of the city the hostile farmers promised that no water secured by the McNally deal would ever be allowed to pass on down the river to the aqueduct. Despite threats of legal action from Los Angeles men, the head gates of other ditches below the McNally intake were soon taking in the extra flow of its water, and the irrigators were happily agreeing that the city purchase had solved a pressing water shortage.

Los Angeles agents in turn retaliated by going into the Bishop farm area and making indiscriminate purchases of land and water. The practice differed sharply from the policy shown on McNally and the ditches of the lower valley, which were bought in entirety by the offer of attractive prices, so that no individual farmers were left with the task of maintaining the entire ditch. It was claimed by the infuriated valley people that the option takers were deliberately "checkerboarding" the area to impress reluctant owners with the futility of resisting sale. City officials denied the charges; but if the "checkerboarding" was not deliberate, it had the same effect and produced the same reaction.

The most strategic ditch involved was the Owens River and Big Pine Canal, whose 100 second-feet of water rights irrigated more than half the lands around the town of Big Pine. Although a younger water filing than the McNally, and hence inferior to it in right of usage, the Big Pine Canal was some sixteen miles downstream from the city's newly won property. The Los Angeles water that was allowed to flow past the McNally Ditch toward the aqueduct intake ran the gamut of every head gate in the Bishop area, and if any was left it found its way into the waiting mouth of the Big Pine Canal. South of this head gate Owens River was as dry as the Mojave Desert during the summer months of 1923; whatever water the aqueduct carried was taken from side streams and wells in the lower valley.

The city's predicament in paying more than a million dollars for something it could not use became a prime joke among valley farmers and a serious problem for the Water Department. Legal proceedings against the diversions might take months. In the meantime Haiwee Reservoir, the main seasonal regulator for the aqueduct, was reduced to a scant 8000 acre-feet by the severe drought. Irrigation water in San Fernando Valley had been shut off for days at a time while crops withered and died. Los Angeles officials were ready for almost any measure that would bring an added share of Owens Valley water down the parched conduit.

City men first invaded the Big Pine area with cash and option papers, but its citizens formed themselves into a "pool" and demanded a total price equal to about $15,000 per second-foot. Refusing this offer, the agents turned to negotiations with the Owens Valley water users as a whole. In July the Board of Water Commissioners—the governing body for the department—met with W. W. Watterson and at his suggestion framed a proposal for a peaceful division of the river. The valley would guarantee that a third of the river's flow should be allowed to pass on down to the aqueduct, and the city would agree to refrain from further land and water purchases. To reach final agreement on this plan, W. B. Mathews and H. A. Van Norman traveled to Bishop for a mass meeting of the valley farmers set for August 13, 1923.

But when the proposal was first revealed to valley farmers, stout objection came from the Big Pine owners. They pointed out that, according to valley custom, water not used by any one ditch belonged to diversion points lower on the river. Undoubtedly the Big Piners, fully aware that they were the masters of the situation, did not want to submit to a general agreement without playing out their hand.

Apparently as a move to weaken the Big Pine position, city agents in the valley sent a crew of men, mules, and scrapers to Big Pine to take what one of them described as "primitive measures." On the same day as the scheduled meeting in Bishop, the Big Piners discovered the city grading equipment and the beginning of a cut opposite the mouth of their canal. Situated at the point of a U-bend in the meandering riverbed, the farmers' head gate would be left "high and dry" if a ditch were completed across that narrow neck of land.

Within a few minutes a carload of outraged men was bouncing out the old Bishop road to the home of George Warren, Big Pine's representative among the irrigation district directors. Warren, shrewd and self-possessed, had served for several years as president of the valley's Associated Chambers of Commerce. Quickly his friends described the emergency.

"We'll have to get an injunction!" one of them concluded.

Warren's view, however, was that the city's officials hoped by this means to precipitate a court decision on its water claims.

"We're not able to fight the city in court," he argued. "What we want is a shotgun injunction!"

Back to town the Big Piners rambled in their auto, stopping at farmhouses on the way to gather recruits. By late afternoon a staunch citizens' posse of some twenty men, armed with rifles and shotguns, headed eastward out of Big Pine. Crossing Owens River, they stationed themselves on the neck of land where the city's men had begun the cut.

Shortly afterward George Warren and another rancher followed a set of wagon tracks leading away through the brush to the place where the city employees were camped. In charge of the outfit was a man whom Warren knew as "One-eyed" Dodson. After an exchange of greetings, the Big Piner stated his business.

"Are you hired to fight for the city?" he demanded.

Dodson announced that he was not.

"Well, we've got our men over there on the river," he was told. "We don't want any shootin', but we're not going to let you make that cut."

One-eyed Dodson decided that he also wanted no shooting.

"We won't go back there till we hear from you," he agreed.

At the bend of the river the guardsmen heard Warren's report with satisfaction. They clinched the victory by throwing the city's grading equipment in the river and settled down to guard the head gate through the night.

With their strategic hold on Owens River maintained by "right of shotgun," the Big Piners sent a strongly backed delegation to the water meeting at Bishop that evening. While Van Norman and Mathews stood ready to sign the proposed agreement, W. W. Watterson presided and outlined it once again to the crowded room of farmers. In addition to the allotment of a third of the Owens River to Los Angeles, it provided for the abandonment of further city purchases, the lifting of the valley's suit against the 100-foot Long Valley Dam, and the construction of water wells by the city in the Bishop area, to be operated by the farmers in time of drought.

After Watterson had finished, it appeared that the city and the valley were ready to mend the crisis that was being emphasized with rifles a few miles to the south. But when the chairman asked if there was any criticism, George Warren stood up in his place with the Big Pine delegation.

"I have some criticism to make," he announced.

Warren then went over the agreement point by point, demanding why the irrigation district should be obliged to give away a third of its water, and in particular why Watterson himself had undertaken to be so generous. Other Big Pine speakers followed and pointedly asked the Los Angeles men whether they intended to complete the disputed cut if the agreement were denied. The city officials were noncommittal.

"I think we'd better have a recess and talk this thing over," decided Watterson, who had turned pale with anger at the unexpected Big Pine opposition.

"We don't need a recess," Warren shouted back. "That agreement is dead as hell!"

The negotiations collapsed. After a short discussion among groups of water users, Watterson reported to Van Norman and Mathews that the district could not allow any water to pass on down the river "so long as it was needed in the valley." Agreement was impossible without the co-operation of the Big Pine ditch owners, who had enforced their position with words as well as guns.

Within two days, during which the Big Pine riflemen relieved each other in a round-the-clock vigil, the city crew struck camp and departed. Up and down the valley the Big Pine affair was hailed as a first victory in the Los Angeles fight. It would stand out, declared the Independence paper, "as one of the prominent things that saved this valley."

"Los Angeles, it's your move now," challenged the Big Pine *Citizen.* "We're ready for you."

But it soon became apparent that the main effect of the Big Pine stand was to force a wholesale purchase by the city. Los Angeles agents had already invaded the area, and formal negotiations were promptly opened by the Water Department. At a stormy meeting on October 15, 1923, the Big Pine owners voted to sell 4416 acres and the water rights to Los Angeles for $1,100,000—a price which made more than one rancher financially independent.

Some of the owners and their families, attached to the land by ties stronger than money, opposed sale at any price but bitterly agreed to the offer rather than be forced to maintain the entire Big Pine Canal themselves. It was such minority farmers, selling against their will, who naturally held a real grievance against the Los Angeles invasion. Yet their hatred was caused more by fear than actual harm; in cases where isolated ranchers did not sell, their full share of water was scrupulously delivered by the Los Angeles Water Department. Nor did the city take a single piece of land or water by condemnation or unlawful means; in practically every case its prices were above the valley market, though not equaling the actual value of the water as applied in Southern California.

The people's principal objection was the atmosphere of uncertainty which the city's opportunist methods cast over the valley. Where indiscriminate buying was employed, individual ranchers feared their neighbors would sell out and leave them isolated. If entire ditches were purchased, the townspeople of Bishop and Big Pine noted with dismay a wholesale exodus of customers they had served for years. In the neglected orchards and abandoned farmhouses the people as a whole saw a stark contrast to the undisturbed scene in Owens Valley before the city came.

Valley hatred was further inflamed when the anti-Watterson forces, led by lawyer L. C. Hall, took steps to prevent the concentration of water rights in the irrigation district. Bonds were issued by the district to buy the stock of the ditch companies, but Hall, presumed to be acting on behalf of the city, was able to disrupt the transaction by legal proceedings in February 1924. This frustration of plans was the final provocation for the upper-valley farmers.

Though their irrigation district had been spiked, they still retained possession of the water itself. Los Angeles men found that in spite of the McNally and Big Pine purchases most of the water they had bought twice was still being diverted into the private ditches in the upper valley. Obviously the farmers were determined that the city should not settle its water problem simply by amputating two ditches from the rest of the district. The generous prices paid for the McNally and Big Pine canals had suddenly impressed them with the value of their water to the city of Los Angeles. By continuing to withhold the water already bought, they meant to make the city officials "buy us all, or leave us alone."

6:   CALIFORNIA'S CIVIL WAR

By early 1924 the valley population was so aroused that unified action came hurriedly and with deadly earnestness. At meetings held in local ranch houses, plans were laid for a long fight against Los Angeles. These sessions developed a leadership which earned a general allegiance. Most dominant, of course, were Wilfred and Mark Watterson, whose personal charm and financial power had already influenced valley affairs for years. Chief among the ranchers was Karl Keough, whose family had first settled in the valley in the 1870s. Ordinarily hearty and easygoing, Keough displayed such steel nerve and cool judgment in a crisis that his leadership was almost automatic. He held the presidency of the Owens River Canal, largest of all the valley ditches, which tapped the river above Bishop and paralleled the main stream some fourteen miles to his own resort at Keough Hot Springs.

Providing invaluable publicity for the cause was Harry Glasscock, the tall, swashbuckling editor of the Owens Valley *Herald*. A brother of the Western author, Carl B. Glasscock, the headstrong newspaperman was indeed the firebrand of the valley's fight. Although Willie Chalfant, editor of the rival Inyo *Register*, was more generally respected and equally as adamant against the city, it was Glasscock whose newspaper and publicity contacts were wholly at the disposal of the valley's leadership.

In addition to a general mobilization, the more extreme element in the Bishop area formed a secret organization to back up the irrigation district's stand with force, if that became

62

necessary. During the summer of 1923, while a revival of the Ku Klux Klan was raging throughout the nation, an organizer was brought into Owens Valley to help form its own band of Klansmen. An inner group of this faction took as its main purpose an underground opposition to the Los Angeles water board and its representatives. Night meetings were held in open fields, where auto headlights were turned outward to prevent the approach of any eavesdropping city agents.

One of this group's first moves was a series of night visitations to homes of those who had opposed the irrigation district. George Watterson, L. C. Hall, and Bill Symons were all told that their further presence in Owens Valley was at the risk of their lives.

The demands were met with equal firmness from the threatened men, who held that they were the real defenders of the valley. All three secured gun permits and began carrying revolvers for self-protection. Bill Symons of McNally Ditch habitually carried a double-barreled shotgun whenever he drove his team into Bishop. When George Watterson was threatened a second time, his husky young son Alfred accosted Mark Watterson in front of the Bishop bank.

"If anything happens to my father," he told him in a rage, "I'll hold you accountable."

More than once L. C. Hall was asked by Sheriff Charles Collins to leave the valley and ease the situation. At length the officer asked the state attorney general how he might secure Hall's departure.

"If he wants to commit suicide," said the official, "you're not responsible."

Finally Hall was prevailed upon to restrict his operations in Bishop. He remained in the upper valley, however, and a few months later—on August 27, 1924—caused a sensation by appearing once more on the streets of the town. A band of determined men met and apparently decided that if their supremacy was to be maintained the time had come to fulfill the threats that had been so openly disregarded.

While Mark Watterson paced back and forth, surveying the scene from across the street, three or four men entered a restaurant where Hall was eating at the counter. Without a word they seized him, snatched the gun from his belt and, while the startled patrons watched in amazement, hustled him out the back door with a strong arm about his neck. He was placed in a car in the alley, and in a moment an escort of four autos raced southward out of Bishop, carrying a grim force of some twenty-five men. Hall was almost unconscious when the grip on his neck

63

was released after a few minutes' drive. It was then made plain to him that he was to be hanged as a valley traitor.

A few moments later the caravan passed a man walking along the road; the fear that he might identify the cars and their occupants caused a sudden disruption in plans. Several stops were made while the leaders hurriedly conversed. Hall was taken out of the car more than once in the confusion, during which he took opportunity to argue his own defense.

"I'm fifty-two years old," he told his captors with as much composure as possible, "and I've done nothing to be ashamed of. You're allowing your prejudice to make you commit a crime you'll have on your consciences for the rest of your lives."

At one stop near a cottonwood tree a rope was produced, and Hall was taken from the car once more.

"Give my regards to the Wattersons," he remarked bitterly. "They're the ones behind this."

When Hall believed his minutes were numbered, he gave voice to a distress signal known to the Masonic fraternity. Several men in the group surrounding him were Masons. One in particular showed evidence that he had been moved by this call from a lodge brother. It was soon apparent that this last resort had saved Hall's life.

More conferences were held, and the caravan then headed southward again under a final change of plans. Hall was taken to Big Pine, where he was released at the home of George Warren with orders to leave the county and never return. Next day, after Sheriff Collins had arrived and advised him to leave, Hall made his way out of the valley that had been his home for most of the past twenty years. He established a law practice in Southern California and lived in retirement at his home in Glendale for many years.

Finding their deed unchallenged by the law, the extremists in the upper valley began extending their threats to Los Angeles employees. The right-of-way and land agent, who had been particularly active in "checkerboard" purchases, was visited by a delegation and told to leave the valley.

His place as the city's chief local representative was taken by Edward F. Leahey, a husky, red-haired Irishman who was respected by most citizens as a man of straightforward methods. Leahey had grown with the Water Department since the days of aqueduct construction and was already acquainted with the valley situation after several years of employment there. A man of quick wit and decisive movements, he was big enough physically to carry a certain assurance in spite of his uncomfortable position on top of the valley powder keg. Inevitably the business of "running people out of the valley" was mentioned to him one day in his Bishop office by one of the Klan members.

"Don't think much of it," snapped Leahey.

"If your life was threatened, what would you do?"

"I'd kill just as many as I could draw a bead on!"

If this challenge was not relayed to Klan headquarters, it at least became common knowledge among Bishop's radical group. Members may have failed to exercise every threat against their enemies, but it was not from a lack of conviction. They possessed a calculated sense of how far their lawlessness could be carried without hurting their own cause.

It was in March 1924 that the withholding of water by the Bishop farmers began to aggravate the drought conditions already prevailing. With consumption in Los Angeles often running higher than the aqueduct's flow into Haiwee Reservoir, Southern California once more faced a dangerous water shortage. Mulholland was in Washington when he was notified of the situation and promptly wired the Water Department to shut off irrigation altogether in San Fernando Valley. Out of the Los Angeles office came a crisp notice: "No water is to be delivered to open lands for field crops until we get a rainfall."

Faced with crop destruction, a party of seven leading San Fernandans headed for Owens Valley to buy 50,000 acre-feet of water. In Bishop they were greeted cordially by valley leaders, were shown the two main canals running brim full, and then were told that "not one drop of water" was for sale. They were informed, however, that the entire area—both land and water—could be delivered in forty-eight hours for a total of $8,000,000, including $750,000 in reparations to placate the Bishop merchants. At last the upper valley had found a strategic opportunity to state its own terms of sale.

Back to San Fernando went the delegation. At an Associated Chambers of Commerce meeting on March 18 they made a discouraging report. Mulholland, having returned from Washington, attended the meeting himself and helped to prevent any serious consideration of the Bishop proposal.

Yet it was soon obvious that the valley's stand would not depend on a single rejection. Starting on April 2, a publicity campaign was actively opened with a series of articles in Hearst's San Francisco *Call* under the provocative title, "The Valley of Broken Hearts." Written by a former Owens Valley newspaperman and a brother-in-law of the Wattersons, the articles reported the aqueduct controversy to all of California for the first time. They spoke in particular of the reversion of unwatered valley lands to desert and of the city's "relentless" land-buying methods. In many instances, it was said, "men and women have blotted their signatures with tears." The city now had the choice, concluded the articles, of building its Long Valley Dam and guaranteeing water to the Bishop users, or proceeding to buy out the entire valley. Of the two, the people now favored an $8,000,000 sale instead of the dam as an end to the "weary problem."

The *Call* series was effective enough in stating the valley's case; what followed gave it an emphasis that could not be overlooked. On May 10 the city filed suit against the remaining valley canals for recovery of McNally and Big Pine water which they were "wrongfully diverting." The move was taken as final legal action to underline the city's water priority in its McNally filings, the oldest on the river. Though the suit was to be expected in consequence of the valley's diversion of all the river water, it nevertheless threw the people into renewed anger.

Whether in retaliation against this new threat or as part of a deliberate scheme, a body of about forty men met south of Bishop on the evening of May 20, 1924, with three boxes of dynamite taken from the Watterson powder house at the railroad station. Someone later complained that there were so many eager volunteers in the plot that they hindered its efficiency.

In a caravan of eleven cars they filed down the valley highway and passed through Independence with lights extinguished and license plates removed, while the town's population stood gaping. A few miles north of the town of Lone Pine they pulled off the road alongside the Alabama Hills and began their work. Part of the crew was detailed to watch for signs of aqueduct patrolmen; another group set about disrupting nearby telephone lines. Three carloads of men drove to a covered spillway gate in the open-ditch portion of the Los Angeles Aqueduct. There they placed the dynamite against the cement gate and attached fifty feet of fuse.

Shortly after 1 a.m., Lone Pine was awakened as if by an earthquake. At the place of explosion great blocks of concrete were thrown high in the air, cutting telephone and power lines, and landing as far as a quarter of a mile away. The spillway gates themselves were tossed fifty feet up the mountainside. Forty feet of the concrete ditch were blasted away, but a great shower of rocks and debris fell back into the hole and prevented more than five or six second-feet of water from escaping.

The dynamiters, scarcely anxious to review their work, were already scattering over the byroads near Independence to find their way back to Bishop later. Within an hour the entire lower valley was alive with activity. City employees discovered the break and began piling up dirt-filled gunny sacks to stop the loss of the precious water. Sheriff Charles Collins and District Attorney Jess Hession arrived promptly, followed by their deputies and investigators.

In Los Angeles, Mulholland and the water board went before the City Council that morning with the news, and $10,000 reward was quickly offered for the authors of the "dastardly" crime. Squads of deputy sheriffs, city police, and detectives rattled northward in open cars and were on the scene by early afternoon in search of clues. Close behind them was the city's newspaper contingent. The *Times* sent a photographer in an Army plane from Clover Field to circle the area and wing southward again with the first shots of the break.

The carload of reporters arriving in the valley found its citizens grimly sympathetic with the dynamiters but sternly silent to any queries about their identity. The first excitement had passed when most of the city newsmen gathered on the steps of the Dow Hotel in Lone Pine to discuss the occurrence with editor Harry Glasscock of Bishop. One young reporter from the Los Angeles *Herald* arrived full of questions about the names of the dynamiters and how they had planned the blow. Though his indiscretion met with icy silence from the bystanders, he continued to press eagerly for answers. At length the exasperated Harry Glasscock accosted him and demanded that he head back for Los Angeles.

"If you don't leave," he warned when the man hesitated, "I'll shoot you!"

At the time Harry wore a revolver in a side holster, and the young reporter did not dally in his departure. Glasscock returned to his conversation and the other pressmen made a mental note of proper valley etiquette.

The hospitality displayed by the Bishop editor, in fact, was no stronger than sentiment throughout Owens Valley. In the streets of Bishop the blowup was the universal topic. Many observed that it was done to warn the city and "protect our homes." E. F. Leahey, the city's representative in Owens Valley, received word to stay out of Bishop—a warning he promptly disregarded without harm. When other city investigators came to Bishop as the most likely source of the trouble, the citizens held a closed meeting, discussed a proposal to run them out of town, and finally voted it down as too extreme. Glasscock's Owens Valley *Herald* openly called the dynamiting "merely the protest of an outraged people."

"There is a limit," he declared, "to what a law-abiding people can stand."

Feeling was further inflamed when Mulholland, outraged at this attack on the water source for which he felt such a responsibility, made public statements against Owens Valley ranchers. Word came immediately for him to stay out of Bishop to avoid being lynched.

"They wouldn't have the nerve," the old man growled defiantly. "I'd just as soon walk the whole length of Owens Valley unarmed."

He afterward traveled through the valley, including Bishop, whenever occasion required. But a cousin, who was stopping at an Independence hotel, discreetly registered himself under an alias rather than sign the name "Mulholland."

If the men who dynamited the aqueduct intended it, as was claimed, as a warning to the city to "speed up action," they were wholly successful. Within five days the valley was invited to send a delegation to discuss the water situation with the Los Angeles Chamber of Commerce. In a matter of hours W. W. Watterson, Karl Keough, and four other representatives headed southward to confer with the Chamber's committee.

Later the Los Angeles group returned the visit and inspected Owens Valley first hand. They went back to the city filled with valley sentiment and turned in a report calling on the water board to buy the remaining property at prices fixed by a board of arbitrators—a proposal which Watterson had assured them would be satisfactory. The valley's indignation was not relieved when the Chamber report was withheld from the public because, as the water board later explained, the committee's investigation "consisted almost entirely of interviewing Mr. W. W. Watterson and his associates."

A few days later the upper valley played host to the editorial staff of the Los Angeles *Record*, a Scripps-Howard newspaper specializing in exposés. When the newsmen departed, Wilfred Watterson had gained a permanent ally in Los Angeles. On June 24 the *Record* startled its readers with the headline, "City's Water Supply in Danger," and the warning, "Blood may color the aqueduct water and a real explosion choke this city with thirst." In a series of front-page articles it described the valley's plight, emphasized the bitter feeling of its citizens, and proposed that the city buy valley land with prices fixed by a disinterested commission.

Next came a three-man engineering board headed by no less a valley acquaintance than J. B. Lippincott. Its purpose was to examine the water resources of Owens River and report to the water commissioners on possible methods of dividing it between city and valley. In an official report on August 14, 1924, the engineers claimed that proper water development would allow permanent irrigation of 30,000 acres in Owens Valley and still provide just enough water in dry years for a full aqueduct. The revelation was at the same time a blow to valley hopes for wholesale purchase and a welcome feeling of independence to the Board of Water Commissioners.

Armed with the water knowledge in the Lippincott report, the entire board, accompanied by Mulholland, Mathews, Van Norman, and a corps of stenographers and newspapermen, arrived in the valley to confer with its leaders early in September. At a public meeting in Bishop, W. W. Watterson told them that the only fair solution was to buy the whole district at a price which included compensation for damages already done. Before the water board left the valley its chairman was ready to promise that everything possible would be done to reach a fair understanding. "There is no question but mistakes have been made," admitted one of the commissioners.

If the valley men believed they had induced the water board to buy their entire irrigation district, they were promptly disillusioned. On October 14 the commissioners announced their long-sought policy on Owens River in a resolution to "keep 30,000 acres green." Acting on the findings in the Lippincott report, they offered to set aside that amount of land free of city purchase and to do all in their power to develop surface and underground water "to at least insure a full supply for said irrigated areas and the aqueduct." They further promised, in compensation for loss of business from previous land purchases, to help build up the valley communities by highway and transportation improvements that would increase tourist trade.

As soon as the text of the resolution reached Owens Valley, Wilfred Watterson called a meeting of the irrigation district directors. In a bitter counterresolution they rejected the proposal as "unacceptable."

On the surface its basic weakness was that it provided no concrete compensation to the townspeople for their loss of trade. But underlying the disagreement was a more subtle clash of purposes. At that time Los Angeles officials needed no more valley water than they had already bought and intended to concede little more than necessary to secure it free passage past the valley head gates and into the aqueduct. Valley people, on the other hand, would not overlook the inroads already made. Their weapon was the water the city had purchased, and they would neither relinquish it nor make a compromise agreement until Los Angeles bought the entire irrigation district in a lump settlement. It was now they, and not the water commissioners, who desired the sale of the upper valley.

The Bishop people were also aware of the city's need for a peaceable population at the source of its water supply. Valley newspapers did not hesitate to mention this factor in their violent reactions to the city's proposal.

"The people here have shown that they can protect their homes," cried Harry Glasscock in his Owens Valley *Herald*, "and they will show it again if it becomes necessary."

The Big Pine *Citizen* added that if the people of Los Angeles could not be convinced of "the seriousness of our situation here we will be compelled to use other means to try and save complete destruction of our homes and businesses."

Evidently the decision to take drastic action was made by valley leaders soon after the water board's announcement. When Van Norman and Mathews reached Bishop to negotiate the agreement early in November, Watterson and his irrigation district spokesmen went through the motions of a formal meeting but neither accepted nor rejected the proposals. Six days after the city men left with negotiations still pending, Owens Valley's citizens took steps to pass over the head of the water board and bring their plight to the forcible attention of the state of California.

On the morning of November 16, 1924, between sixty and a hundred men, led by Mark Watterson and Karl Keough, left Bishop in a cavalcade of automobiles and paraded southward through Independence with drawn shades. A mile north of the spot previously dynamited they pulled up at the Alabama Gates, one of the main points provided for turning floodwaters out of the aqueduct. Without delay they climbed up the hill, took possession of the control house, and turned the wheels that opened the gates beneath. A flood of some 290 second-feet of water churned down the spillway, splashed across the highway, and made its way over the valley floor to the dry bed of the Owens River. Not a drop continued down the great cement trough of the Los Angeles Aqueduct.

The gatekeeper came running to protest, but he was simply ignored. Sheriff Charles Collins, who had seen the caravan pass through Independence, arrived soon after and went through the futile motion of asking the men to desist. When he began to write down a list of those present, they crowded about, each one insisting that he "put my name down." He was told that the party would keep possession of the gates "until we gain our point."

When news of the seizure was conveyed to Ed Leahey,

the city's representative in the valley, he disregarded a warning to stay away from the gates. Driving southward from Bishop, he stopped at Independence to demand that the county authorities accompany him to the scene. When this was refused he wheeled down to the Alabama Gates.

Leaving his car at the foot of the hill, Leahey started hiking up the slope beside the roaring spillway to the wheelhouse above. Through one of its windows a noose suddenly appeared and dangled before his eyes.

Leahey could do nothing but assume that the macabre warning did not exist. When he reached the top Mark Watterson, Keough, and four others came out of the house.

"You armed?" someone asked.

The city official threw open his coat to show that he was not. There was an embarrassing pause, during which someone asked if Leahey would "have some coffee."

"Who's in charge here?" he asked abruptly.

"We're all in charge," returned Mark Watterson.

"You can't contend we have no right to this water," he told them. "It's not hurting anybody going down the ditch."

"Don't you realize," Watterson retorted, "that, whether people are damaged or think they are, the effect is the same?"

"You can tell Mathews and Mulholland that we're going to stay here till they settle with us," added someone else.

The city representative realized the demonstration was no sudden outbreak, but a calculated effort to bring Los Angeles to terms.

"If you try to close these gates we'll make our own gates," warned Watterson as Leahey made ready to leave.

The last was a veiled reference to a cache of dynamite understood to be hidden in the hill behind the gates. Though the men displayed no guns, they were determined to hold off any attempt to recapture the aqueduct.

Leahey immediately phoned Mathews in Los Angeles. Two carloads of detectives and investigators were hurriedly dispatched from the city. When the valley people heard of their coming, a band of embattled settlers gathered in Bishop to demand arms from the Watterson hardware store. Sheriff Collins, frantically trying to prevent bloodshed, rushed southward and met the Los Angeles men below Lone Pine.

"If you go up there and start any trouble," he warned, "not one of you'll get back to tell the tale."

It is said that the investigators left Owens Valley without a look at the Alabama Gates.

But the next contingent of Los Angeles men was more warmly received. By nightfall a squad of newsmen arrived to find the seizure operation working efficiently. Two aqueduct searchlights had been commandeered and now converged on their auto as it approached. Barbed wire had been spread at the base of the hill, where a sentry challenged them on the single path that led up to the gates. But when Harry Glasscock came down and vouched for them, they were roundly welcomed at the wheelhouse and allowed to sleep there through the night among the forty men who guarded the gates, while the aqueduct water continued to thunder down the cascade toward Owens River.

But already the city water board was taking hurried action. Up from Los Angeles on the night train came S. B. Robinson, able assistant to Mathews in the Water Department's legal counsel. Ed Leahey met him with an auto at Lone Pine, and while passing the spillway the two were stopped by a crew of guardsmen, who allowed them to pass after a few apprehensive moments.

Next morning at Independence, Robinson demanded an injunction against the spillway gang from Inyo's respected superior judge, William D. Dehy. A temporary restraining order was issued, but when Sheriff Collins served seventy-five copies of it at the spillway, the group gave him a polite but firm refusal. To his chagrin several of the men threw the documents into the rushing spillway.

"No, Sheriff," said one of them, "we won't leave here until the state troops come in and put us out. We haven't been treated right and we're going to stick until we have let the state and the country know the facts."

To show him they felt no ill will at his official act, several of them jokingly picked up the dignified officer as he was leaving and carried him in a sitting position to his automobile.

With the injunction ignored, Robinson demanded that Judge Dehy issue warrants for the arrest of the men at the gates. The magistrate then replied by declaring himself disqualified to act "by personal interest." The move also invalidated the injunction he had issued, and the men were left without any legal restraint whatever. The same day Karl Keough gave emphasis to the situation with an announcement to the press.

"We are here to keep this spillway open. We will stay here until we are driven out or dragged out."

By noon on the seventeenth more than twenty women had arrived from Bishop and were serving their husbands a picnic lunch. From every community in the valley people were arriving all day long, either to stand by and view the scene with

72

satisfaction or to take an active part in supporting the original contingent. Soon the spillway seizure became a grand Owens Valley reunion. Ranchers and businessmen gathered about the campfires in cheerful conversation while their wives brought hot meals from homes in Independence. Even the minister of the Bishop Baptist Church was on "the hill" with the rest.

"I am here because most of my congregation is here," he explained.

In Bishop, where practically every store was closed, a large sign had been placed on the flagpole in the center of town: "If I am not on the job, you will find me at the Aqueduct."

On the eighteenth, more than seven hundred persons were constant participants in the demonstration; stoves, tents, and beds were erected for a more permanent camp. Movie star Tom Mix and his company, then on location in the Alabama Hills, visited the gathering and contributed an orchestra.

Next day the crowd had a huge barbecue, supplied with food by Bishop butchers and grocerymen. Fifty Bishop housewives each made a pie and arrived at the spillway with their children to officiate at the picnic. Mrs. Harry Glasscock came later after running off the weekly issue of her husband's paper, which carried a rousing news story on the seizure. Everyone in the valley was invited, including S. B. Robinson and the city's employees. Even Sheriff Collins joined the throng which gathered on the hill to enjoy Owens Valley's best barbecued beef.

But behind the carefree atmosphere was an earnestness of purpose in their presence at the Alabama Gates. Late in the day the crowds gathered wearily about the campfires, the women sitting beside their husbands, holding the smaller children. The Baptist minister produced his church hymnbooks, and soon the heavy strains of "Onward, Christian Soldiers" issued from several hundred throats and swept across the valley. Below them the water continued to roar down the spillway for the fourth consecutive day. On the edge of the aqueduct near the wheelhouse a woman was silently watching the flow when someone pointed out the tiny blades of grass that had begun to sprout along the edge of the stream.

"Yes, that is the lifeblood of this valley," she observed thoughtfully, "and if they'd just let it circulate the valley would come back to life."

It was no coincidence that the seizure occurred at a time when Wilfred Watterson was in Los Angeles to outline valley grievances to the city's banking organization, the Clearing House Association. In a meeting on November 18, the third day of the aqueduct seizure, he addressed the bankers for an hour on the water dispute, recommending the purchase of the irrigation district for "between $12,000,000 and $15,000,000."

The Clearing House members then told Watterson with ill-concealed anger that there could be "no talk of conference and compromise" while he stood there "defending the lawlessness of the Bishop mob." It is said they also told him that if he did not get the gates closed they would shut off his bank's credit.

At the same time the Los Angeles newspapers were outraged at what the *Examiner* called the "big card" in a "gigantic holdup scheme." The *Express* accused the ranchers of "pure vandalism" in wasting Los Angeles water and joined the *Examiner* in demanding that they be tried and punished. But the *Record*, whose policy had favored the valley for months, insisted that the ranchers were "fighting for their homes and the right to exist." It was the *Times* which struck a middle attitude:

"These farmers are not anarchists nor bomb throwers, but in the main honest, hardworking American citizens." Admitting "a measure of justice on their side of the argument," the paper called for restraint from the ranchers and generosity from the city. "There must be no civil war in Southern California."

But the story of "California's little civil war" was already being headlined across the nation, covered by an article in the *Literary Digest*, and featured in newspapers as far away as France and Sweden. California's own press, while deploring a resort to force, was generally supporting the ranchers and demanding that Los Angeles submit the case to arbitration.

Before long the unfavorable publicity was affecting farm immigration into Southern California, and a Los Angeles commercial group sent circulars to 750 California editors asking them to call off the attack. That this pro-valley campaign may not have been spontaneous in every case is suggested by the claim of the Wattersons a few months later that "we have spent in actual cash, for publicity and otherwise, over $30,000" in the fight against Los Angeles.

But the city water board would not be high-pressured into a change of policy as long as its water supply remained in hostile hands. Haiwee Reservoir was already low from another year of drought, and a prolonged loss of water would eventually be felt in the city itself. To lawyer Mathews the board gave the peremptory order to "get the aqueduct back in the possession of Los Angeles. . . ."

The Los Angeles county sheriff was then prevailed upon to get in touch with the sheriffs of Kern and Ventura counties and assure their help if needed in the crisis. To the harassed Sheriff

74

Collins of Inyo County came a wire describing the force available in Southern California to aid in dispersing the mob.

Collins was too busy to answer the offer. For three days he had been carrying on frantic correspondence by wire with Governor Friend W. Richardson to secure the state militia which the spillway mob seemed to desire.

"Confident party will disperse and bloodshed be averted," he telegraphed, "only by arrival of state troops."

"You have abundant power to control the situation," answered the governor. "Do your duty bravely and in the end you will receive commendation."

Collins wanted troops, not commendation. He repeated his request in a second telegram: "Please send them forthwith."

"I hope you will do your duty fearlessly," returned Governor Richardson. "People elect sheriffs to stand up and prove their courage."

That kind of courage, Collins knew, would not withstand the next valley election. Inyo's District Attorney Hession then stepped into the dispute; after being driven at top speed to Mojave, he caught a train for Sacramento and appealed to the governor personally for a corps of militia. But Richardson had already sent a special investigator and considered that action sufficient. This one element in the well-laid plans of the aqueduct seizers was a significant failure; a cool-headed governor would not give their act the publicity of a dispersal by state militia.

But on the night of the nineteenth word from another quarter made a heavy impression on the spillway people. Wilfred Watterson had sent a telegram from Los Angeles to his brother at the Alabama Gates:

"If the object of the crowd at the spillway is to bring their wrongs to the attention of the citizens of Los Angeles, then they have done so 100 per cent. . . . I have the assurance that strong influence here will be brought to bear on the situation to see that justice is done."

Shortly afterward Watterson himself arrived in the valley and met with a twelve-man delegation from the spillway at his soda works at Keeler on Owens Lake. There he explained that the Los Angeles Clearing House Association had finally agreed to use its "best efforts with the business interests of this city to bring about an equitable settlement" if the ranchers would give up the aqueduct.

The group then returned to the spillway and early on the morning of the twentieth turned the great wheels in the control house that lowered the Alabama Gates. The four-day stream that had flowed across Owens Valley to the river was made dry, and once more the full flow of the aqueduct went hurtling on its way down the cement ditch to Haiwee Reservoir.

Early in the day people began arriving from both ends of of the valley for a final barbecue to celebrate the end of the long vigil. Some fifteen hundred persons assembled on the hill, joined in community songs, and listened with moistened eyes to encouraging speeches from W. W. Watterson and others. Before sundown the crowd broke camp and left historic Alabama Gates, which stand today to the left of the highway four miles north of Lone Pine.

To District Attorney Jess Hession at Sacramento, tired Sheriff Collins dispatched a wire urging that the governor be asked to see that the Los Angeles banking group carry out its intentions: "The farmers assert that the city officials never have kept a single promise and if the Clearing House fails to keep faith I look for hell to pop!"

Nine days after the gate closure W. W. Watterson submitted to the Clearing House Association a written statement of valley grievances and three alternate proposals for settlement: 1. Keep 30,000 acres green, but give damaged property owners $5,300,000 in "reparations." 2. Buy the entire irrigation district for $12,000,000, including reparations. 3. Buy the district at a price set by a disinterested board of arbitration.

The Water Department then submitted its own version of the Owens Valley controversy to the association, answering Watterson's charges paragraph by paragraph. As for the main grievance against land purchases, it was pointed out that top prices were paid to valley owners without condemnation or compulsion: "If the city did wrong in buying, they did wrong in selling." But against the claim that the shrinking population had damaged the trade of the townspeople, the city had little reasonable defense. Its only argument against reparations was a cold statement of nonresponsibility:

"Such losses, while very regrettable, are among the hazards which all must take in buying property or establishing a business, and cannot be the basis of a legal claim for compensation."

This aloof attitude over the plight of the valley townspeople was probably the most ill-considered decision of the water board. Its members seemed to believe that because the city could not legally be made to pay reparations it was justified in disclaiming any interest in the valley whose life it had affected root and branch.

Undoubtedly the idea was born of a distrust of the Watterson brothers and a feeling that the issue was a battle of wits between them and the water board. Reluctance to concede to

76

these archenemies made the city officials unreceptive to the idea of any compensation. Though the Watterson reparations figure of $5,300,000 was certainly too high, the Los Angeles men apparently made no effort to negotiate an equitable settlement.

Either because of the arguments of the water board or a falling out which developed between Watterson and the chairman of the Clearing House Association, that body soon abandoned its efforts for a solution. The bitter assumption in the valley was that the association's promise to arbitrate had been given only to gain back the aqueduct.

There remained as an opportunity for settlement the efforts of the governor's special agent, State Engineer Wilbur F. McClure, who reached the valley on the last day of the spillway seizure. As McClure had been a Methodist minister in Owens Valley in the early 1900s, his appointment as state investigator in the water crisis was not considered unfortunate by its citizens. After a month of investigation and a meeting with the the Los Angeles water board, he sent a hundred-page report to Sacramento completely endorsing the ranchers' stand.

"The valley does not desire to be big-brothered," he summarized, "but go its own way, and insists that if the parental idea plan is to be insisted upon, the would-be big brother should be willing to pay well for the privilege of exercising such domination."

But aside from its publicity value McClure's report had little concrete effect. Governor Richardson must have believed the crisis was over with the closing of the Alabama Gates. So, apparently, did the Los Angeles water board, whose chairman is said to have exclaimed on hearing of the gate closure, "The publicity stunt has failed!"

Even W. W. Watterson, realizing that in the spillway seizure Owens Valley had reached a high tide of unity, afterward chastised himself for closing the gates prematurely. Never again would they have the city at the same disadvantage.

7:    "WE WHO ARE ABOUT TO DIE"

The efforts toward negotiation after the gate seizure had now failed. Obviously it was time, as Sheriff Collins had feared, for "hell to pop!" But before valley leaders could take the initiative, circumstances forced the Water Department to make a sudden and agreeable change of policy.

Los Angeles—and all of Southern California—was in the midst of its greatest boom. During the drought of the twenties the city found itself engulfed with a flood of Easterners that doubled its population to more than 1,000,000. An oil boom in Long Beach and a motion picture boom in Hollywood were underwriting the Southland's prosperity. New luxury hotels, a coliseum, a giant city hall were rising to make Los Angeles look the part of a metropolis. Great new suburbs and cities sprang up as Los Angeles moved westward to the sea.

This was a time for the "reward of approbation" of which Mulholland had spoken; it was a boom that simply would never have been—without the water of Owens River. Yet the dry years had revealed a limit to the growth allowed by the aqueduct. Mulholland's search for water caused him to turn his eyes four hundred miles eastward to the Colorado River for long-range needs. For the immediate future, the city must gain possession of water it had already bought in Owens Valley, but which the unrelenting farmers were still diverting into their own ditches.

After visiting Inyo County to investigate land values, Harvey Van Norman went before the water board with a new proposition.

"The only way to settle things up there," he told the commissioners, "is to buy out the rest of the valley."

"My God!" cried one of the members. "How much will that cost?"

"Five or six million dollars," was the cool answer.

Such a figure was far above any former water investment. It meant a tacit admission of past mistakes and a partial concession to the proposal of the Watterson group. But W. B. Mathews joined Van Norman in convincing the board that such a move was the only means of gaining security at the source of the city's water. Early in 1925 the commissioners announced they were ready to buy all land tributary to the Owens River, leaving no isolated pieces.

The proposal caught the valley people by surprise. For the first time the city had agreed to one of their major points of contention. It meant that bargaining between valley sellers and city buyers would be conducted on an equal basis and not on city terms. But it also meant that the ranchers must abandon the reparations cause of the townspeople. Theirs had been made a long and separate struggle by the water board's stout refusal to pay damages.

Wilfred Watterson himself was in Los Angeles a few days after the board's announcement, offering to sell the 1200-acre Watterson ranch and twenty-two others under the Bishop Creek Ditch. Soon a price of $700,000 was agreed upon and the

78

transaction closed. When it was announced in Bishop on March 7, 1925, valley people were astounded that the Wattersons were selling independently of the powerful irrigation district "pool." Walter Young, a leading figure in the valley group and a close friend of the Wattersons, encountered Wilfred on the streets of Bishop and asked for an explanation.

"Why is it you're selling when you're asking everybody else to hang on?"

"We have to get money to carry on the valley," was the banker's reply.

Young dropped the matter but wondered why the Wattersons needed money when mortgages were being paid off regularly by individual ranchers selling to the city.

Evidently the brothers felt the tension their move had created. On the night the sale was announced, Watterson met with Karl Keough and the owners of the Owens River Canal—last of the big ditches—and, after explaining his position, secured their unanimous consent to the sale. A few days later Wilfred and Mark Watterson published an open letter in Bishop newspapers justifying the deal and were thus able to gloss over the act without losing the valley leadership.

By the end of March the "majority" farmers of Bishop Creek Ditch sold their lands as well, and the entire holding fell to the city. So also did control of the irrigation district, for Los Angeles gained the third director out of a total governing board of five. But the main acquisition was more than 100 second-feet of water from the Bishop Creek system, which lay below the head gate of the Owens River Canal and hence was safe from diversion by the last main ditch still holding up the city's full use of its purchased water rights.

"We anticipate joy in San Fernando Valley," wrote Harry Glasscock with sarcasm, "when they hear that the long-promised relief is so much nearer."

Once again Owens Valley was watching the spectacle of migrating families, vacant farmhouses, and neglected fields. Many of the Bishop Creekers moved across the Sierra to San Joaquin Valley, answering advertisements placed in Inyo newspapers by eager Central Valley real estate men. A majority of the sellers stayed in the valley because of the city's policy of leasing back land minus water rights. Others, like the Wattersons, still had holdings in the Owens River Canal or other ditches. But the following year both voting registration and school enrollment showed that a quarter of the Bishop area population had left in the four years of city land purchases.

For the merchants of Bishop the new emigration meant another drop in business and another raise in reparations demands. In four years of city land buying, several Bishop stores had lost a third of their trade, while some of those dealing in farm supplies had suffered worse reverses. Such concerns as gas stations and restaurants enjoyed a growing tourist business from Los Angeles, but this offered little comfort for the majority of storekeepers, who depended on community customers.

By the spring of 1925 a valley committee was lobbying at Sacramento for a reparations law which would remove the objections of Los Angeles officials that there was no legal basis for damage payments. The bill was signed into law on May 1, making cities which took water out of its drainage basin liable for damages to business or property values. Valley people then formed a reparations association and within a few months compiled more than $2,270,000 in compensation claims for presentation to the water board.

At the same time a renewal of the valley struggle was also apparent when city officials turned to buy the Owens River Canal. They found its owners demanding a figure considerably advanced over prices paid for Bishop Creek lands. The stalemate might have remained peaceful, however, if there had not been an evident attitude among some of the farmers that the city was obliged to meet their figure. Ed Leahey, the city's representative in Owens Valley, soon became aware that the radical leadership of the Klan was still in control.

Since the aqueduct seizure he had employed a corps of Pinkerton detectives in the valley to keep him informed of extremist movements. These "gumshoes," as they were derisively called by the people, conducted a campaign of eavesdropping under windows, shadowing suspected persons, and other melodramatic activities which served mainly to amuse valley citizens. More effective were several local parties who were in touch with the radical element and informed city men of its movements.

On July 31, 1925, a woman in Bishop who had been reporting to Los Angeles agents gave the warning that a fresh plot was being made to dynamite the aqueduct. A note was intercepted between two elements of the radical group, revealing that the blow was aimed at the outlet at Haiwee Reservoir. Such a calamity would disrupt the city's entire water supply.

Ed Leahey quickly notified the Water Department, and within a matter of hours several machine guns from the Los Angeles police force were rushed across the Mojave Desert to the crest of the Haiwee Dam. Right behind them came the usual carload of newspaper reporters ready for the fireworks. Leahey managed to send a grim note to the radical leaders back through the same channel his operators had interrupted:

"It would be a terrible situation if you sent men with rifles to Haiwee, because I've got three machine guns there."

Evidently the warning and the defense were enough to bring a hurried change of plans. When the Los Angeles newsmen pulled into Lone Pine, they met Harry Glasscock on the main street and asked him what was supposed to happen at Haiwee.

"No, there isn't anything doing around there," Glasscock replied cautiously. "Besides, they've got a lot of guns down there!"

Most Angelenos never knew how narrowly their water supply had been saved from serious disruption. "As far as the people here were concerned," Glasscock's paper said innocently, "they had not even heard of any trouble, but it appears that W. B. Mathews and others . . . of the City are undergoing a case of 'nerves' that got the best of them. . . ."

For several months afterward the valley situation smoldered while the reparations committees finished compiling claims and the Owens River Canal ranchers awaited further negotiation. To reach a figure that might be considered fair, the Water Department got an appraisal on remaining property in the Bishop area from three well-respected Inyo officials, two of them experienced tax assessors. Their detailed figures, announced early in December 1925, were accepted by a West Bishop "pool" but turned down by the Owens River Canal, or "Keough pool."

The talks that followed between the canal ranchers and two city negotiators, Ed Leahey and H. A. Van Norman, were marked by rising bitterness. In a meeting early in April 1926, with only $141,000 separating the city offer from the $2,500,000 demanded by the canal owners, the tense negotiations suddenly gave way to angry quarreling. Heated words passed between the Watterson brothers and one of the city men, who threatened that the Water Department would open a rival bank in Bishop.

In a moment the other representative stepped between them to prevent an exchange of blows. Negotiation was ended and the opponents departed with the ragged edge of discord exposed once more.

On the night of April 3 the people of Bishop were awakened by a rattling of windows that announced another dynamiting. A mile west of town on the former Watterson ranch a city water well had been "shot" with only minor damage. A resolve to do the job right must have motivated a more successful blast the next night at another well, where the shaft house was blown into small bits.

The attack was promptly interpreted by the Owens Valley *Herald* as another "notice" to Los Angeles agents. Glasscock could not resist adding that there still existed the probability of "bloodshed at any time if the city's officials get too arrogant."

In the following weeks the fighting editor stepped up his attack to correspond with the reopening of hostilities. On April 21 he claimed that the city was "forcing people from their homes with veiled threats of ruin, left-handed bribery, and in fact using every means possible to crush them down." Two days later the water board, exasperated at his continued attacks, debated for several hours whether to have him prosecuted on charges of criminal libel. When Glasscock heard of it, he stormed down to Los Angeles and issued an open letter to the water commissioners—with copies to leading California newspapers—challenging them to try him for libel.

"They are afraid to carry out their threats to have me arrested," cried Glasscock, claiming that the board feared the world would know the facts in Owens Valley. "I defy them!"

Defiance was not confined to Harry Glasscock. On the night of May 12 another heavy blast was fired in the side of the aqueduct just below the Alabama Gates, a hole some ten feet in diameter being blown in the cement wall. Los Angeles repairmen and detectives rushed to the scene and within twenty-four hours the wound was repaired. To the Inyo *Register* came a telegram from the valley's reparations committee, then in negotiation with officials in Los Angeles:

"Interest of valley seriously menaced by acts of violence. Hope hotheads can be persuaded to desist."

"These repeated occurrences," added editor Willie Chalfant, "do more harm to the valley than to the city."

The admonitions were apparently effective, for the dynamitings were suspended for the rest of 1926. But the valley reparationists were still unable to make headway with Los Angeles water officials. In December they were told that any action by the city would have to follow a test case to determine the constitutionality of the reparations law.

A suit for damages should then have been brought by a valley claimant. The Wattersons, who were asking about $170,-000 in compensation, were the logical ones to take such a lead. But, like most valley men, they claimed to be afraid of long-drawn litigation and continued to press for a board of arbitrators. To such a proposal the city would not submit, and the rankling problem dragged on unsolved.

By early 1927 the long deadlock on both reparations and the Keough pool caused farmers and townsfolk to join interests once more. From the upper valley came unmistakable signs that all forces were being summoned for a final effort to bring the city water commissioners to terms. Throughout March 1927 a series of rallies, steered by Mark Watterson, Karl Keough, Harry Glasscock, and other leaders, was held throughout the valley. At the final mass meeting in Bishop one speaker announced for the benefit of the city's agents that the organization now being formed was "the most radical group the country had ever had."

Feeling ran so high that a few days later on the main street of Big Pine a city employee called the speaker to account for his remarks and precipitated a two-man battle. It was said that the "radical" was leading on points at first but that the city man was holding him by the hair and pounding his head when the local deputy sheriff separated them.

By the time the formation of the new "Owens Valley Property Owners Protective Association" was announced it was plain that a headlong offensive was looming against Los Angeles. Calling the movement "The Last Stand" of the valley, Harry Glasscock's paper warned that "what it has in store" for the city's representatives "is yet to be seen. . . . This is the last fight that will ever be made by the people of Owens Valley," he announced dramatically.

On March 19, 1927, the opening publicity shot of the campaign was fired with all of California as a target. Full-page advertisements had been placed in leading newspapers throughout the state, describing the valley's struggle under the provocative heading, "We Who Are About to Die."

The real direction of the drive became apparent when the editor of the Sacramento *Union* was welcomed to Inyo County for a personal investigation late in March. After conferring with local men and viewing some of the farm communities affected by city purchase, he returned to write a series of articles against Los Angeles that made impressive reading for legislators at the state capital. They were printed in pamphlet form by the valley's Protective Association and mailed by the thousands to citizens throughout California.

Action had, in fact, already opened in the legislature. A resolution had been introduced in the Assembly, condemning Los Angeles for its policy and demanding that the city restore the valley or buy it all. In mid-April a committee of assemblymen visited Inyo County to inspect conditions at first hand. After being shown through the valley by a Bishop delegation, they returned with a scorching report of local conditions. On April 19 several members of the Water Department, having requested a hearing of their own case, were questioned in Sacramento by the

Assembly committee. W. W. Watterson was also present with a delegation to emphasize the valley viewpoint, and the session waxed hot with charges and countercharges.

W. B. Mathews, ordinarily a model of self-possession, grew so exasperated under cross-questioning that he made a defiant but ill-considered admission: Los Angeles would get water any place it was available, he said, even in San Joaquin Valley.

Next morning the Los Angeles group broke off its sessions with the committee, which then secured passage of the Assembly resolution condemning the city's course in Owens Valley as "against the best interests of the state of California." The bill was killed in a Senate committee, but the valley delegation was able to return with its quest for publicity satisfied. Newspapers up and down the state had not failed to catch the story of the Assembly's condemnation. With the offensive succeeding according to plan, Mark Watterson was voicing optimism by early April.

"I feel we have the city on the defensive," he wrote to one newspaperman, "and we must strike hard and often now and not give them time to recover themselves."

The realization that they faced a showdown in the battle for the Owens River caused city officials to make a stern decision. The only way to end the campaign was to subdue the power of its financial source—the Watterson banks. They looked upon the struggle not as one between city and valley but between themselves, as public servants responsible for a city's water supply, and a group of opportunists entrenched at the source of that water.

Ed Leahey first went to officers of the Bank of America and asked if they could be interested in an Owens Valley branch. When they assented he suggested further that the Wattersons should first be approached for an outright sale, "just so they won't say we're freezing 'em out." Leahey then opened negotiations with the Bishop bankers through a third party, who would not reveal the identity of his clients. He found the brothers in an awkward position. They wanted to sell out but were reluctant to disclose the chaotic condition of their Inyo County Bank.

At length the negotiator reported to Leahey and asked if he would also take the Watterson business enterprises and $700,000 in notes. The city official then learned that the brothers had siphoned bank money into their private concerns—the National Soda Works at Keeler, the tungsten mine on Mount Tom, and other enterprises—without accounting for its transfer. Immediately he pressed the negotiations further in an attempt to get a commitment from the bankers. The moment they agreed to sell, as Leahey put it, "they'll be saying 'good morning' to the judge."

84

The Wattersons soon ended the discussions, possibly with the suspicion that the city was involved. But Leahey was now aware of their weakness. He conferred with Bank of America men once more, and steps were taken to get a state charter for a branch in Owens Valley. It was agreed that application should be made by a substantial group of valley men, who would be able to explain the local situation to the banking commissioner and to justify a new financial house in Inyo County.

Ready to join the venture were five valley men antagonistic to the Wattersons, including their uncle, George Watterson. Late in March 1927 they journeyed to Sacramento and laid their application before the California banking commissioner, Will C. Woods.

But W. W. Watterson and several valley supporters appeared at the hearing in full force, stoutly denying charges against the financial integrity of the existing banks. Commissioner Woods tentatively refused to grant the charter.

Watterson returned to Inyo with a temporary victory but with the shadow of a rival bank still threatening his financial control. Evidently he determined that this challenge would have to be met with severe reprisal.

One of the five bank charter applicants was George Warren, the Big Pine rancher who had clashed more than once with the Bishop group. Early in April word passed through the valley that the Protective Association intended to wait upon Warren and demand his departure. At least one of the members was notified by W. W. Watterson himself. On the morning of April 12, Walter Young, a close friend of the Watterson brothers, was stopped by Wilfred at the door of the Inyo County Bank.

"A bunch of the boys are going down and run George Warren out of the country," he confided and asked if Young would join them.

The rancher wanted to know if the banker himself would be present.

"No," answered Watterson, "it wouldn't do for me to go."

Walter Young agreed that he would "be there"; later that morning at a hill two miles below Bishop he joined a group of forty men, including Harry Glasscock, Karl Keough, and representatives from every community in the valley. There was no mention of Warren's connection with the bank application, but it was said that he was "interfering with plans for a settlement with the city" and must be made to leave the valley.

Two men acquainted with Warren were sent to bring him from his house just north of Big Pine. There the stolid ranchman refused to go with them but agreed to receive a seven-man committee at his home. Early in the afternoon the specified group reached Warren's place and was invited into the house. From his back yard a spokesman for the delegation grumbled that they could say everything right there.

"Since you refused to meet with us all," he was told, "your orders are to get out of the county inside of forty-eight hours."

Warren then asked what he had done but was given no explanation beyond that of "interfering with reparations plans." As the rancher began to argue his position, the men turned to leave.

"Am I to understand," he called, "that I have to either get out of the county inside of forty-eight hours or prepare to defend myself?"

There was no answer; the man's defiant spirit flared.

"If you've come to tell me to leave without saying why," Warren shouted, "you can go back and tell your bunch to go plumb to hell—I'm not going anywhere!"

The declaration was provocative enough, but the men stalked out to their car and allowed their ultimatum to stand. Late in the afternoon of the fourteenth, after Warren's allotted time had expired, a string of cars left Bishop and paraded down the highway along the Sierra foothills. Just north of Big Pine they drew up at George Warren's house, intent on making good their threat.

But from Warren's garage, from the rocky hill above his ranch house, more than twenty Big Piners looked upon the interlopers with poised rifles. Inside the house Warren was trying to comfort his plucky wife but at the same time stood ready to defend his position.

The Bishop men surveyed the scene but made no hostile move. Conferences were held behind the cars, and at length they wheeled about and headed northward. Warren and his friends watched them go in jubilation.

Next night, and for several thereafter, a string of headlights moving south from Bishop warned the defenders of another visit. But each time the mob's determination was frustrated by the commanding position of those rifle barrels.

Los Angeles newspapers picked up the story when the siege was several days old. Quickly the news of this latest outbreak of lawlessness reached the state legislature in Sacramento, where friends of the valley were trying to press through the resolution condemning Los Angeles. From their chief exponent in the Assembly came a hurried telegram to officers of the Valley Protective Association:

"Absolutely demand any semblance of disorder in Owens

Valley stop. This legislature should not be embarrassed. I am working hard for favorable settlement and insist drastic actions hinder your cause."

After that the night visitations ceased. Violent threats were still heard through the upper valley, for the group could not reconcile itself to an embarrassing defiance of orders. But the siege at last was lifted and a "Battle of Big Pine" averted. Warren's guards were reduced to a skeleton force; the rancher had made good his promise that he was "not going anywhere."

But already the rush of events was making the Big Pine affair a preliminary skirmish in a full-scale conflict. In March the Los Angeles Water Department had suddenly decided to set a deadline for land purchases. Ed Leahey knew the continuing negotiations with Owens River Canal was all that had preserved peace in the valley.

"If you do that," he warned, "they'll start dynamiting again."

But on March 23 advertisements in the Bishop papers notified valley residents that the water board would buy all land offered at appraisal prices until May 1, 1927, "and not thereafter." The deadline was pointedly ignored in Owens Valley. Five days after its expiration the water commissioners announced a final denial of the townspeople's reparations claims. Valley wrath was now complete.

Early in May the ominous signs of violence were no longer concealed. Lack of punishment for previous assaults, and a sort of frontier bravado which still prevailed among many men in this mountainbound valley, brought the return of lawlessness. Glasscock's Owens Valley *Herald* solemnly declared that the aqueduct "would run red with human blood before this trouble was settled." Later testimony and recollections have indicated that the Watterson bankers were able to use their financial influence in bringing a final outbreak of dynamitings. A valley citizen named Perry Sexton, whose testimony may or may not be credited, told of owing a note to the Inyo Bank and of stating to Mark Watterson that he could not pay it until the city sent him some money he had claimed. Mark observed that Los Angeles would never settle with him.

"If they don't pay me," confided Sexton, "I'll shut the water off for them at the intake."

"If you do that, Perry," answered Watterson, "we'll give you all the time you want on your note."

Meanwhile night meetings in the open fields near Bishop were resumed once more. On May 11, a valley rancher arrived at the Hercules Powder plant in Martinez, California, and bought eight cases of blasting gelatin—enough to carry on a prolonged attack against the aqueduct. A final letter was sent by the Owens Valley Protective Association to Los Angeles officials and civic organizations, charging that a continuation of the water board's policy would "inflame real American citizens to violence" and asking them to reply whether they would "take definite action. Should the few remaining property owners be forced to the breaking point we shudder at the possible results."

No answer had been received in about two weeks. One of Leahey's informers in Bishop tried to warn him of an aqueduct attack, but for fear of being caught he delayed making the contact until it was too late.

In the early morning darkness of May 27, 1927, ten armed men drove into the canyon at No Name siphon, one of the largest pipe sections of the aqueduct, ten miles south of Little Lake. Descending on the nearby repair house, they surprised the two aqueduct watchmen.

"We'll take you for a walk," the leader snapped. "There's going to be a dynamiting here."

While four of the intruders marched the guards up the canyon out of blasting range, the other six went about their work with deadly efficiency. A string of explosives was wrapped about the great tube at its lowest point and a waterproof explosive container with a lighted fuse was dropped into the roaring aqueduct stream at the north entrance of the pipe.

A few moments later, with a thunderous blast, the entire bottom section of No Name siphon ripped into space. The vibrating canyon was showered with rocks, steel, and water. Out of the bleeding trunk of the north pipe the aqueduct's full flow gushed with such speed that the steel collapsed into the vacuum like a punctured tire tube.

The dynamiters had at last accomplished a major piece of destruction on the Los Angeles Aqueduct. Without delay they hurried to their cars and drove northward while almost 400 second-feet of water roared into the Mojave Desert.

As soon as the alarm was telephoned to Haiwee Dam, the flow was shut off with a total loss of about 500 acre-feet. Harvey Van Norman, stopping at Lone Pine at the time, hurried down to No Name siphon and before nightfall on the following day had 150 men working on repairs and an order given to a Los Angeles steel company for some 450 feet of new pipe. Up from Los Angeles came W. B. Mathews and William Mulholland, who bitterly replied to press queries that he could not comment on the dynamiting "without using unprintable words."

Before the Water Department had time to recover from the

No Name "shot," another blast the following night shattered a 60-foot pipe section leading to the city's power plant on Big Pine Creek. From the valley below a repair crew was immediately dispatched. While 600 reservists were assembled at the central police station in Los Angeles, a detachment of detectives drove northward armed with Winchesters and tommy guns. Their orders were to "shoot to kill" anyone loitering near the aqueduct.

Up and down the valley the names of the dynamiters were apparently as well known as they were well guarded by the population. Some of the conspirators made little effort to conceal their participation from their neighbors. One boasted, "We blew up the aqueduct again" and added that they "would continue to blow it up until the city came to terms."

After a week of silence the dynamiters moved out once more on the night of June 4. According to his later testimony, Perry Sexton was driven from Bishop to a section of the aqueduct opposite Owens Lake near Cottonwood Power House, where he was dropped off with a gunny sack of blasting gelatin. While a guard paced along the edge above him, he placed a charge in a drainage tunnel under the conduit; after waiting two hours, he ignited the fuse and stumbled back to the highway to be picked up by another car.

The explosion shook every home and building at the power plant. Scarcely had the dust cloud settled when a crew of city employees came running to the break. At least a hundred and fifty feet of conduit wall had been blown apart, and the water was already spilling crazily down the hillside. Word was flashed up to the Alabama spillway, and the gates were opened to drain the ditch and allow repairs.

This time the Water Department prepared for open warfare. Some fifty sawed-off shotguns and rifles, with ammunition, were bought for shipment to valley employees. On the night of June 10 a special Southern Pacific train rattled out of Los Angeles northward with two coaches and a baggage car loaded with a hundred armed aqueduct guards—mostly World War I veterans.

Their coming was saluted the following night by another blast in the side of the aqueduct just below Lone Pine—an act which brought new reinforcements hurrying up from Los Angeles. The lower valley along the line of the conduit was virtually thrown under martial law. While searchlights mounted along the ditch scanned the highway at night for suspicious movements, the guards flagged down automobiles and inspected their occupants by flashlight. From Bishop came the threat via Glasscock's paper that "it is more than likely that some real cold lead will be pumped into them some night as a way of warning them. . . ."

Already the upper valley was rumored to be arming for battle. Nearly sixty Winchester carbines were shipped from Los Angeles wholesalers to the Watterson brothers' hardware store in Bishop, where they were hurriedly passed across the counter to willing hands. When the Los Angeles *Times* called the Bishop store and asked what they would do with the guns, a Watterson employee growled back, "Use them, of course!"

"There isn't any particular demand for rifles at this season of the year, is there?" pressed the inquirer.

"You'd think so if you were up here," was the grim reply.

But actual violence was confined to a weekly "jolt in the ribs" of the aqueduct. On June 19 a small explosion knocked out sixteen feet of conduit about three miles below Lone Pine in the lower end of the Alabama Hills. Five evenings later another tremor shook the lower valley and a squad of city guards went scurrying southward, followed by part of the eager population of Lone Pine. Near the same spot the dynamiters had attempted to block the ditch by blasting loose a giant boulder perched on the hillside above; tons of rock and dirt were lifted skyward and deposited in the cement conduit, but the water continued to flow onward. One of the guards came within a hundred feet of being engulfed by the avalanche. The boulder itself was shaken loose but failed to reach the aqueduct.

"Through some miscarriage of justice," as Glasscock boldly described the event, "it did little harm. We hope the boys will do better next time, as it is a shame to go to all the trouble of setting off a lot of dynamite . . . and then have the work for nothing."

But the main purpose of the dynamitings—that of gaining publicity for the valley's cause—was succeeding well enough. The story of this all-out battle in California's water war was carried in newspapers and magazines across the nation; the No Name blast even made the front page of the Parisian *Le Temps*. Throughout California, of course, the drama was covered and editorialized on in most newspapers. Though they deplored the resort to violence, they generally condemned the city for its policy.

The San Francisco *Chronicle* pointed out that if Los Angeles officials claimed the water was worth more in Southern California they should have reimbursed the valley for its full value. "The city paid only a small part of that and left the rest of the value of the Valley to wither and die." Even the Los Angeles *Times*, agreeing that "the city has made mistakes," admitted a justifiable grievance on the part of valley merchants, "who have seen their customers, one after another, sell out and move away. . . ."

90

At the same time the ranchers themselves were pushing the campaign with direct appeals. They ran a large advertisement describing their plight in the Los Angeles *Record*, which was already giving their cause plenty of publicity in articles and cartoons on "Old Bill's Aqua-Duck." A Los Angeles reformer named Andrae B. Nordskog championed the valley cause in lectures before women's and service clubs, in talks with the mayor and state officials, and in the columns of his weekly newspaper, the *Gridiron*. For this supposedly altruistic crusade he was to receive $3500 from the Wattersons, of which $2000 was actually sent him.

By the end of June Governor C. C. Young, armed with a firsthand report on the Owens Valley situation, visited Los Angeles to seek out a settlement of the water war. After conferring with city officials, he returned to Sacramento and invited a delegation of valley men to a meeting there on July 1. What their people should do, he advised, was to open a test suit in court to determine the constitutionality of the reparations law.

For two weeks the dynamitings were suspended along the aqueduct; valley committees conferred on the governor's suggestion and on July 14 sent a reply rejecting it as one that "would be very welcome to the Water and Power Board and for that reason is looked upon with fear and distrust by our people."

Next night a blast one mile south of Lone Pine shook the town, broke out a section of the aqueduct wall, and sank a repair barge. Ninety minutes after city guards had rushed down to the spot, another heavy report was heard four miles north of Independence. A well-placed charge had blown out a timbered side gate, opened sixty feet of conduit wall, and released the full aqueduct flow until the main intake gates were closed at Owens River. The dynamiters had resumed action once more with a double-barreled charge.

The continued attacks under the very noses of the Los Angeles guards brought mounting tension and jittery nerves in the lower valley. When one patrolman saw a mysterious object floating down the stream, he shouted a warning, leaped off the embankment, and promptly ran into a barbed-wire fence. Cooler examination showed the thing to be an empty kerosene can and gave valley citizens a chuckle at the city's expense.

One night another guard had turned an aqueduct searchlight on a car moving along the highway when the driver abruptly stopped and climbed out. It proved to be Fred Eaton's son Harold, traveling from Los Angeles to his Long Valley ranch.

"Turn off that light!" he hollered.

The blinding spot continued to frame him. Eaton took his revolver from the car and, drawing a bead on the searchlight, fired two shots. He missed the lamp, but the light was promptly extinguished. The rancher drove on with the dubious distinction of having fired the only known shots in the Owens Valley war.

Through the early summer of 1927 the outdoor sport of "shooting the duck" was a leading occupation and a main topic of conversation in Owens Valley. On August 3, Harry Glasscock spoke darkly of a time "when many will give up their lives in order to make their rights regarded" and expressed the possibility that "there will be more bloodshed than anyone looks for at the present time." Even Willie A. Chalfant, although he opposed the dynamitings in his Inyo *Register*, declared, "Only violence would have called our plight to the attention of the state."

Although lawlessness, together with the publicity it engendered, had come to be the only weapon of the valley extremists, it made their cause vulnerable to a counterattack from Los Angeles officials. With the aqueduct under fire and the water supply threatened, city men were fighting back with more than armed guards. It was the series of dynamitings that eventually gave Ed Leahey the advantage he needed in his struggle with the Watterson bankers. Securing a financial statement of their outside business firm, Watterson Incorporated, he discovered a number of unspecified money disbursements to Harry Glasscock and other leaders in the water war. On August 2 he accompanied W. B. Mathews to Sacramento and talked with the state corporation commissioner.

"We have reason to believe," Leahey reported solemnly, "that corporate funds are being used for dynamiting the aqueduct."

The startled commissioner looked at them in amazement.

"Would you repeat that?"

Leahey made the charge again and added details on the condition of the Watterson finances.

"I suggest you send an examiner over there to look at the situation in those banks."

That night, at the request of the corporation commissioner, Will Woods of the state banking office put an investigator on the train for Owens Valley. When he arrived at the Inyo County bank on August 3—two months before his expected periodic visit—Wilfred Watterson had reason to turn white with shock.

Giving his brother Mark orders to close the bank next day, Wilfred left Bishop immediately for Los Angeles. There he sought out the bankers with whom he was on friendly terms and pleaded for a substantial loan to meet his crisis. One of them went to the water board and suggested that at least $200,000 would have to be lent to the Watterson banks. He found that such a proposition was scarcely welcome in that quarter.

Hoping the loans might come from Los Angeles banks in time to save him, Watterson withdrew reserve funds from personal safety-deposit boxes in the city and headed back for Owens Valley.

At noon on the fourth, the five Watterson banks in Inyo County were closed. At the doors of each, groups of citizens gathered to read a curt notice, signed by the Wattersons:

> We find it necessary to close our banks in the Owens Valley. This result has been brought about by the past four years of destructive work carried on by the city of Los Angeles.

Owens Valley was stunned. The Watterson brothers had been the very pillars of Inyo County, had held the complete confidence and friendship of almost every resident. The closure of their banks was at first believed to be only a temporary difficulty, though Chalfant's *Register* called it "the darkest blow that the valley has received directly or indirectly from the work of Los Angeles."

City Water Department officials were furious at the Wattersons' attempt to blame them for the bank debacle. It was labeled by the Los Angeles *Times* as "a last frantic falsehood."

Meanwhile the examiners were checking the books and discovering monumental shortages. In the vault there was more than $33,000 cash missing. A superficial perusal of the books showed some $190,000 in account with the Wells Fargo Bank of San Francisco, but a check with that institution showed it had received none of the amount.

Mark Watterson, left in charge of the bank in Wilfred's absence, was consumed with despondency. On the afternoon of the fourth he left Bishop and headed up Pine Canyon, taking refuge at the Watterson tungsten mine on the side of Mount Tom. There he rested alone, trying to collect his thoughts and foresee some future beyond the calamity that had overtaken them. But that evening when Wilfred returned, Wilfred sent his son and Walter Young, Mark's lifelong friend, up to the mine; they encouraged him enough to secure his return.

On the same day Banking Commissioner Woods reached Bishop after being notified of the shortages by his examiners. In a meeting at the Inyo County Bank that night the two brothers were brought to account by the banking officials and District Attorney Jess Hession. What, in particular, asked the examiners, had happened to the $33,000 cash shortage?

"We took that money," Wilfred answered, "and we used it for our own personal obligations."

"That's right," agreed Mark.

One of the state men asked about the bonds which depositors had placed with the bank for safekeeping.

"Well," admitted Wilfred, "we had to use some of those too."

But though Watterson was at bay he was not yet beaten. All his persuasive powers were mustered to convince Woods that disaster could be averted if he would take his men out of the bank and give it a chance to make up the shortages. The banking commissioner relented but gave the brothers only five days. When the hoped-for loans from Los Angeles had not arrived by August 10, Woods made formal charges of embezzlement. The two brothers were arrested and released on $25,000 bail each, which was put up by several Bishop friends.

Meanwhile some forty upper-valley men met near Bishop and determined to raise the shortage money among Inyo citizens. So great was public confidence in the bankers that nearly $1,000,000 was pledged by valley people within two days. One Lone Pine woman offered to deed over her unencumbered ranch property if it would help in the emergency. Superior Judge William Dehy wrote from Independence that he had a few bonds and securities which the brothers were welcome to use.

In a series of meetings the Wattersons explained their actions to the people, claiming that the city's invasion of the upper valley in 1923 had forced them to assume leadership in the community, that the bank funds had been channeled into mining and other Watterson enterprises to make them replace the loss of farming as a valley industry.

"We stood by you," said Wilfred, "and we have been forced to be a sacrifice."

But discoveries still being made by the banking examiners showed an enormity in embezzlement that could scarcely be laid to actions of the city. While the other Watterson branches were in good condition, a total of $2,300,000 was missing from the Inyo County Bank in Bishop and the Watterson corporations. When it was revealed that securities placed in safekeeping by trusting friends had been sold, that many mortgages and loans paid off by thrifty farmers had never been canceled and were still on the books, that at least two biennial banking reports had been falsified to cover thefts, a terrible awakening swept over the valley. The total loss of more than $400,000 in irrigation district bonds added strength to the belief that, instead of their losses being caused by the water struggle, it was the Wattersons' desperate need of money which motivated many of their actions in that struggle.

Not the least shocked was Harry Glasscock, whose newspaper had been devoted to the cause led by the Wattersons. His expenditures, including trips to Sacramento and Los Angeles in the water cause, had been partly paid with Watterson drafts; for these he had signed notes on his presses and equipment—merely as a formality, as the Wattersons had told him. But when the bank went down, his notes were on the books and his entire business was in jeopardy.

Disillusioned by the men he had championed, Glasscock left his office and went on one of his periodic drinking sprees for several weeks while his employees turned out the Owens Valley *Herald*. When at last he reappeared in charge of the paper, he ran an editorial on August 31, relinquishing the stand he had made for years in support of the Wattersons. He would never, wrote Glasscock, "make excuses or apologies for people who have violated the confidence" of Inyo citizens; "we cannot longer, under the circumstances, ask the people of Owens Valley to continue under their past leadership."

Before the year's end his equipment had been attached by the bank's assignees and his paper was defunct. A few months later, while staying in a Los Angeles hotel, the beaten crusader was overcome with despondency. After telling a fellow newspaperman over the phone that he was "going on the great adventure," Harry Glasscock took a fatal dose of poison.

Most tragic effect of the debacle was the almost complete financial prostration of the valley's people. All business had been transacted through these five banks, and their closure had left merchants and customers alike with nothing but small change on hand. Lifetime savings of the people—in many cases the entire payment gained from the city for the sale of homes and ranches—had been wiped out. Practically isolated by mountains from the rest of California, the valley found its trade paralyzed for lack of currency. Los Angeles water employees were paid a month in advance to bring some relief, but it was impossible to prevent one business after another from closing its doors.

By mid-September a Bakersfield bank opened branches in the valley and helped to relieve the stagnation. At the same time the charter for the Owens Valley Bank sought by the city's agent was granted by the state; a few months later the Bank of America used it to open a valley branch. But the new banking facilities could never compensate for the loss of fortune which nearly every resident suffered.

The trial of the Wattersons opened in Independence early in November, with a crowd of solemn valley people filling the courtroom. District Attorney Hession, acting in the painful role of prosecutor of lifetime friends, introduced his evidence of shortages with methodical repetition, constructing an undeniable case. The only defense of the Wattersons, as stated in their testimony, was that the money had been taken as loans which they had intended to pay back. But Hession pointed to the false credit with Wells Fargo that had been used to cover up shortages: "Now, if that isn't stealing . . . I don't know what it is."

The full impact of the tragedy was driven home by Hession in his final jury address on November 11, 1927: "It is their neighbors," he reminded the court, "men and women whose confidence they won, whose faith was unbounded, who are the victims of these men." Before he had finished the prosecutor was exhibiting brave tears, the eyes of the jurymen and many of the visitors were wet, and even the judge himself took out his handkerchief and valiantly wiped his nose.

Six hours later the jury returned a verdict of guilty on all counts. The hushed court began to stir with relief at the end of the last tragic act in the Owens Valley drama. When the session was adjourned, some remained to offer consolation to the two brothers. Others, torn between bitterness and lifelong friendship, hurried away without knowing what else to do.

Within a few days the Wattersons were given from one to ten years' imprisonment at San Quentin. Paroled in 1933, they resided in Los Angeles for the rest of their lives, occasionally visiting Owens Valley.

The fall of the Wattersons ended the active fight against Los Angeles. No longer did its aqueduct rock with blasts from embattled valley ranchers. As the tension relaxed, a voluntary confession came in November 1927 from one dynamiter, Perry Sexton. At the same time city detectives had traced dynamite purchases to another valley citizen, who had already been arrested. But at a hearing held in Bishop the following spring this combined evidence was rejected by a local justice of the peace and six defendants were released. As for Sexton's full confession implicating the others, the judge simply would not believe it.

It appeared that, whatever else they had lost, the valley people were resolved to protect their defenders to the last. Disillusioned and beaten, their only possession now was an unalterable resolve, as one Inyo newspaper expressed it, that "we will yet, somewhere, somehow, find a way to rise out of the dust and make our beloved Owens Valley as sweet a place to live as it was in years gone by."

96

But they could not help knowing that the fate of the valley had passed from their hands. In the long struggle for control of Owens River the Los Angeles Water Department had suddenly won a more complete victory than it had intended.

8: OF FLOOD AND DROUGHT

Los Angeles was still reeling from the battle of Owens Valley when nature and bad judgment combined to deal the city an overwhelming blow. The underlying cause was the same drought in the early 1920s that had brought on the struggle for the Owens River.

Even while the city was being pushed to desperate lengths for water, it became aware of an undue waste caused by its power plants in San Francisquito Canyon, some twenty miles north of San Fernando Valley. Unlike water, electric energy cannot be stored in large quantities. It must be sent over transmission lines and used in homes and factories at the instant it is generated by the turbines. The constant flow of water at the two San Francisquito plants was too much for the San Fernando reservoirs to hold. Much of it was dumped into the canyon bottom, there to find its way into the Santa Clara River and eventually to run past the Ventura County towns of Fillmore and Santa Paula on its way to the ocean. This loss in a drought season was deplored by the Water Department and taken into court by at least one irate San Fernando Valley farmer.

Obviously a great new reservoir site below at least one of the power plants was needed to help the two San Fernando lakes in storing water for the city's use. William Mulholland first proposed a dam in Big Tujunga Canyon at the east side of the valley. Condemnation of the reservoir site was begun, but the owners fought for an extravagant price in court. Mulholland, refusing to allow the city to be held up, had the proceedings ended. An alternate reservoir site was bought in the San Francisquito Canyon, below Power House No. 1, and construction was opened in August 1924.

By May 1926 the Water Department had completed the great, arch-shaped concrete structure and christened it St. Francis Dam. When filled to capacity a year later, the reservoir held some 34,000 acre-feet—almost equaling the combined volume of the two San Fernando basins.

Faced with continuing drought, Mulholland had doubled the city's water storage none too soon; another dry season in 1927 made the new reservoir a veritable lifesaver for San Fernando crops.

Yet the heat of the emergency had caused Mulholland to overlook ordinary engineering precautions. Along the San Andreas Fault much of the Coast Range was crossed with cracks; at the San Francisquito site, where the canyon walls were formed of mica schist and conglomerate, these faults brought unusual water leakage. Before the end of 1927 the abutments against which the dam rested had been soaked enough to swell slightly. In January 1928 two cracks appeared on the face of the dam, beginning at top center and slanting downward to the sides. Since the structure rested on solid bedrock, this indicated that the two sides had been moved slightly upward by the swelling. Water leaked through these seams, but they were soon calked up; some leakage is common in many dams.

Downstream near Power House No. 2 lived thirteen city employees and their families, who watched the passage of waste water with some apprehension. One nervous individual was continually predicting that the dam would break. Early in March the water turned muddy—a danger sign that abutment ground might be giving way.

On March 12, Mulholland and Van Norman inspected the dam to check these reports. They found leakage, but to their relief noted that the muddy water was caused by some nearby road construction. The dam, they believed, was in no immediate danger.

Late that night the abutment anchoring the east end of the dam collapsed under the weight of the water it had absorbed. Several minutes before midnight a whole section of ground broke off, slid past the face of the dam, and thundered into the canyon floor. With it crashed the abutment itself, overpowered by the tremendous pressure of the reservoir water.

In the next moment both wings of the dam crumbled under the terrific outpouring of water. While the whole canyon shook, a giant flood hurtled out of the reservoir on either side of the central section. On the crest of a hundred-foot wall of water, huge blocks of concrete rode down San Francisquito Canyon. Several, weighing thousands of tons apiece, were carried as far as half a mile. The canyon had suddenly been turned into a great trough for an overwhelming mountain of water.

At Power House No. 2 the families were asleep when the giant thundered down upon them. The man who had predicted disaster awoke at a dog's bark. Hearing the awful roar, he jumped out of bed with a yell of warning and climbed furiously up the hillside. He barely escaped the flood that engulfed the others, smashed the power plant, and rumbled past.

Down the canyon it swept, stripping the sides of all vegetation, houses, and power lines for sixty feet above the stream bed. Pieces of aqueduct siphons were carried off like straws, interrupting all water supply north of San Fernando Valley. As the deluge poured out of the canyon, it shot past Saugus for a mile before turning at the command of gravity and flinging itself into the Santa Clara River.

At a rate of eighteen miles an hour the giant thundered westward, carrying an ugly burden of uprooted trees, houses, and debris. Castaic Junction was overwhelmed under a sixty-foot tide; only a handful of survivors, warned by the terrifying roar, escaped to higher ground.

Eleven miles farther, at a construction camp of the Southern California Edison Company, 140 men slept in the path of the monster. It was almost upon them when the night watchman heard the rumble. Shunning his own safety, he ran through the tented streets shouting the alarm. Many of the men awoke, but not one escaped into the open before the deluge struck. Suddenly each tent house was turned into a bedlam of frenzied, clutching men. The canvas flaps had been tied shut against the cold March nights, and the victims fought to tear their way out of the sides. Some of the tents were sealed so tight that they floated on the crest of the flood like half-filled balloons—a trick of fate which was all that saved most of the survivors. One man rode an empty trunk down the torrent; another sat astride the company water tank. Survivors were eventually washed up on higher ground as far west as Piru, but eighty-four were lost, among them the heroic night watchman. Fifty automobiles and tons of electrical equipment were washed away or buried in sand.

Onward through the rich Santa Clara Valley the monster rolled, leaving no life in its path. Orange groves almost ripe for picking, apricot and walnut orchards, alfalfa and bean fields were wiped from the land and a blanket of white sand left in their places. Highway bridges were splintered by debris and washed out. Scores of farm families along the river were caught sleeping, with no chance to escape. Those on higher ground had time to scramble for safety in their nightclothes, abandoning home and farm animals to the deluge. Others found house and all suddenly picked up by some terrifying force and carried madly along, until crushed by the torrent or smashed against the stump of a broken bridge. A woman with her three small children—one of them a month-old baby—clung to a feather mattress for two miles down the torrent; the top of a tree caught and held them until they were rescued later.

More than one household was aroused in time by the frantic

howling of the dog. Others heard the flood's terrible roar, later described as that of an Eastern tornado. One rancher blasted a hole in the roof with his shotgun as the water engulfed his house. The family was crawling through when the building began to move. It sailed downstream, caught in a group of sycamores, and floated there with its passengers until the flood subsided. Another family of fourteen tumbled into a single car and headed for safety with the roar ringing in their ears. On the way they stopped while the father ran to warn another household on a hillside. When he returned, his car and family had disappeared in the flood.

The town of Piru had no more warning than the ranchers. Most of the community was sheltered by a hill, but settlers near the willow bottoms were swallowed up before they could flee. Seven miles beyond lay the larger town of Fillmore; nine miles farther, the chief settlement of the valley—Santa Paula. Telephone lines had been washed out, and all hope of warning them seemed lost.

The first alarm came from the Los Angeles power bureau, which had investigated the cause of electricity failure from the plant in San Francisquito Canyon. At 1:15 a.m. the warning was phoned to the sheriff's office at Ventura on the coast. Calls were immediately relayed to Santa Paula and Fillmore. A squad car swung out of Ventura and roared up the valley with siren blaring. It reached Santa Paula as local officers were turning out to rouse the town and sped on for Fillmore. There the driver pulled up at the firehouse and began ringing the bell. The telephone operator was already warning one family after another with frantic calls. Soon the cry was all over town: "Flood is coming; get back to the hills!"

For half an hour the fire bell and two sirens kept up their ominous wails, while American Legion men routed the people in the lower part of town. Ignoring every plea for her own safety, the telephone girl remained at her switchboard, warning isolated farmhouses.

An hour after the first warning the rising roar came out of the east and sent the remaining citizens hurrying for higher ground. In a moment an irresistible wall of water struck the lower part of town, and the bridge across the river went out with a crash that was heard for miles. From the main street of Fillmore the people watched while the fury passed. Then they followed the water's edge as it receded—some to pick treasured belongings from the rubble.

Nine miles beyond, Santa Paula lay in the direct path of the flood, unprotected by hills. As soon as the alarm arrived from

Ventura, the whistle at the nearby Union Oil refinery began to sound steady shrieks of warning. People rolled from their beds, expecting a fire; seeing none through their windows, many turned back to sleep. Others found the electric lights were dead and realized something was wrong. Most of them rushed out of doors and joined the excited crowds in the downtown streets. Trucks and autos were dashing by, carrying load after load of people to the safety of the hills. Here, too, the telephone girls stayed at their posts to warn the valley, not knowing when the flood might strike. Two motorcycle policemen roared from house to house in the lower residential district, pounding on doors.

"The dam has broken," they shouted. "Flee for your lives!"

About three-thirty in the morning, two hours after the alarm, the roaring monster descended on Santa Paula. A twenty-five foot wave billowed through the streets, overturning houses and autos, carrying some of them downstream in its teeth. Onward it raged past the threatened settlements of Saticoy and and Montalvo. Then shortly after five o'clock it flung itself with its burden of debris headlong into the sea.

As soon as the crest of the flood had passed, the people of Santa Paula scrambled back into the valley with lanterns and flashlights, searching the wreckage for survivors. Hundreds of Ventura County Legionnaires, alerted an hour after the dam broke, took over the work of rescuing the living and recovering the dead. There were few injured survivors; the deluge had made a relentless sweep of the valley, destroying anything caught in its way. People were either whole or they were lost.

Scarcely an hour after the flood the local American Red Cross had set up its first emergency canteen in Santa Paula. In three more hours it was fully organized and serving hot breakfasts to long lines of refugees. Ventura County Boy Scouts were helping with first aid, running messages, guarding property.

In the early morning all Southern California heard the news; radio stations sent out appeals for help, and volunteers were hurrying northward. The Southern Pacific ran free trainloads of rescue parties as far as the Santa Clara riverbed, where its tracks were washed out for miles. Southern California fuel and truck companies promptly donated gas and equipment without charge for the emergency. Scores of relief cars from the Southern California Auto Club were rushed to the valley, while sixty Los Angeles policemen patrolled the area to keep out sight-seers.

By 10 a.m. an emergency meeting of civic leaders was held in Santa Paula to organize for the disaster. A Citizens Emergency Committee was formed, headed by Charles C. Teague, veteran valley rancher and one of the most respected men in

101

California. Through its efforts hundreds of refugees were sheltered in a huge abandoned packing house, while others were taken into the homes of friends and relatives.

In Los Angeles, William Mulholland, builder of St. Francis Dam, was prostrated by the news. The tired old man, his face lined with remorse, shuffled into the office of the water and power commissioners and reported the calamity. "I envy the dead," he said later.

By the next day the entire nation was extending its sympathy to the stricken Santa Clara Valley. That morning the national officers of the Red Cross reached the scene, and a telegram of condolence arrived from President Calvin Coolidge. To the people of the nation, many of whom had experienced the slow-rising floods of Midwestern rivers, this unexpected giant in the night was a strange and terrifying thought. There was yet no way of knowing its death toll, but it was later fixed at 385 persons, with 1250 houses and 7900 acres of rich farmlands destroyed—altogether one of the worst disasters in American history.

From the beginning the city of Los Angeles accepted full blame for the appalling catastrophe.

"Los Angeles cannot restore the lives lost," declared Mayor George Cryer, "but the property damages should be paid. . . . The responsibility is ours."

A committee was immediately formed by the city to share the relief work with the valley group under C. C. Teague, and the City Council advanced $1,000,000 as an earnest of its responsibility. Soon other joint committees were set up to work out payments for damages.

"No question of the legal status of claims should ever be raised," they were directed by Van Norman of the Water Department. "The moral obligation to repay damage in the valley is sufficient."

As a result Los Angeles paid without question every claim established by the committees—a total of $15,000,000. More than a thousand homes were rebuilt by the city; the lower section of Santa Paula blossomed as a model community of modern houses. Despite the number of ambulance chasers who flocked to the valley and promised huge settlements to individuals, not one damage claim against Los Angeles was taken into court.

For the next few weeks after the disaster San Francisquito Canyon was alive with engineers and geologists investigating the cause of the disaster. Five different reports were rendered to state and local governments; all were agreed that the concrete in the dam was faultless but that it had failed because of poor rock foundations. The coroner's jury, sitting in Los Angeles a few days after the tragedy, concluded that construction and operation of a great dam "should never be left to the sole judgment of one man, no matter how eminent, without check by independent expert authority, for no one is free from error."

That one man—William Mulholland—was felled by the calamity; but he would not shrink from the responsibility. Broken in spirit, he feebly took the stand at the coroner's inquest and gave his forthright testimony. When it was suggested, by way of diverting the blame, that he often left engineering details to subordinates, the Chief raised his tired head in protest.

"Fasten it on to me if there was any error of judgment—human judgment," he said in a voice deep and trembling. "I am that human."

In spite of the dreadful liability placed upon him, that upright admission earned Mulholland the sympathy of Southern Californians. A flood of editorials and letters gave him ample assurance, if any were needed, that the community which owed its growth to the water he had brought was standing by him in his dark hour.

The disaster had struck Mulholland at the height of his career. Through the mid-twenties he had been able to turn over much of his duties to his chief assistant, H. A. Van Norman, but he still filled the post of superintendent and the unofficial title of "grand old man" of the department. Recently Mulholland Dam and Mulholland Drive had been named in his honor by a grateful city. In February 1927 he had been the guest of honor at a brilliant banquet celebrating the silver anniversary of the city Water Department. All the notables of Los Angeles were there; after serious speeches by Van Norman and others, the Chief had been presented with a loving cup in the midst of appropriate eulogies and a thundering applause.

True to form, he had opened his speech with sly jibes at previous speakers, launched into some anecdotes at their expense, and soon had the guests howling with delight. One distinguished crony after another jumped up and exchanged stories with Mulholland while the audience roared. In his lovable way the old Chief had broken the ice, had turned a dull evening into a hilarious reunion, and had shown that at seventy-two he could still lead the field in a battle of wits.

But now that irrepressible spirit was gone. The tired and sensitive old man could not withstand the shock of the St. Francis disaster. For six months he turned within himself—a stony figure who would not speak, whose friends and family hesitated to address him. Usually a hearty eater, he scarcely touched his meals. At night he tossed in bed or walked the floor. In November 1928 he resigned as superintendent and left an active career with the department after fifty-one years. Though he was retained as chief consulting engineer, time weighed heavily on him; he was the kind of man who had never taken a day off except when forced by his associates.

"I took a vacation once," Mulholland recalled. "I spent an afternoon at Long Beach. I was bored to death from loafing and came back to work next morning."

On his seventieth birthday in 1925 the water board had "directed" the chief to take a vacation. At first he said nothing, as though he could not tolerate such an idea. But in a few days he notified the board that he "desired to be absent from the city for about a week" and headed north on his first vacation in thirty-five years. At Oakland and Sacramento he stopped long enough to serve on two consulting boards of engineers and was tied up in work again when a birthday telegram reached him from the Los Angeles board, reminding him that he had intended to take at least one day off. He finished his consulting work just in time to catch a southbound train at the week's end and appear at his old desk next morning.

Mulholland's retirement now plunged him suddenly from this strenuous life into one of lonely leisure. When an unexpected rain struck Los Angeles, he would still hurry to the department offices to join his comrades in reassessing the city's water supply. But ordinarily he found himself strangely lacking in his old enthusiasm for life. Even his hobbies of geology and nature study no longer held interest for him. More than a year after the dam failure he was taking a ride in San Fernando Valley with his daughter Rose. Suddenly he realized that the entertainment he usually gained from the sights along the way was now lost.

"What's the matter with me?" he exclaimed abruptly, then slowly gave his own answer. "I see things, but they don't interest me. The zest for living is gone."

By the end of the 1920s it seemed that the same disaster which broke Mulholland's spirit had also affected the entire Los Angeles Water and Power Department. Like a beaten giant, it turned with compassion to a final settlement in the Owens Valley controversy. It found a community equally distressed—prostrated by the fall of the Watterson banks.

Resentment in the valley still ran high against Los Angeles. Although their leaders had been proven false, nothing could erase the memory of years of struggle with city officials, and nothing could hide the neglected fields and empty farmhouses remaining on lands acquired by the city's purchasing agents.

It was time for understanding by negotiators on both sides. In the generous payment of St. Francis disaster claims Los Angeles had learned that the good will of the people involved was worth far more than the money that might be saved by taking a coldly legal view of responsibilities.

Two problems remained for final settlement in Owens Valley —sale of the Keough pool and other ranch properties, and compensation for loss of trade for town properties. These were the issues which had inflamed valley men to violence in 1927. That violence had ended only in defeat for the settlers, but the city now moved to fulfill the conditions they had sought.

In the summer of 1929, Los Angeles agreed to a three-man arbitration committee—one of the old valley demands—for the fixing of prices on remaining ranch property. Each side selected a representative, and the two then chose a third, impartial member. After going over thirty-eight pieces of property, they fixed a series of appraisals which were largely favorable to the valley. Both sides accepted; the Owens River Canal ranchers did not get the full price demanded, but they had profited by waiting. Time and arbitration had gained them what dynamite could not.

When it came to the town properties, the Los Angeles men refused to consider reparations. They agreed, however, that the city could buy the land and improvements outright and lease them back to the occupants. In September 1929 a committee of valley representatives met with city officials at Independence to work out this proposal. Heading the Los Angeles group was Judge Harlan J. Palmer, then president of the water board, whom valley people respected as a fair arbiter. He proposed a generous formula for prices which was thereupon accepted.

The following year Los Angeles voted the necessary bonds— over $12,000,000 to "clean up Owens Valley." According to agreement, the city paid peak 1923 prices for town properties during the depression years which followed, yielding far greater values for sellers than they could have made on the open market. Los Angeles was making an expensive try at gaining the good will of the valley and bringing the long struggle to an end.

But though Los Angeles owned practically all of Owens Valley by the mid-thirties—from farmlands to store buildings—it had solved the rankling problem only in a mechanical way. Owens Valley remained a tenant community dependent on a single landlord. Those who had sold town property signed away all right to sue the city for reparations; those selling farmlands leased them back minus the water rights and irrigated their crops only through short-term agreements or the sufferance of the city. Los Angeles had brought an end to the Owens Valley question, but only insofar as its own purposes were concerned. So long as an unwatered Owens Valley remained, such a settlement was California's loss.

Through the dry years of the early 1930s valley agriculture reached its lowest ebb. Besides draining every drop of surface water into the aqueduct, Los Angeles dotted its land with wells and pumped water out so determinedly that underground levels sank to depths which made ordinary farming impossible. The settlers still selling to the city had no reason for remaining on their lands and were soon engaged in the third exodus from Owens Valley. In the lean years from 1929 to 1936 school enrollment dropped thirteen per cent. Hardest hit were the towns of Big Pine and Independence, which for many years exhibited vacant store buildings and empty highway lots.

Through this period, as in the middle twenties, families were piling autos high with household belongings, taking a last look at the old farmhouse, and heading down the highway to Southern California or San Joaquin Valley. They had not been driven from their homes, as some have claimed. But with the sale of their property they had left behind a part of their lives in as beautiful a pastoral valley as California possesses. Their feelings at this uprooting process were expressed in a series of prose sketches appearing in the Inyo *Independent* during the early thirties.

"It is not the loss of the home, or the garden . . . or the growing business which has been the test," said one; "it's the loss of the years, and the hope and the endeavor. . . ."

Stronger words than these were hurled at the city in a simultaneous outburst of critical writing. It seemed that all the pent-up feelings created by the Owens Valley war were suddenly released in a torrent of words. Willie Chalfant, unrelenting editor of the Inyo *Register*, turned out a revised edition of his *Story of Inyo* in 1933, unleashing a terrific diatribe against Los Angeles. Since Fred Eaton's original reconnaissance trip to the valley in 1904, Chalfant had witnessed the whole drama and had recorded it in his weekly newspaper. Like a prosecuting attorney, he now marshaled his evidence, drawing his conclusions without quarter.

> With adequate storage of flood waters [he declared], there would have been little occasion for interference with the streams that were the very life-blood of Owens Valley; there would have been no destruction of homes and farms; Owens Valley towns would have continued to grow; there would have been water for all; millions of dollars would have been saved to the city; and Los Angeles would not have created for itself a repute that generations may not forget.

At the same time outside writers were seizing the Owens Valley story and extracting from it the last drop of pathos and sensationalism. A Southern California newspaperman named

Morrow Mayo far surpassed Chalfant's accusations in his history book, *Los Angeles*. Under the provocative chapter title, "The Rape of Owens Valley," he tackled his subject with obvious relish. Some of the legitimate complaints of valley people became the basis of wild charges and inaccurate history.

"The city of the Angels moved through this valley like a devastating plague," he charged. "It was ruthless, stupid, cruel, and crooked. It deliberately ruined Owens Valley. It stole the waters of the Owens River."

To refute his statements one by one would seem unnecessary if they had not been believed and repeated by later writers. He claimed, for example, that the Owens Valley project was conceived by the men who bought land in San Fernando Valley for the purpose of reaping huge profits at public expense; that Los Angeles "forced the ranchers to sell to the city at condemnation prices and get out"; that it took water from the river forcibly without legal right, "with armed men patrolling the aqueduct and the river day and night."

Even the Owens Valley people made no such claims as these. Fred Eaton and no other conceived the Owens River scheme. In practically every case ranchers sold to the city because they were offered highly attractive prices. Los Angeles took extreme care to establish legal water rights from the beginning; for several years, in fact, it was prevented from exercising part of these rights because of forcible diversions by some of the ranchers. And the aqueduct guards were not mounted to take water from the river but to protect the ditch from dynamitings by some of the valley men.

Unfortunately Mr. Mayo's book was unchallenged for many years and stood as the prime source on the Owens Valley story for other writers. The distorted claims were tacitly accepted as fact. Many Angelenos believed that their city "robbed" Owens Valley of its water and used it for nothing else than to fatten San Fernando Valley.

Certainly the Owens Valley episode was bad enough without burdening Los Angeles with such imaginary crimes. It is true that some city officials used questionable political methods to kill federal development in Owens Valley, gain rights-of-way, and hold water filings; that they failed to build a reservoir at the head of the aqueduct which would have prevented the need of desolating Owens Valley; that for several years they had no settled land-buying policy, causing loss of confidence among valley citizens; and that they hurt business in the towns by the purchase of farms but refused to assume responsibility for such losses. These are the grievances of valley people.

Without these injustices there would have been ample reason for good feeling between city and valley. Los Angeles had shown examples of good will which in other circumstances would have earned the friendship of the settlers. Construction of the aqueduct had brought Owens Valley its long-sought rail connection with Southern California. City power plants provided electricity for Lone Pine and Independence. While exempted by law from paying taxes in Inyo County, Los Angeles voluntarily paid them anyway and helped to push through a legislative bill legalizing the process. It exerted efforts to get a paved highway into the eastern Sierra.

But the spirit of co-operation which might have been engendered by these neighborly deeds was turned into hatred and violence by the results of one tragic mistake. From the city's failure to build Long Valley Dam stem most of the other costly events; through it Los Angeles could have had enough storage capacity to tide itself through dry years in the twenties and thirties and still leave surplus water for Owens Valley farmers. Without it the drought forced city purchases in the upper valley and loss of trade to its townspeople. When Los Angeles failed to meet demands from the settlers, their answer was written with dynamite.

Ironically, Los Angeles tolerated this glaring mistake throughout the Owens Valley war. Only after the crisis had passed and the entire valley lay in its control did the city turn to remove the root of the trouble.

It had long been known that Los Angeles could acquire Long Valley whenever it would meet Fred Eaton's price, which was a million dollars or more. Mulholland, believing Eaton was attempting to hold up the city, had refused to deal. But by the middle 1920s, when drought was threatening their water supply, Los Angeles officials were ready to ignore Mulholland's feud with Eaton. Ed Leahey, the city's valley representative, had begun buying land in upper Owens Valley at extravagant prices and believed the same liberality should be extended to Long Valley.

"Eaton has never been connected with the dynamitings," he told Mulholland. "We should give him as good a deal as the dynamiters."

The Chief agreed, and negotiations were opened with the man who ruled Long Valley. But Eaton was quick-tempered and stubborn; after trying for twenty years to get his price on the property, he would not compromise now. He knew Long Valley was far more valuable as a reservoir site than as a cattle ranch and believed that if the city resorted to condemnation it would have to pay a reservoir price. Leahey dickered and argued with him time after time, offering as high as $750,000. To Eaton the amount was unthinkable; he finally developed such a violent reaction at the mere mention of the figure that the Los Angeles agent had to forget it. At one time, while negotiating with Eaton at the California Club in Los Angeles, Leahey offered to submit the property to Dun & Bradstreet for appraisal. The old man was outraged.

"You call yourself a friend of mine," he shouted, shaking his cane, "and suggest a commercial-firm appraisal of reservoir land?"

But other events were crowding in upon Eaton to force a crisis on Long Valley. Though he owned a controlling share in the Eaton Land and Cattle Company, there were other interested parties who urged acceptance of the city's offer. About 1926, while Eaton was in Los Angeles, the Watterson bankers loaned $200,000 to the Eaton company through some of its other officers and took a mortgage on Long Valley. The transaction should have been invalid without Eaton's knowledge, but before he could take necessary action the Wattersons sold the paper to the Pacific Southwest Trust and Savings Bank—a Los Angeles firm. Soon afterward the Watterson banks crashed. With them went the $200,000, which had supposedly been on deposit.

The loss was the beginning of disaster for Fred Eaton. He was left with a mortgage on his Long Valley lands and no way to pay it off. For years he battled the Pacific Southwest Bank in the courts, claiming that he could not be held by a note he had not signed. But in 1932 the bank won its case and foreclosed the mortgage. Long Valley at last went under the hammer to satisfy the debt; Fred Eaton's twenty-seven-year fight had ended in calamity.

Los Angeles bought the property on December 8, 1932. It might have profited by Eaton's desperation but paid an appraisal price of $650,000. Two thirds of this was absorbed by the bank note, interest, and fees. Eaton and his associates split the rest and had little left after paying an accumulation of debts. It was bitter fruit after a million-dollar dream.

At last the city had bought Long Valley at its own price, but the few hundred thousand it had saved were a costly economy. Many millions in Owens Valley land purchases might have been spared and a water war averted if Long Valley Reservoir had been bought and developed in the early twenties.

As for Eaton, the long years of struggle toward a single material goal had taken a relentless toll. Always shrewd and willful, Eaton grew bitter as old age crept upon him. The million-dollar price he demanded became a fetish with him. Some time after

109

the Watterson debacle left him hopelessly in debt, the old rancher suffered his first stroke. Thereafter he walked only with the help of a cane and aged rapidly.

Not long after the foreclosure and sale brought an end to the tension, Eaton moved to heal the break with his old friend Mulholland. In younger days the two had been hearty companions, had shared many a trip afield and many a laugh around a desert campfire, but it had been thirty years since the two men had forsworn each other. When a message now came to his home that Eaton would like to see him, Mulholland put on his hat and hurried out without a word. At Eaton's house he was ushered to the side of his onetime friend, greeting him with a "Hello, Fred."

They were the first words that had passed between them in years. The two were left alone to compress years of conversation into a few minutes. When Mulholland left, the old enmity had been healed, and Eaton had absolved himself of rancor. A few months later, on March 11, 1934, Fred Eaton died. That night a brooding Mulholland made a strange disclosure to his daughter.

"For three nights in succession I dreamed of Fred," he mused. "The two of us were walking along—young and virile like we used to be." Then, with a pause, "Yet I knew we were both dead."

The startling experience was almost a prophecy. Mulholland, younger than Eaton by one day, followed him in death by little more than a year.

Los Angeles now had Long Valley, but there was one more obstacle to wipe out before it could build the dam that would write the end of the Owens Valley episode. Ever since the city's entrance into the Sierra country in 1905, it had been hampered by a private power filing in the rapids of the Owens River gorge. Situated below the Long Valley reservoir site, the gorge was an ideal power location. As the Los Angeles Water Department extended into the electric field, the site became one of the biggest factors in its expansion plans. After 1920, when the property was acquired by the Southern Sierras Power Company, Los Angeles tried to condemn it in the courts. But the private concern was already operating as a public utility, transmitting power as far as Imperial Valley. When the Supreme Court finally ruled that the property could not be condemned, Los Angeles bought it outright in 1933 and ended the long battle.

With both reservoir and power sites in its hands, the city plunged into active work on Long Valley Dam in April 1935. By 1950 it had completed the dam, tunnels, and powerhouses to

110

harness the remaining energy locked in the depths of the Owens River gorge.

Meanwhile a continuing drought through the early 1930s had made Los Angeles desperate for new water sources. Into Mono County, north of Inyo, went the city's purchasing agents, buying water rights on all the headwaters of Owens River—McGee Creek, Horton Creek, and a dozen others fed by jeweled lakes in the snow-clad Sierra. North of the Owens River basin they tapped every stream as far as Leevining Creek, which flows into the saline expanse of Mono Lake.

These waters were brought into the head of the Owens River by a giant eleven-mile tunnel under a row of extinct volcanoes, the Mono Craters. After an exasperating battle with underground water and carbon dioxide gas deposits, the great bore was completed in six years. On April 24, 1940, the first waters were turned through the Mono Craters Tunnel to the head of Owens River, to join the aqueduct at the growing reservoir at Long Valley.

It was a gigantic feat, even for the master dreamers and doers of the Los Angeles water system. By their energies the southern metropolis now taps almost the entire east slope of the High Sierra—a mighty water source extending a hundred and fifty miles from Mono to Owens Lake. To make full use of it, they added fifty per cent to the capacity of the Los Angeles Aqueduct with a "second barrel" completed in 1969.

Beginning in 1936, a series of wet years helped to bring a rebirth in Owens Valley. From despair and disillusion its remaining settlers turned to new hope as the community shook itself out of slumber. Little attempt was made at farming, but the city's withdrawal of its water wells caused the native grasses to appear in the valley once more. Gradually there rose a flourishing cattle and sheep business. One of the original industries of Owens Valley, stock raising had long since been supplanted by agriculture through the magic touch of irrigation. Now the settlement was starting over again, retracing the same steps of development which civilization itself has followed.

But this time the valley was no longer isolated by mountain fastnesses. Good paved highways made its scenic beauties available to all Californians, and especially to the people of Los Angeles. Owens Valley, gathering strength for its comeback, took new heart and enthusiasm in the task of selling itself to prospective vacationers.

Leading the movement was Father John J. Crowley, who had come to Owens Valley as a young Catholic priest in 1919. Toward the end of the water war he had transferred elsewhere;

111

but in 1934 he returned, broken in health but hoping to rebuild himself in the invigorating mountain climate. Perceiving the despair of the valley's people, he determined to make its rejuvenation his crusade. In little more than a year he joined editor W. A. Chalfant and other businessmen in organizing the Inyo-Mono Association and set about publicizing the vacation wonders of eastern California.

In helping Owens Valley back to life, Father Crowley rebuilt his own health. He lived to see his parish grow into a vacationer's paradise, saw new auto courts, gas stations, and chain groceries spring up in the towns of Lone Pine and Bishop. By 1940 a million tourists a year were pouring through the valley, leaving some $5,000,000 in trade. Even some of the old-timers who had left Inyo in its dark days were drifting back as the community returned to life.

Most of this vacation traffic was coming from the great metropolis to the south, which had been mushrooming for twenty-five years on a foundation of Owens River water. Thus the lost product was bringing its own indirect return. Angelenos who would scarcely admit their address when visiting Owens Valley in the bitter twenties were now welcomed as customers in the valley's leading business—the tourist trade.

Nor was this the city's only aid to Owens Valley. New water and power projects brought added employment and heavy payrolls to the eastern Sierra country. By 1941, Harvey A. Van Norman's crewmen had finished Long Valley Dam and thereby corrected the mistake that had sparked the Owens Valley war. Standing 118 feet high, the earth-fill structure stored 183,000 acre-feet—not far from the amount originally demanded by the farmers when the matter reached a crisis in 1922.

On October 19, 1941, the final phase of the Owens Valley drama was opened with a celebration, attended by over six hundred Owens Valley and Los Angeles people, at a spot overlooking the giant new reservoir in Long Valley. It was the dedication of Crowley Lake, named in honor of a country priest who had helped to stir Owens Valley out of its despair. Father John J. Crowley had not lived to witness the event, but his tragic death in an auto accident the year before had left the valley people determined to fix his name to the waters of their hope.

Among the speakers at the ceremony was Willie Chalfant, old and embattled editor of the Inyo *Register*. His comment on the Long Valley achievement brought an official close to the struggle he had witnessed for thirty-five years:

"It is a promise of the end of dissentions, and we welcome its implied pledge that hereafter, City and Eastern Sierra shall

112

work hand in hand. . . . We cannot but regret that this enterprise was not constructed long ago; there would have been less
of history to forget. . . ."

Poetic justice would be served if it could be reported that
the Long Valley Dam has made possible the rebirth of Owens
Valley—that the farmers have returned to the land and are pushing back the sagebrush with orchards and green fields. It is
tempting to declare that the million dollars Fred Eaton had demanded for this reservoir site would have been cheap compared
to the millions paid for Owen Valley property.

But the relentless growth of Los Angeles has blasted such
conclusions. Even with the aqueduct's second barrel, and with
the capacity of Crowley Lake reservoir expanded to 285,000 acre-
feet, the city's insatiable thirst still leaves too little water for a
guaranteed supply to Owens Valley farms. What little farming
is attempted depends upon short-term leases which permit the
city to withhold the water at any time. Though early construction of the Long Valley reservoir might have averted a water
war, Owens Valley farming would eventually have been sacrificed on the altar of Los Angeles boosterism.

Supported by the dollars brought by vacationers—largely
from Los Angeles—Owens Valley now numbers more permanent
residents than it did before it came under the shadow of the
monolith. But it is no longer the home of frontier farmers
breathing the exhilarating air of self-reliance. It is a tributary
province to the city it helped to build.

That city's enormous growth in population and wealth, made
possible by this bounteous river of water, was once the unques-
tioned goal of Angelenos. Today this feast of material achievement is turning to ashes in their mouths. It has brought with it
pollution, congestion, and most all the discomforts that the Eastern millions had sought to escape in Los Angeles. Compared to
this paradise lost, the pastures and the sun-tipped crags of Owens
Valley are paradise enough, even without the water.

Photographs

Downtown Los Angeles about 1902, looking east from the Courthouse near Temple Street and Broadway. *LADWP Photo*

William Mulholland, builder of the Los Angeles-Owens River Aqueduct.
LADWP Photo

Watershed area of the eastern Sierra Nevada. *LADWP Photo*

Diversion point of Owens River into Aqueduct at Aberdeen. *LADWP Photo*

Early steam shovel digging a section of the Los Angeles Aqueduct.
LADWP Photo

A section of open lined canal under construction on the Aqueduct. *LADWP Photo*

52-mule team transporting pipe section. *LADWP Photo*

Construction of a major siphon on the Los Angeles Aqueduct. *LADWP Photo*

120

Castaic Cascade section of the Los Angeles Aqueduct. *LADWP Photo*

Wreckage of No Name Siphon after dynamiting by Owens Valley ranchers, May 27, 1927. *LADWP Photo*

121

Jawbone Siphon. *LADWP Photo*

122

Entrance to Elizabeth Lake tunnel on Los Angeles Aqueduct. *LADWP Photo*

123

Crowd at auction of lots on official opening of Van Nuys, Feb. 22, 1911.

Arrival of crowds for opening of Los Angeles Aqueduct, Nov. 5, 1913, near San Fernando. Mulholland is on left side of rear seat of center auto.
Los Angeles Times *Photo*

124

Arrival of first Owens River water in Los Angeles through Cascades in San Fernando Valley, November 5, 1913. *LADWP Photo*

Mohave Conduit section of Second Los Angeles Aqueduct. *LADWP Photo*

Jawbone Siphon section of second aqueduct. *LADWP Photo*

Concreting at Hoover Dam, 1934.

Hoover Dam. *LADWP Photo*

Power Plant at Hoover Dam. *LADWP Photo*

San Jacinto Tunnel construction, mid-1930s—one phase of the Colorado River Aqueduct project. *MWD Photo*

Miners cutting San Jacinto Tunnel encountered a very active spring system. At worst times, up to 40,000 gallons of water a minute had to be pumped from the tunnel. *MWD Photo*

Parker Dam, completed in 1938, forms Lake Havasu, forebay and desilting basin for the Colorado River Aqueduct intake. *MWD Photo*

Section of Colorado River Aqueduct canal crosses the Colorado Desert. *MWD Photo*

Julian Hinds pumping plant, 126 miles from the intake, is the last and highest lift on the Colorado River Aqueduct system. Water is raised 441 feet. *MWD Photo*

Oroville Dam, completed 1967, and lake, part of the California State Water Project. *DWR Photo*

California Aqueduct near Patterson. *DWR Photo*

135

Part 2

9: THE DESERT BLOSSOMS

More than anything else, the Owens Valley story epitomizes the basic conflict over water among the peoples of the Southwest. In most of the arid country of America development has been limited by water supply. But Southern California has refused to recognize such limits. It is here, therefore, that the West's fundamental water problem has rankled deepest and has driven cities and farm communities to the furthest extremities. Its economic development has risen out of its water development—first from irrigation along its own limited streams and finally through diversions from far-off sources for both farm and city use. Certainly its growth has not been held back by other disadvantages. Like most arid regions, its soil is as fertile as any in the world.

"Where the mesquite grows," runs an old desert saying, "you can make fence posts bloom if you bring water."

The lordly Colorado, as the one great river worthy of the name in the far Southwest, has provided its most spectacular water projects and its most far-ranging water conflict. One of America's three great water systems, it drains parts of seven states from Wyoming to the Gulf of California. Winter snows on the summits of the Rocky Mountains—the "white gold" of the West—make up its source. The sandy beds of its lower tributaries, from Utah southward, load its currents with mud, helping it through countless ages to scour out a deep gorge along most of its length.

For decades after the white man's entry into the Southwest the Colorado kept its secrets locked behind these impenetrable

139

canyon walls. Then in 1869 the first full-scale exploration was made by Major John Wesley Powell, a Civil War veteran turned geology professor. Starting in Wyoming on the Green River—longest of the Colorado's upper tributaries—he headed downstream with eleven men and four wooden boats. Four months later, after a harrowing passage through the rapids of the Grand Canyon, the expedition reached the Gulf of California. Powell's reports of this and later expeditions helped to unlock the mysteries of the Colorado and prepare it for the use of man.

Outposts of the American frontier had already begun to tap the Colorado system for meager supplies of irrigation water. In 1854, a party of Mormons, the West's first American irrigators, settled in Wyoming's southwest corner and began diverting water from the Green River to their crops. After Powell's expedition other settlements sprang up along mountain-bound tributaries in Colorado, as fast as the region was made safe from Indians.

In the early 1880s farmers began to cultivate the Uncompahgre Valley, southeast of Grand Junction, and proceeded to put three times as much land under the hoe as the river could irrigate. Then began a long struggle to secure relief from the deep-gorged Gunnison River several miles away; it did not end until 1909, when the United States Reclamation Bureau completed one of its first and most spectacular projects with a six-mile tunnel from the Gunnison to the Uncompahgre.

By this time, however, the lower basin of the Colorado was outstripping the mountain region in irrigation. The Southwest's first water diversion from the Colorado had been made in 1877 by Samuel Blythe, for whom the California town of Blythe is named. He was soon irrigating crops in the Palo Verde Valley, one of the few spots along the deep canyon of the Colorado where water can be turned onto the land by gravity ditches.

On the Arizona side, irrigation first began in the Yuma Valley in the early 1890s. When the Reclamation Service was formed, it made this one of its first projects and in 1909 completed Laguna Dam—the first dam on the Colorado. From the beginning Yuma was a model project for other government irrigation efforts throughout the West. But having begun its life in 1902, the Reclamation Service was about three years too late for the most spectacular development of all.

On a blistering day just before the dawn of the twentieth century five men drove their wagon into the sterile depression known as the Colorado Desert; from a spot near the present Calexico, they surveyed its barren expanse.

One of them was Charles Rockwood, a huge, powerful young

man with a bulldog appearance and an enthusiasm for sharing in the great task of reclaiming the arid West. In his mind was a plan to turn this treeless inferno into an agricultural empire of 1,000,000 acres. The magic ingredient was water. Rockwood believed he knew where to get it.

Another was George Chaffey, one of the world's leading reclamationists. Founder of Ontario and other California settlements, builder of pioneer irrigation projects in Australia, this quiet, gray-bearded engineer had carved empires on two continents by the simple formula of applying water to the earth. Rockwood was now urging him to build the canal which would bring lifeblood into this uninhabited land.

Chaffey caught the vision, for he was also a man of big dreams. But his practical side rebelled at the expense of constructing the necessary fifty-mile canal. Turning to Rockwood, he told him it was no use. They headed back to the town of Yuma while Rockwood nursed his disappointment.

Ever since he had first seen this land in 1892, he had tried in vain to finance its development. Born in Michigan, Rockwood had come West as a young engineer and had lived in arid regions long enough to know that this was a project of magnificent promise. As chief irrigator for the vast Yakima development in Washington—one of the first reclamation schemes in the Northwest—Rockwood had gained experience and fame. Now, through the greatest part of the nineties, his potentialities as an engineer had been buried in his visionary Colorado Desert plan.

The physical features of the idea were obvious. They involved the law of gravity and the waters of the mighty Colorado River, passing scarcely sixty miles away unused.

Like any other muddy river, the Colorado formed a delta of earth where it entered the ocean. Second only to the Tigris as a carrier of silt, it sent down enough soil every year to refill the Panama Canal. But in the ancient process of building its bed out into the Gulf of California, the river played a unique geological trick. It completely spanned an ocean inlet which once extended as far north as the present Indio, in Coachella Valley. A third of the gulf was thus cut off; its water evaporated in the sun, leaving a dry basin below sea level known as the Salton Sink.

But the silt-laden river, building up its own bed on the delta at the rate of a foot a year, remained unstable in its course. Several times in past ages it had left its channel to the sea and turned northwest into the sterile depression it had created. For years at a time it had poured into this prison, until the new bed had been lifted high by depositing silt. The stream was then obliged by gravity to switch southward once more into the gulf. The inland lake evaporated, to await replenishing ages hence, when the indecisive river changed its mind again. It was one of the most remarkable geologic phenomena in all of nature.

How long since the river had paid its last visit was unknown to Rockwood. Native Cocopah Indians told a legend of the inland sea which once filled this "palm of the hand of God." Certainly there remained as a telltale record the ancient shore line around the rim of the basin. In canyons along that shore line, myriad groves of palm trees stood as survivors of a once tropical climate.

Even in the four hundred years of white man's acquaintance the Colorado or one of its tributaries had periodically flooded enough to overflow into this sink, forming a temporary lake in its lowest depression. Today experts can examine the earth on the different mesas of Imperial Valley and identify the particular Colorado tributary—Gila, Salt, Williams, or Virgin rivers—whose floodwaters rushed in and left a deposit of silt. It is these layers of fine soil, spread by flash floods, which have covered the alkali floor left by the sea and made the valley fit for cultivation by man. Its position several hundred feet below the Colorado River has laid the entire region open to gravity irrigation.

Others, before Rockwood, had visioned the latent power of the Colorado Desert. Chief of these was Dr. Oliver Wozencraft, prominent forty-niner who first conceived the idea of reclaiming the region with Colorado River water and consumed the last forty years of his life trying vainly to promote it.

Rockwood himself—first called to the Colorado delta to build an ill-fated irrigation scheme in Sonora, Mexico—remained to tackle the more inviting problem of the Salton Sink. By 1896, after repeated financial disappointments, he joined Anthony H. Heber and several other associates in forming the California Development Company. During the next four years he haunted Eastern financial circles in an effort to raise real capital for the venture. But to prospective investors the Colorado Desert was as remote and uninspiring as the Sahara. Capitalists laughed at him, saying that even if water could be brought to the land it would never yield any crops.

"Why, it will be absolutely worthless anyhow," he was told. "Alkali will come up."

Late in 1899, with the California Development Company facing defeat, Rockwood was closing up his New York office when a telegram reached him from California: George Chaffey, the great irrigationist, had agreed to examine the project.

Hurrying westward, Rockwood met Chaffey and accompanied him into the Colorado Desert. But after two months of investigation, the famed empire builder pronounced the scheme impracticable. Rockwood returned to New York all but beaten. By February 1900, with a delinquent-tax suit threatening the company, he wrote to Anthony Heber in despair.

"I feel very much inclined to jump the whole business and go into something else," he said, "but will stick to it for a month yet. . . ."

George Chaffey, in the meantime, had not been able to dismiss the Colorado scheme. During a visit to Yuma he decided to investigate a new aspect of it which had crossed his mind. Taking an Indian guide, he explored the Colorado delta in detail, finding a series of ancient watercourses into the Salton Sink which could be used to cut canal costs to one tenth of the estimate.

Chaffey returned from three weeks of desert hardships which eventually caused him permanent deafness; but also with him was a fresh enthusiasm. He now saw Rockwood's project as an unsurpassed opportunity to reclaim an empire. When he reached Los Angeles, his son Andrew pointed out the financial risks and begged him to stay out of this shaky California Development Company. George Chaffey would not listen.

"Let me do one more big thing before I die," he said.

Andrew relented, and the old irrigator sent a hurried wire to Rockwood in New York that he would join the scheme.

Chaffey's entry into the project proved its turning point. Early in April 1900 he contracted to build the canal and deliver the water at the upper end of the valley in return for a quarter of the company's stock. Instead of the formidable name "Colorado Desert," he proposed another which reflected his British background—"Imperial Valley." Immediately the name, together with the luster of his own, gave the project a new reputation.

Spurred by lavish boom literature, eager settlers were soon driving in from San Diego, Arizona, and all the Southwest. Excursion trains from Los Angeles were run over Southern Pacific tracks to the northern end of the valley. From there the newcomers were whisked southward by dust-caked stagecoach to the heart of Imperial, where land was free with the purchase of company "water scrip."

In spite of intense heat, the valley looked inviting that summer. The spring overflow from the Colorado River had left much of the countryside green with grass, on which thousands of horses and cattle were contentedly grazing. By early 1901 the population had jumped from zero to 1500, and the town of Imperial was mushrooming as fast as mule teams could bring in the lumber. In March the Imperial *Press*, first newspaper in the valley, blossomed with the jubilant slogan, "Water Is King: Here Is Its Kingdom."

But what of the water? Until now the land had been settled in the promise of it, and farmers were plowing their first furrows in anticipation. The only thing still lacking was the same thing that had always been lacking—water.

The cause for delay, as usual, was financial. Rockwood and his associates had kept Chaffey from knowing the company's rickety condition, fearing that if he abandoned them the last chance to reclaim the Colorado Desert would be gone. Aside from the unpaid taxes, the company had failed to buy the key property through which the canal must run.

Chaffey was outraged to find he had been used to rescue a tottering concern. But with settlers pouring into Imperial Valley on the strength of his participation in the scheme, he resolved to go ahead. Out of his own pocket came the money to pay off debts, buy the necessary land, and set the company on its feet.

Late in November 1900 his crewmen attacked the big canal with dredge, plows, and a battery of shovels. Near the promontory of Pilot Knob, just above the Mexican border, he built his wooden head gate to control the inflow of river water. An intervening range of shifting sand, the "walking hills" of the Colorado Desert, blocked his direct path to Imperial Valley. Swinging below them through Mexico, Chaffey carved his canal parallel with the Colorado River for over four miles, connecting with the ancient overflow channel known as the Alamo River. For the next fifty miles westward his task was merely to clear the brush and unnecessary bends from this ready-made canal. Finally, just below the point where it recrossed the border on its way to Salton Sink, he built another control works to divide the water into the valley's various irrigation canals.

Scarcely five months after he broke ground, Chaffey completed this bloodstream to the thirsty lands of Imperial Valley. On May 14, 1901, the old man went to his head gate near Pilot Knob to make the great diversion. Until this crucial test, no one could know for certain whether the giant experiment would succeed. But to his son in Los Angeles, Chaffey was able to send a simple telegram of cheer:

"Water turned through gate at 11 a.m. Everything all right."

Immediately the expectant valley sprang to life. At last the Imperial *Press* and its "Water Kingdom" could receive their king. Through the summer of 1901 crops of wheat and barley were sown as fast as water canals could be extended. By

144

the spring of 1902, when George Chaffey withdrew from the project after an eventful two years, 400 miles of distributing canals had been built to serve up to 100,000 acres of land.

At the same time enthusiastic citizens decided their new empire needed the Iron Horse; they promptly founded the Imperial and Gulf Railroad to connect with the Southern Pacific at the valley's northern end, boasting openly that the move was a bluff "to force the S.P. to build the road."

Imperial's paper railroad kings did not wait long. Before the end of May the Southern Pacific stepped in according to plan and laid tracks into Imperial town by February 1903.

Trainloads of settlers, responding to a new deluge of advertising, poured in to bring the valley its first real boom. New towns—Brawley, Holtville, El Centro—sprang up out of the barren ground, first put together with boards and canvas, later with brick and mortar. Some 5000 people reached the valley that year, more than tripling its population. Crop acreage, standing at 25,000 in the spring of 1903, jumped to 100,000 by December.

To these incoming empire builders it was America's last farm frontier. Once again they were suffering under the same pioneer hardships of a generation before. At first they lived in tents and rude huts, lighted by candles or coal oil, without telephones or running water. During the winter they braved bitter frosts to tend their crops; by summer they sweated in the fields through desert heat that reached 125 degrees in the shade. The battle to bring civilization to this forbidding region was an American epic, fought with the characteristic courage and unyielding tenacity of the frontier farmer.

But the builders of Imperial Valley were soon encountering other enemies beside the elements. The federal government, its enthusiasm for public irrigation projects fortified by the new Reclamation Act, was moving into the Southwest with a clumsy tread. Distrusting any development by private companies, it began to throw every possible obstacle in the way of Rockwood's scheme. In the fall of 1901 a pair of overzealous experts from the Department of Agriculture came into the valley, armed with hand augers and mortars for testing the soil. Their report, widely heralded and eagerly awaited by valley farmers, fell at last as a bombshell in January 1902. Over half the land in the valley, it calmly declared, "contains too much alkali to be safe, except for resistant crops. . . . For the worst lands," it concluded, "the best thing to do will be to immediately abandon them."

To most of the valley farmers the report was absurd. Some of these very soil tests had been made in fields of shoulder-high

145

grain. It was true that alkali lay under the rich topsoil washed in by Colorado floods, but it was too deep to affect production for many years to come. Melons, tomatoes, lettuce, cotton, grapes, and almost every farm product were growing in abundance, yielding prime market prices because they matured ahead of the national harvest.

But for prospective settlers, the report loomed like a detour sign. Newspapers used it to attack Rockwood's California Development Company as a gigantic fraud. Land sales fell off, and the entire project faced disaster. Finally the company's president, Anthony Heber, journeyed to Washington and discredited the report before the Secretary of Agriculture. A reinvestigation was promptly made which restored the valley's reputation before it was too late.

Imperial was booming once more when the government turned its guns on the project's legal title to land and water. Suddenly the fact developed that the original land survey had been erroneous; every title in the valley was therefore faulty, and until the matter was cleared the government claimed it all as public land.

Then the C. D. Company fell into a squabble over water rights with the newly established Reclamation Service, which claimed that the federal government had sole jurisdiction over the Colorado River. In an argument with J. B. Lippincott, then chief engineer for the service in the Southwest, Anthony Heber made a regrettable boast: the 10,000 second-feet claimed by the company, he declared, was enough to hold practical control of the whole river.

"You are taking the water illegally," retorted Lippincott, "and we can stop you in a moment."

"I don't think you will do it—will you?" challenged Heber. "Because it would certainly injure those people very much, and if you do we will have to lean upon the Mexican Government. We will certainly connect the river . . . below the line, which we can do in twenty-four hours' time."

The question was left unsettled; and when the Imperial people heard of the conversation, alarm spread through the valley. Mass meetings were held over this threat to their water supply; telegrams were dispatched to Washington asking recognition of the project's rights. With its credit sinking and its settlers clamoring for action, the C. D. Company moved in self-defense. Heber hurried to Washington early in 1904 to urge a bill in Congress legalizing the diversion of Colorado water. The Interior Department fought him before the legislative committee, whereupon Heber made his famous threat:

"It is my earnest desire to worship at our own altar and to receive the blessing from the shrine of our own government, but if such permission is not given, of necessity I will be compelled to worship elsewhere."

True to his word, Heber stormed out of Washington when his request was denied and made his way to Mexico City. There he asked for a water concession below the border but found authorities unwilling to grant it without a stipulation that up to half of any water taken through the canal should be used on the Mexican side.

The terms were hard, but Heber could do nothing but submit. Without an unclouded right somewhere on the river his company would be ruined, and Imperial Valley must wither and die.

Besides, a new difficulty was also forcing abandonment of the American intake. The initial four miles of the canal, constructed without sufficient grade for a swift flow, had become so filled with Colorado silt that in low periods the valley found its lifeblood practically choked off. With the farmers already suing the company for failing to deliver enough water, Heber was desperate. In July 1904 he signed the concession and ordered Rockwood to make the Mexican cut.

Plans for a controlling head gate on the proposed intake were quickly submitted to Mexico City for approval. But after months of exasperating delay Rockwood found the fall irrigating season approaching with the Mexican cut still unbuilt. He hesitated to make the opening without a head gate for control, but after checking on the river's flood history, he was satisfied to take the chance.

In October 1904, Rockwood completed the short ditch between the river and the canal at a point four miles south of the border, opposite a prominent island in the channel. Water was soon flowing through it toward the valley, to the relief of its farmers. In one stroke Heber and Rockwood had foiled the government's attempt to deny their water rights and had bypassed the silt-choked portion of the Imperial Canal.

But the C. D. Company had reckoned without the unpredictable Colorado. For endless millennia the great brown current had wound through its tree-lined channel like an endless snake, gliding in apparent calm during its low stage but rearing its angry head to threaten everything within reach in time of flood. For four years it had flowed on in silent wrath while man had toyed with its power, drawing off part of its body into the ancient inland basin.

Did these canal builders want more water in Imperial

Valley? Very well; the brown serpent had been building up the bed of its channel for decades, preparing once again to switch its course away from the gulf and into the blind sink to the north.

10: RUNAWAY RIVER

Beginning early in February 1905, desert cloud bursts sent a series of floods pouring down the Gila River, the Colorado tributary whose branches drained most of Arizona. Laden with logs and debris, its reddish waters emptied into the main stream at Yuma and hurtled onward toward the gulf.

The first two freshets swirled by Rockwood's Mexican cut, merely silting up part of its opening. Such floods were unusual and short-lived; Rockwood was unconcerned, intending to dam up the breach before the spring floods of the main Colorado.

But early in March a third freshet raged down the channel with twice the volume of the other two. Swinging headlong through Rockwood's cut, it eroded the entrance to an alarming size. The engineer now found his main problem was not to get enough water for Imperial farmers but to keep out more water than was needed.

Immediately a makeshift dam was begun across the gap. A floating pile driver pounded three rows of poles in the swirling water while hard-working crewmen filled the spaces between with brush and sandbags. Only a six-foot gap remained when the Gila rose in its fourth flood. It struck the Mexican heading on March 18, washing out Rockwood's miserable dam like a pile of straw.

Imperial Valley was in serious trouble now. There was no record of such winter floods in the river's history. Although the settlers were unaware of it, this was the moment in geologic time when the Colorado was making another of its periodic switches from the gulf into its northern basin. Man's fumbling work was merely hastening the process.

One more desperate attempt was made to close the gap before the regular spring floods. But in May 1905 the rising tide of the Colorado found the workings still unfinished. Long and sustained in contrast to the sudden winter flashes out of the Gila, the annual spring flood slowly undermined the entire dam. Rockwood abandoned it to the river's fury in June. With almost half of the Colorado pouring through the hole toward Imperial Valley, the distraught engineer could only stand by in helpless insignificance and wait for the flood to pass.

148

But in the valley itself continual flooding of the Alamo channel brought general alarm. All at once the people realized that the river was out of control. Already the Salton Sink at the valley's lowest point had been turned into a vast and sparkling Salton Sea, rising several inches a day. If the breach could not be stopped, they feared, it would keep on growing till it reached sea level—and the whole of their bright new empire would be submerged like some lost civilization.

Frantically Heber and Rockwood appealed to the Southern Pacific, which had already been forced to move its valley tracks to higher ground by the encroachment of the Salton Sea. They pointed out that the railroad was doing a promising business in Imperial Valley and could not afford to let it die. When its California officials hesitated, Rockwood went to New York and approached Edward H. Harriman, the railroad's iron-fisted president.

While still in his forties, the dynamic financier controlled enough railroad to make him the dominant figure in American transportation. Without hesitation he agreed to loan $200,000—a sum which dwarfed other river investments—but on condition that the Southern Pacific take temporary control of the California Development Company.

Rockwood jubilantly returned to the valley in mid-June, confident that the river would be tamed. But his spirits were soon shattered by another trick of the devilish Colorado. When the summer flood subsided, the island opposite the Mexican intake showed itself above the surface; before the valley engineers could stop it, the entire right half of the Colorado had been deflected into the Imperial Canal.

Confined in this narrow passage, the river was forced to grind its way deeper into the soft ground, forming a deep canyon which soon cut itself back upstream to the north end of the island. Then the flow on the Arizona side abandoned its course and swung headlong into the Mexican cut. When Rockwood arrived to find the entire Colorado River leaving its channel and driving straight toward Imperial Valley, he realized that this was as serious a problem "as had ever before confronted any engineer upon the American continent."

Down from his headquarters in Tucson, Arizona, came Epes Randolph, the engineer whom Harriman had named as the new president of the C. D. Company. Builder of most of Southern California's Pacific Electric Railway system, Randolph had been Harriman's shrewd and active lieutenant for several years. At sight of the runaway river he telegraphed his chief that no $200,000 could save the valley. There was no telling the ultimate cost, he advised, but warned that it "might easily run into three quarters of a million dollars."

From New York came Harriman's answer: "Are you certain you can put the river back into the old channel?"

"I am certain that it can be done," Randolph replied.

"Go ahead and do it," concluded the railroad president.

The decision was made. Harriman meant to stop the river without regard to cost. Rockwood thereupon threw himself into the task once more; between the northern end of the island and the Mexican shore he began building a new brush dam in July 1905, determined to deflect the entire river down the Arizona channel. Starting at the island, a floating pile driver pounded logs into the riverbed, while a crew of Mexican laborers struggled to fasten a brush mattress in place.

Against this obstruction the river began to deposit a bank of silt, helping to form its own barrier. But after a half-mile sandbar had been formed, the concentration of the channel in the last 125 feet made the torrent too unruly. Logs and brush mattings were no sooner rammed into the breach than they were uprooted and swallowed up by the current.

Rockwood gave up at last. The Mexican shore, little more than a log's length away, was in reality as distant as ever. Some $30,000 had so far been spent without effect.

With the autumn irrigating season approaching once more, Rockwood conceived a plan to stop the river and still leave a controlled flow of water into Imperial Valley. At a point down the canal from its opening he would build a bypass containing a wooden head gate, through which the water could be diverted while a heavy rock dam was flung across the crevasse. Then the flashboards of the gate could be closed, the water would find its path barred, and gravity would force its return to the regular Colorado channel. Rockwood's gate would remain, however, to permit a certain flow into the canal for the crops in Imperial Valley. After getting Randolph's approval of the scheme, Rockwood left the details to others and turned to his office tasks as general manager for the C. D. Company.

Into his place at the river came the Southern Pacific's chief bridge-building engineer, F. S. Edinger. Distrusting Rockwood's head-gate scheme, he abandoned it and began raising another dam, between the island and the Mexican shore. Once again brush mattresses were woven between log pilings, but on this foundation were dumped tons of heavy rocks which gave promise of stopping the river. By the end of November, with only three feet of water flowing over the dam, the river fighters were ready to deliver the final blow that would divert the Colorado out of Imperial Valley and back into the Gulf of California.

150

On the twenty-ninth the Gila River came hurtling out of Arizona with 100,000 second-feet of floodwater and a grinding cargo of logs and debris. It washed out miles of Southern Pacific tracks west of Yuma and rolled onward for the Imperial intake. All night long it battered Edinger's nearly completed dam with its irresistible mass of driftwood.

Next morning, with the fury spent, the engineer found only the stumps of pilings showing above the river's surface to mark the grave of his broken dam. Two thirds of the island had been washed away by the flood; through the crevasse, now grown to 600 feet, the Colorado was pouring unchecked into the Imperial Canal. One observer commented bitterly that they "might as well attempt to plug an open faucet with a postage stamp as to stop this flow by brushwood mats."

A few days later Epes Randolph arrived at the Mexican break to view the disaster with Edinger, who resigned as engineer-in-charge. Rockwood was also there, angrily pointing out that it was Edinger's abandonment of his head-gate plan that had brought on the debacle. To his delight Randolph ordered him to proceed with his head gate.

The veteran river fighter promptly dropped his office chores and threw himself wholeheartedly into the new construction. In mid-December 1905, after hurriedly gathering men and equipment, he broke ground for his gate in a proposed bypass just north of the canal opening. When this was completed he meant to build a rock-fill dam across the canal itself to divert the Colorado through the bypass and its controlling gate. But Rockwood knew he must hasten; the entire process must be completed before the Colorado's spring floods arrived to throw too great a strain on the head gate.

Work therefore proceeded at a furious pace. In the bypass his crewmen laid a great wooden platform, upon which a row of massive A-shaped frames—the backbone of the gate—gradually took shape. Yet in spite of night and day shifts, Rockwood found construction falling behind schedule.

Early in April 1906 the gate was complete enough to allow the river to be diverted through it; but before he could begin dumping rock for his diversion dam across the canal, Rockwood saw the Colorado rising once more. The annual spring flood had caught up with him—just soon enough to prevent operation of the gate. Already twice as much water was rushing through the canal as the head gate was built to control. There was nothing to do but wait for weeks while the flood raged on and then subsided. Once again the relentless Colorado had thwarted its would-be captors.

Still Rockwood knew that this delay was inviting disaster. Even now the silt-laden waters were gouging out the banks of the crevasse, widening it to half a mile. From the delta country came word that the river was already overflowing the canal banks and spreading over the land. The inland body known as Volcano Lake was filled completely, with the surplus spilling northward to the border. Mexican families, homeless and bewildered, were fleeing before the blanket of water.

Rockwood had spent practically all of the $200,000 advanced by Harriman of the S.P., and the situation was more alarming than ever. The only remaining hope was that the financier could be induced to cast aside the rules of business and throw more good money after bad.

But on April 18, 1906, disaster struck in another quarter. The earthquake on that fateful day was scarcely felt in Imperial Valley, but from the north came ugly word of catastrophe. San Francisco, standing in the path of the San Andreas Fault, was shattered and set afire. For the men fighting the river below the border the main tragedy was the demolition of this heart of the Southern Pacific rail system. Traffic was paralyzed; trains were backed up to Cheyenne in one direction, to Los Angeles in another. Harriman and Randolph both hurried to the bay to take personal charge. In the face of this tragedy, further Southern Pacific help in fighting the river now seemed a forlorn hope.

But Harriman, having tackled the Colorado, was not inclined to retreat. With all San Francisco prostrate about him, with his rail system taxed to the limit in rescue work, Harriman yet remembered Imperial Valley. Before the end of April he gave $250,000 to stop the break in the Colorado River. Behind that was as much more as was needed.

Even with Harriman's help there was no hope of stopping the river until the spring flood subsided. One of the highest annual rises in the river's history was pouring headlong into Imperial Valley; now it was the settlers' turn to fight the monster and protect their homes and crops.

Out of the delta country below the border the floodwaters came hurtling into the valley through two ancient channels—the New River and the Alamo. At the north end the Salton Sea was rising seven inches a day, placing a salt refining works sixty feet under water by June 1906. Time after time the Southern Pacific found its tracks awash and hurriedly moved them to higher ground. Below the border its Mexican line was completely submerged for miles.

All at once the valley people discovered a new threat from the treacherous Colorado. As its volume rose to 70,000, then

152

100,000 second-feet, it began to gouge out more elbowroom in the channels. At every bend the silt-laden current struck angrily against the banks, undermining whole blocks of soft earth which cracked off and plunged into the roaring current.

Worse still, the flood in New River began to scour deeper into the bed itself. Starting at its mouth in Salton Sea, a cataract was formed in the stream bottom where the muddy water gouged into the silt. The cutting action against the lip of the waterfall forced it to move steadily backward and upstream, toward the Imperial farm settlements and border towns. Within a few days the cataract grew to twenty feet in height, at the same time widening the channel to massive proportions. If it reached the regular Colorado channel at the Mexican break, all hope of damming the madcap river would be lost.

Over on the Alamo channel the same appalling phenomenon had occurred. A waterfall was cutting southward at more than half a mile a day, and by early June was bearing down on the Southern Pacific railroad bridge east of Brawley on the Los Angeles line—the only remaining route out of the valley. Frantically the Imperial farmers turned to their ripening cantaloupe crops. If that destructive cataract destroyed the trestle before the melons could be harvested and shipped, financial ruin would be added to the threat of inundation.

On June 14, 1906, with the Alamo falls scarcely a day away from the bridge, every farm family in central Imperial Valley was in the field stripping the cantaloupe vines. From all directions a stream of wagons trundled into the railway station at Brawley, where busy packers loaded the melons into crates and filled the waiting boxcars. Next day, after working through a sleepless night, the people saw the last trainload pull out for the Alamo crossing. The cataract had reached the bridge, but Southern Pacific crewmen had braced it enough to stand the strain. Cautiously the final cars were shuttled over the torrent and sent safely northward to the Los Angeles market.

Farther south toward the Mexican break the rising floodwaters were even more threatening. Near El Centro the torrent broke through the levee of the Central Main Canal, putting the streets of Imperial town under water and drowning out the surrounding farmlands. Here again every family turned out—this time to fight the water itself. Crews of desperate men, working feverishly to dam the flood, threw sandbags and brush mattresses into the breach. When gunnysacks gave out, local merchants emptied flour and grain bags, and housewives sewed more out of any cloth available. After three days of battle they plugged the gap, forced the angry current back down the canal, and rescued most of the nearby farms.

At the border, where New River ran through the edge of
Calexico and Mexicali, the monster was taking worse toll. With
the river undercutting its banks and widening by the hour, it
was soon threatening to engulf the very buildings of the towns.
In Calexico the people threw up a sandbag levee and fought to
maintain it against the flood. But in neighboring Mexicali, located on the very banks of the river, native families were already
fleeing before the waters. By the last of June house after
house was toppling into the current. As the river undercut its
banks, great chunks of the soft ground broke off, carrying with
them whatever structures they supported. Larger buildings were
first undermined gradually, then, after teetering on the brink,
would be shocked by a heavy wave and sent thundering into the
maelstrom.

After the first excitement the townspeople turned to watch
the river's advance with philosophical abandon. Standing near
the edge of the bank, their view almost obscured by clouds of
dust rising from the crash of earth, they watched with fascina-
tion while the brown serpent slowly devoured Mexicali.

With the Southern Pacific depot threatened, engineer Jack
Carrillo hurried up from his losing fight to protect company
tracks below the border; his first sight of the situation told him
no human effort could save the town so long as the flood raged.
From Los Angeles came H. V. Platt, general superintendent of
S.P. lines from the coast to El Paso. Debarking at Calexico, he
strode across the line to find Carrillo lounging in the shade of
an adobe wall, joining the rest of Mexicali in cool resignation.
His nonchalance, even while the S.P. freight station was being
undermined, infuriated the officious Platt.

"What the devil are you doing to stop this?" he demanded
excitedly.

Carrillo lit a cigarette before answering. "Not a God damn
thing. What do you suggest?"

A few moments later, while the S.P. superintendent watched
helplessly, the building crumpled and slid over the bank. With
a roar and a shower of water it struck the surface and floated
onward in pieces. The Southern Pacific officially surrendered to
the inevitable.

Farther down New River, crews of men were dynamiting the
cataract which was cutting its way upstream in the bed of the
channel. If this process of deepening the walls of the river
could be accelerated, the cutback might reach Calexico in time to
lower the level of the floodwaters and save the town. Into the
turgid stream they would send a boat, from which dynamite
charges were planted and exploded upstream from the waterfall.

154

Whole blocks of earth broke up and toppled forward, causing the cutback to move upstream at a hurried pace.

The people of the border towns waited expectantly for the approaching cataract, while the flood continued to engulf Mexicali. A brick hotel followed the railroad station into the current. Thousands of acres of nearby farmlands were destroyed. Early in July, with the waters lapping at the S.P. depot on the American side in Calexico, the cutback roared past the town. The flood tide dropped fifty feet into the chasm it created, and as the cataract pressed onward upstream, the cutting of the banks ceased. More than half of Mexicali and practically all of Calexico were saved.

Now the immediate problem was to stop the cataract itself, before it reached the break in the Colorado and destroyed any chance of stopping the flood. In the delta swamps of Lower California the crews worked furiously to curb the same cutback they had been trying to hasten. Brush dams were thrown in the path of the waterfall; at first it merely swallowed them and thundered onward. At last the river fighters broke the single channel into smaller fingers, and one by one succeeded in stopping each cutback with brush weirs. Once again man had beaten the river, but not before it had lowered its bed by many feet, left thousands of farm acres without hope of water, and devastated thousands more by flood.

The raging Colorado, pouring its full flow into the Salton Sea, still hung as a threat over Imperial's very life. At the first sign that the flood crest had passed, the Southern Pacific moved once more to dam the Mexican break. Charles Rockwood, whose blundering cut had first brought on this calamity, had resigned as engineer in charge when the 1906 flood had begun to rise in April. Epes Randolph, president of the C. D. Company, then sent for Harry T. Cory, one of the crack construction engineers for the Southern Pacific.

A Midwestern college professor while still in his early twenties, young Cory had made a brilliant name for himself in active railroad engineering. He brought to the Colorado fight the rare combination of painstaking theoretical planning and bold leadership on the ground. Having already seen the Mexican break on several inspection trips, Cory was thoroughly acquainted with the situation when Randolph called him to his Tucson office and placed him in charge. Before he left, Cory remembered the question of finances.

"The expense," he inquired. "How far can I go?"

"Damn the expense!" roared Randolph, who commanded almost unlimited S.P. funds. "Just stop that river!"

Cory returned to the Mexican break in July 1906 and immediately stirred the camp into action. First a nine-mile branch of the Southern Pacific was built by Jack Carrillo, chief of the railroad operations, to provide a reliable line of supplies to the break. Blasting was begun at the quarry near Pilot Knob to supply rocks for the dam construction. From the Union Pacific, another Harriman line, Cory borrowed three hundred special dumping cars known as battleships. Faced with a labor shortage, the engineer recruited a small army of Indian laborers from half a dozen desert tribes, who soon proved themselves the only humans capable of such strenuous work in midsummer heat.

On August 6, 1906, when the Colorado flood receded to a mild 24,000 second-feet, Cory opened his attack. Across the current, now narrowed to a maximum of seven hundred feet, he began building a wooden railroad trestle. Two pile drivers worked from opposite banks toward midstream, pounding in ninety-foot logs as fast as Carrillo's locomotives could supply them. Ahead of each driver floated a barge from which gangs of Indians laid a brush mattress in the current as a foundation for the poles. A pair of single-stacked, stern-wheel steamboats, the *Searchlight* and the *St. Vallier*, churned up and down the canal bringing piles of fresh-cut arrowweed and willow brush for the Indian mattress weavers.

Through this pandemonium the Colorado flowed quietly on, apparently unaware that man was laying a trap to end its yearlong spree in Imperial Valley.

At the same time Cory was strengthening Rockwood's massive head gate, which had lain unused in the proposed bypass north of the crevasse. Largest gate of its type in the world, it was designed to permit a regulated flow into the canal after the trestle dam was finished. The farmers of Imperial, having watched the entire Colorado pouring in upon them for so many months, would find their very existence cut off were the flow stopped altogether.

In mid-August the railroad trestle completely spanned the channel. Long lines of battleships, laden with granite boulders, rumbled past Rockwood's gate and onto the trestle. Directing the rock dumping was lean, hard-bitten Tom Hind, Cory's engineer in charge of construction. Under his orders the cars were arrayed on the trestle like a firing line. Into the brown current on the upstream side the great boulders were dumped by straining men with crowbars. With each new attack the pilings trembled and the river sent sprays of water over the workmen, sometimes dampening the fireboxes of the locomotives.

Night and day the work went on, with Hind's crews fighting to dump rock faster than the river could carry it away. At

156

length the great submerged dam began to raise the level of the current; foot by foot, while the thunder and tumult of the rock barrage gave the scene an air of battle, Tom Hind's dam reared upward under the trestle's feet.

By the end of summer the trap was almost ready to be sprung. Still no one knew whether Rockwood's gate would hold against the Colorado's force. The flow had scarcely dropped to the top capacity of the gate and might vary widely from day to day. Cory, however, could not afford to wait. The entire process of capturing the river in the gate and diverting it back toward the gulf must be finished before the Gila River rose in one of its rampaging fall floods.

Late in September he cut open the mouth of the bypass and turned the river through the Rockwood gate. But before he could prevent it, the sides and bottom of the giant structure began to erode away. Quickly he built another trestle across the bypass a few yards upstream from the gate, making ready to dump rock and dam this final channel if the head gate weakened.

On the morning of October 11 the driftwood accumulating against the new trestle suddenly battered out two rows of pilings. The tracks sagged and toppled several cars off the bridge. Three hours later the lashing of the torrent and debris buckled the Rockwood gate. With a great crashing and splintering the mammoth structure uprooted itself and rose with the current. While Cory and his men watched aghast, two thirds of it broke loose and swung ponderously downstream.

Within two hundred feet it struck against the original trestle which crossed the bypass on its way to the dam. A work train stood south of the trestle at the time, its line of retreat imperiled by the battering of the head gate. With whistle screaming and throttle jammed forward, the doughty engineer took the long chance. His cars thundered over the trestle to the north side just before it collapsed into the maelstrom.

With all control of the bypass gone, the entire Colorado promptly deserted the submerged dam and swung full force through the gap, scouring out a complete channel for itself. The top of the dam, over which several feet of water had been passing, now stood entirely dry.

Once again the brown serpent had slithered out of man's grasp. The work of months had been destroyed by the diabolical Colorado in a few minutes' time.

Epes Randolph came down from Tucson and surveyed the wreckage. Joining him on the banks of the angry torrent, Harry Cory vented his exasperation.

"Let's quit fooling with gates," he shouted against the roar. "What this feller needs is rock, and more rock, and more rock."

157

Randolph and Cory inspected the rock barrier across the old canal mouth and found it staunch and solid. In nineteen months of battling the river this trestle-and-rock method had alone proved successful. There was nothing to do but follow Cory's plan. The river would be dammed without a head gate, and the farmers of Imperial might lose their precious water.

Still there was a possibility of opening up the silted four-mile channel from the original Chaffey gate on American soil, where the railroad had recently installed a new concrete intake. The river tamers resolved to blast open this choked canal with dynamite and close the lower heading forever. To the people of the Southwest, awaiting the verdict of these men, Randolph made a public statement before returning to Tucson.

"The collapse of the wooden head gate," he told the press, "does not mean that the company will fail to control the river. It merely means a delay."

Quickly Harry Cory flung himself and his organization back into the battle. They must make haste, for if the Gila loosed one of its floods before the dam was finished, the entire works would again be swept away.

This time laborers were recruited throughout the desert country, and a thousand men were turned against the river. Six work trains were soon shuttling over the spur tracks, bringing tons of materials for the fight. First Cory repaired the damaged trestle below the site of Rockwood's gate and sent another out into the channel beside it. Four thudding pile drivers, working from both sides toward the middle, pounded poles through the brush mattresses laid in the stream by Indian crews. Even by night, while a string of lanterns spanned the channel, men and machines grappled with the torrent in midstream.

Late in October the two railroad trestles were finished across the channel. Immediately Hind began dumping rock in the space between them as fast as trains could arrive from the quarries. Boulders too big to be rolled off the cars were broken up with "shots" of dynamite. Rock was soon raining into the stream at the rate of a carload every five minutes.

The angry current, unable to wash away the barrier faster than it was built, slid over its top and passed on. Harry Cory knew from his calculations the exact number of days required to lift the river to the level of the old channel, thus sending it once more on its way to the Gulf of California.

By October 29 ninety per cent of the flow had been diverted back to the original Colorado bed. Six more days of continual rock dumping brought almost the whole length of the dam to the level of the main Colorado's surface. All night long on

November 3 the rock crews fought against the river's final throes. Just at dawn someone paused enough to notice a change in the stream.

"Look!" he shouted. "The water has stopped rising. The river is stationary!"

The frustrated waters were indeed swirling back into the ancient channel, their eighteen-month spree at an end. For the rest of the morning, under the insistence of Hind and Cory, the river fighters toiled on to pack the dam and insure their victory. By noon the cautious engineers announced to the men that the battle was won. Then from one end of the trestles to the other rolled a long, heroic cheer. Epes Randolph, on hand to witness the triumph, promptly wired a sober report to Los Angeles.

"The channel leading to Salton Sea is closed. . . . The old channel is carrying the normal flow to the gulf."

All Southern California, which had stood by in helpless concern for eighteen months while the Colorado threatened its lower valley, now turned to its regular cares with relief. The farmers of Imperial rejoiced, with hearty words for the Southern Pacific. Even while permanently closing the break, the company was also blasting out the silted portion of the original Chaffey canal. By early December it was bringing in water through the new concrete head gate north of the border. Not a crop in the valley was lost for lack of water that season.

The menace of flood remained, but this was fast being curbed by mop-up work under Cory's direction. For three weeks his mule teams and scrapers, rail cars and dredges made the dirt fly along the Colorado's banks. Gravel and clay were poured into the cracks of the rock dam and dampened with fire hoses. On both sides of the former break, for nine miles paralleling the river, the great earth levees were extended to hold the waters at the next flood.

The river tamers had not long to wait for the test. Cory and Hind were in Yuma when a sudden Arizona cloud burst filled the arms of the Gila. On December 5, 1906, the Colorado rose from 9000 second-feet to a raging 45,000 below the Gila's mouth. It swirled down the channel toward the gulf, licking at the banks of Cory's levees as it passed. Close behind came the alarmed engineers, leaving Yuma on an early morning work train and reaching the lower Mexican heading before dawn. A quarter mile south of Tom Hind's dam they found three new breaks in the levee. To their utter dismay they realized that one was already beyond control. The brown monster was eating its way through the banks and at any moment would completely bisect the levee and its railroad tracks.

Remembering the grading crew still working on the defenses several miles to the south, Cory sent the steamboat *Searchlight* chugging down the river to rescue them before the shifting Colorado left them stranded. The chubby stern-wheeler had picked up the men and was steaming up the tree-lined channel when the flood suddenly ran dry. To the northward, where the anxious engineers watched from the banks, the river had elbowed out a wide crevasse and was pouring headlong back into the Imperial Canal. The frustrated *Searchlight* was abandoned in the dry channel—an incongruous creature in the midst of the barren Colorado Desert.

Once again the mighty river was hurtling downhill toward Volcano Lake, New River, and its inland prison, the Salton Sea. Cory and his engineers stood by in helpless fury—with $1,500,-000 and the work of months swept away in twenty-four hours. "The battle is on once more," wired a correspondent of the Los Angeles *Times*.

This time the breakthrough proved to most observers that the Colorado had, in the course of centuries, reached the stage of leaving the gulf once more and swinging north into the dead sea its delta had created. The inevitable process had merely been hastened by Rockwood's original Mexican cut. For the first time the engineers realized the full magnitude of the geological forces they had been fighting. The menace of the river, now made more threatening with each passing year, could not be left to the paper protection of the C. D. Company's sand levees. Nothing less than twenty miles of rock dams packed tight with clay and gravel would safely control it—perhaps.

Cory could do nothing immediately; the crews and equipment gathered for the first closure were now scattered over the Southwest. Epes Randolph, hurrying down from Tucson, joined him in relaying the tragic news to Harriman in New York. The Southern Pacific chief, who had already poured a fortune into the river, had reached the end of his magnificent patience. He notified his lieutenants that this new break was not the responsibility of the railroad. If Imperial Valley was to be saved, the burden must be borne proportionately by other interested parties, including the settlers and the government.

When the valley people heard this decision, they gathered in a mass meeting at the town of Imperial on December 13. The Southern Pacific, they were told, would use its organization and equipment to stop the runaway river if money could be raised to pay the bills. The alarmed farmers, facing renewed danger to their valley, had little choice. Before the conference was over nearly a million dollars had been subscribed from the people present.

160

On the same day, at the other end of the continent, E. H. Harriman sent a telegram to the White House. Describing the threat to all of Imperial Valley, including considerable government land, Harriman concluded that "it does not seem fair that we should be called to do more than join in to help the settlers."

For years Harriman had been a close friend of Theodore Roosevelt. Recently, however, the President had turned on the railroad magnate in his furious anti-trust campaign. Back from Washington came a terse reply to Harriman's telegram:

"I assume you are planning to continue work immediately on closing break in Colorado River."

Harriman shot back his refusal, and for a week in mid-December the titans fired telegrams at each other while the Colorado rolled on into the Salton Sea. Cory and his engineers occupied the time in assembling the vast machinery and manpower necessary for the job they knew must be done. Fifteen hundred laborers were recruited throughout the Southwest at top wages. Rock quarries were opened as far away as five hundred miles. Hundreds of cars were commandeered, and the line from Yuma to the break was double-tracked under the direction of Jack Carrillo. Pile drivers and barges, tents and commissaries were hastily assembled. Tom Hind was placed in charge of strengthening the levee system on either side of the crevasse, while the actual task of closing the gap was given to C. K. Clarke, an experienced S.P. engineer. With him Cory hastily conferred over charts and diagrams, planning to extend the Hind dam with two parallel trestle structures which would wall up the break forever. Then the ponderous organization of men and machines waited on the banks of the runaway river while the two presidents settled finances in their "battle of the telegrams."

On December 19, Harriman answered that he had already thrown in $2,000,000 and did not feel justified in spending more. After conferring hastily with Washington officials, Roosevelt wired back that nothing could be done by the government without an agreement with Mexico and an act of Congress.

"Incumbent upon you to close break again," he pleaded.

Harriman wearily answered that the S.P. was not responsible for the debacle. "However," he added, "in view of your message I am giving authority to the Southern Pacific engineers in the West to proceed at once with efforts to repair the break. . . ."

"Am delighted to receive your telegram," sent back Teddy, promising to urge financial aid from Congress. On the same day Harriman flashed the long-awaited signal to his staff at the front: "Turn the river at all costs!"

Instantly Cory's gigantic machinery shifted into action. To a score of sidings and quarries throughout the Southwest he wired a single order, "Go!" Waiting wheels began to turn, and Jack Carrillo's rock cars rumbled southward for the Mexican break. The first trainloads were dumped in rapid succession on the Hind dam, widening it for the double-track extension.

Then across the new 1100-foot crevasse C. K. Clarke started his trestle. Pile drivers swung into motion from each bank, with the lower crewmen supplied by cross-channel barges. They found the current faster, more turbulent than ever before. But Cory could not wait for the Gila's flood to subside. If the spring rise of the Colorado caught the works unfinished, all their efforts and expense would be destroyed.

The slow process of mattress weaving was discarded, and the two ends of the trestle inched out into the torrent with no foundation but the sandy bed of the crevasse. Men fougnt to steady each ninety-foot pole against the powerful current, while a creaking cable hauled the pile hammer to the top of the driver's frame. Then it dropped with a crash that all but toppled the rig into the river, leaving the beaten pile quivering like a bowstring. So great was the danger of overturning the pile drivers that rowboats were stationed downstream to pick up any man who might slip into the river.

Three days after Christmas the Gila turned itself loose again with another flash flood from the Arizona mountains. Part of the torrent carried past the break down the old Colorado channel and provided enough water to refloat the stranded steamer *Searchlight*. The stubby puffer plowed its way upstream to join the river tamers at the crevasse.

But the main force of the Gila's second freshet had rampaged through the break into the canal. The last piles were being driven on Cory's trestle when the debris-laden flood struck it headlong. Out went a part of its pilings; a third of the trestle sagged, ripped off, and disappeared down the channel. Laboriously the crew set about to mend the broken ends as soon as the flood began to subside. Into the brown current the pile drivers pounded their shafts once more.

But in the first weeks of January 1907 the Gila continued to pour a battering ram into the crevasse with every desert cloud burst. It was one of the wettest winters on record in the Southwest, and Cory's weary workers were getting the brunt of it on their backs. Twice more, when the trestle was nearly finished a Gila freshet roared into the break and tore part of it away. Cory was using up pilings so fast that a frantic telegram finally reached him from S.P. headquarters:

"We have exhausted all available supply of piles in San Diego and Southern California."

Yet by mid-January 1907 the trestle was nearly finished for the fourth time, with enough piles on hand to complete it. Epes Randolph was on the scene with Cory, watching his men struggle to place the last of the poles in thirty feet of rushing water. The two engineers hoped desperately that the current would recede before the time came for rock dumping. Otherwise, they feared they could not pour rock and gravel into the river faster than it would be washed away. But on the twentieth their telegraph operator took a message from Arizona: "Gila is rising." Randolph turned away in resignation; it seemed that the fates and the Gila were conspiring against them.

"No rock dumping until next week," he calmly announced.

Through the fourth week in January his crewmen watched the flood roll by, sometimes fighting to clear the driftwood as it lodged against the trestle. At length the current subsided with the works still intact. By the twenty-seventh the last poles were in place and the first trestle was completed.

Before nightfall, with the screeching of whistles and the chugging of locomotives, Jack Carrillo moved his rock cars into the attack. From quarries throughout the Southwest they rumbled over S.P. rails with only a few minutes' headway between them. Until the break should be closed, Harriman had placed his company's entire freight system at Cory's disposal. Both the Santa Fe and the new Salt Lake Railroad curtailed regular shipments to send rock cargoes from quarries along their routes. So much rock-dumping equipment was borrowed from the new Los Angeles harbor, then being built at San Pedro, that construction there was practically halted for several weeks. Along transcontinental routes crossing the Southwest, freight and passenger traffic was shunted into sidings to make way for the strange and hurried procession of rock cars. Never in railroad history had so great a cargo been delivered at one point in so short a time.

Below the border on Cory's battlefield an army of workers was flinging this ammunition into the river as fast as it arrived. While rock dumping began on the first trestle, the second was completed alongside it. Henceforth whole trainloads of battleships rattled over both trestles continuously, night and day. At the signal of whistles their cargoes of boulders crashed into the swirling waters, sending fountains of spray over the cars down the length of the trestle. Against the battle's roar rose a cannonading of dynamite shots which broke the rocks too big to handle. From nearby banks or from the engine's cab Cory and Clarke shouted their orders above the din.

Within three days the rock barrier showed itself above the surface, forcing the water to cascade over the top and down the rock embankment on the other side. As the bombardment continued, the level rose perceptibly. A small part of the current found its way back down the old Colorado channel. Gravel and clay from nearby quarries were then poured on the rocks to plug the cracks. According to Cory's calculation, the river would be completely turned when it had been lifted eleven feet.

But the monster bared its teeth once more before it would submit. By February 2, 1907, the irrepressible Gila was rising in still another flood. On the crest of its first waves rode the usual cargo of heavy driftwood. It charged into the crevasse and piled against Cory's first trestle, taking out three rows of piles. The rock barrier then gave way and battered against the second trestle. Its pilings held firm, but the entire structure soon bent out of shape with the river's full force pouring through the gap.

Cory rushed his pile drivers into position and began pounding logs into the first trestle. All night long they fought the river, one gang breaking up the driftwood with poles while another drove in the pilings. Then they dumped rock as fast as puffing locomotives could deliver it. By morning the rock barrier was restored. The Gila dropped its flood level and the danger faded. But in the railroad tracks along the second trestle an unmistakable kink still revealed the spot where the Colorado had made its last stand.

For the next eight days and nights the rock pouring was almost ceaseless. Having nearly lost his dam in the teeth of the runaway river, Cory was hurrying to bridle it before it could snort and rear again. By February 10, with the Colorado's level raised over ten feet and most of the flow already diverted to the original stream, the assault reached a furious crescendo. That night at eleven o'clock the wearied men stopped the last remnants of the river. The Imperial Canal was dry, and the entire flow was coursing down its ancient channel to the Pacific Ocean. For the second time Harry Cory and the Southern Pacific had beaten the Colorado.

There was still no time for celebrating. The grim engineer, intent on nailing down the river for good, kept his shifts coming on the job and pouring rock. By late afternoon of the next day Cory was certain enough to announce that the break had been closed. Randolph and a party of engineers rode the steamer *Searchlight* for several miles up and down the river, returning to report that it was veering to the south and away from the break all along the line.

Newspapers throughout the Southwest headlined the story to a relieved public. Across the nation the leading publications of the day, from engineering journals to popular magazines, hailed

Cory's feat and the saving of 1,000,000 acres of American soil. In rescued Imperial Valley the people rejoiced openly and prayed in thanks. On the same day of the final closure the new concrete head gate north of the border was reopened to allow a continuous, controlled flow of Imperial's lifeblood into its veins. The empire conceived by Rockwood and enlivened by George Chaffey had been saved from self-destruction by Harry T. Cory.

But the engineer knew this single victory had not harnessed the river. As long as the same sand levees remained, through which the creature had already burst from under him once, it could not be trusted for a moment. For the next few months he kept his trains and mule teams busy along the river building twenty miles of staunch rock levees—extensions of the dams with which he had stopped the flood.

Even this obstacle, he knew, was a precarious expedient. The mighty Colorado was bent on revisiting the Salton Sink and filling it to its brim—a process it had repeated at intervals through past ages. Undoubtedly the greatest geological change in the world's recorded history had been frustrated here by the hand of man. The Colorado would not submit to this indignity without a sullen intention to rebel.

11: DIVIDING THE WATERS

Following the closing of the break, Imperial Valley found itself living in uneasy peace during the Colorado's spring rise of 1907. That year the river flung a record flood against the new Southern Pacific levees. Patrols watched the swollen current day and night as it rose toward the top of the embankments. But in early summer it receded, having given the new defenses a thorough test and the Imperial settlers another fright.

By this time, with the flood battle ended, Congress was finally moving toward action on the river. Beginning early in 1907, measures were repeatedly introduced to provide funds for government levees in Mexico and for reimbursing the Southern Pacific for part of the $3,000,000 which Harriman had thrown into the Colorado. But though the repayment was urged by most of the California congressmen and Presidents Roosevelt and Taft, it suffered a lingering death in Washington. After four years the bill came out of a House committee with approval, but a minority report helped to kill it with the charge that it was "an attempted raid on the Federal Treasury."

Harriman took this repudiation with philosophical calm. Shortly before his death in 1909 he made an inspection trip to the Colorado levees; while stopping in Imperial Valley, he was interviewed by a newspaperman, who reminded him of his unappreciated efforts in turning the river.

"Do you not, under the circumstances, regret having made this large expenditure?"

"No," returned Harriman. "This valley was worth saving, wasn't it?"

"Yes," the reporter agreed.

"Then we have the satisfaction of knowing we saved it, haven't we?"

By 1910 the river was rampaging once more. Leaving its old bed, the Colorado turned into another ancient channel on the delta—Bee River. It was soon emptying into Volcano Lake, which began to fill and threaten an overflow northward toward the valley.

This time the Southern Pacific would take no hand in the fight. New levees were hastily thrown up by Imperial farmers, and pleas for help were rushed to President Taft. Congress quickly appropriated $1,000,000 for flood control—its first sign of concern over the destructive powers of the lower Colorado.

Using the old S.P. technique of a trestle and rock dam, the government engineers turned the Colorado once more and built the twenty-five-mile Ockerson levee to keep it in place. But with its very next flood the diabolical river knifed through the government levee, poured back into Bee River, and wiped out $1,000,000 in federal funds. At least the river had no partiality concerning whose money it wasted.

By now Imperial had little chance of turning the river back into its old channel. The most that could be hoped was that it could be prevented from getting any closer to the valley. Accordingly, the settlers built new levees against any overflow from Volcano Lake, forcing its excess waters southward to the gulf.

After that the Imperial farmers, who for years had allowed the fate of the valley to rest in outside hands, moved to take control themselves. In 1911 they organized the Imperial Irrigation District, the largest single agricultural unit in the world. Ownership of their water canal and protective levees in Mexico still resided in the pioneer California Development Company, which by this time had been forced into bankruptcy by repeated floods and other misfortunes. The Southern Pacific Railroad, having controlled the C.D. Company since the great flood, bought it at receiver's auction in February 1916 and promptly sold the property to the Imperial Irrigation District for $3,000,000. Along with the canal, levees, and equipment came company manager Charles Rockwood, "grand old man" of Imperial, who took over the duties of chief engineer for the district.

Valley settlers had gained control of their own water supply none too soon. The Colorado was now alternating between drought and flood, requiring desperate measures to control it. In 1915 the river was so low that for over a month Imperial irrigators diverted its entire flow through their head gate by the use of a temporary dam across the channel. But that winter a flash flood of the Gila sent 200,000 second-feet of water roaring past Yuma—a record volume for the Arizona tributary. When it began piling up against the brush and rock dam at the Imperial heading, water was backed several miles up the river.

Imperial's citizens scarcely felt the flood, but their Arizona neighbors at Yuma were soon fighting for their homes. North of town the river broke through the levee on January 22, 1916. Immediately the alarm was sounded, and Yuma farmers came rushing with their teams to move their household belongings out of town.

They were too late. Brown Colorado water swirled down Main Street, pouring into the buildings. In the lower section one adobe building after another melted like sugar and dropped into the torrent. Frantic citizens were soon paddling through the streets in rowboats, with the flood standing four feet deep in the main hotel. "The water in the bank," recalled one apprehensive resident, "was four inches below my safe-deposit box."

Farther down the Yuma Valley the river made a second break and destroyed many acres of alfalfa. Even after the settlers plugged the holes in the levees the water remained in their valley to plague them for several months. So much sediment had been deposited over the land that for years much of it was unfit for crops.

The Yuma people then turned on the dam at the Imperial heading as the cause of their disaster. When the Imperial Irrigation District started to rebuild it late that summer, an irate Yuma delegation went down and ordered Rockwood's engineers to stop. If another rock was dumped on the dam, warned the Yuma men, they would "go in there and blow it and you to Halifax."

But the Imperial group was not convinced until the Yuma Water Users Association brought an injunction against them in August 1916. Then the I.I.D. obliged by dynamiting enough of the dam to relieve the flood menace, and the two agricultural sections lived in neighborly peace thereafter. The injunction stood from year to year, permitting Imperial to rebuild the dam only on the promise that it would be destroyed before the Gila's winter flood season. Yuma's residents, prizing water as much as any Southwesterners, were equally aware that there was such a thing as having too much.

Still the flood menace was as close as ever for Imperial farmers. Below the border the Colorado, riding nervously on top of its delta cone, grew more threatening every year. Its bed in Bee River channel was building up with silt at the rate of a foot a year, causing the I.I.D. to keep raising the levees by the same amount. One corps of Imperial engineers was surveying for new levee construction along the Colorado when the freakish current suddenly broke out of its banks and spread for miles over the delta country. Every man took to the mesquite trees, perching in the thorny branches for three days until one of them swam to higher ground for help.

Against this treacherous creature the Imperial Irrigation District built up a formidable standing army of river crews, equipped with work trains and sixty miles of levee tracks. In flood seasons a quantity of rock was kept ready at the quarries in California, to be loaded and sent rolling at a warning phone call from the patrols on the levees.

The continuing struggle against the Colorado was made doubly tedious by the location of the canal and levees below the border in Mexico. Every set of plans for improvements was subject to interminable delays by officials in Mexico City. Local authorities in Lower California insisted on tying the district's hands with red tape, taking advantage of the fact that an American group was dependent on Mexico for water and flood control. Each carload of rock bound for the Colorado levees was stopped at the border for customs duty. During one period every member of the I.I.D. levee crew was stopped daily at the border on his way to work and asked at least fifty questions by the customs officers.

At one of the crucial flood times a force of three hundred men was fighting the river along the levees below the border. After they had worked feverishly for long hours, night and day, without sleep or food, the I.I.D. made up a load of about a thousand lunches for them. "We rushed them to the customhouse in a truck," as one valley farmer bitterly recalled, "and they made us set every one of those lunches out and counted them individually and made us pay tariffs on them afterwards amounting to more than they cost."

Part of the trouble rose out of the valley's original Mexican water concession of 1904, which reserved up to half of any water passing through the canal for lands in Mexico. Over 830,000 acres below the border—including nearly all the irrigable delta lands—had been owned since the turn of the century by a band of Los Angeles investors. Chief of these was Harry Chandler of the *Times*, although the syndicate included others of the same group which had subdivided San Fernando Valley. When it was

168

discovered that cotton would grow successfully on these lands, they were leased out to Mexican and Chinese tenants, who irrigated them with an assured water supply from the Imperial Canal. Cultivated land below the border jumped to 118,500 acres by 1918, as compared with 367,000 in Imperial Valley. The American farmers began to fear that there would be far too little water for all users in the next period of drought.

Under these conditions Imperial Valley could not hold its destiny in its own hands. As long as its lifeblood depended upon the whim of a foreign authority, it had no security in its water supply or in its defense against floods. By 1917 the I.I.D. was talking of a new canal which would tap the Colorado at Laguna Dam above Yuma and skirt along the border on the California side till it reached the valley. It would have the formidable walking hills to cross, but Imperial engineers believed a canal could be maintained through them in spite of shifting sands. The valley was determined, in any case, to uproot itself from the grasp of Mexico.

The idea of an "All-American Canal" north of the border was not new. Since 1912 a resolute Imperial farmer named Mark Rose had been trying to get a water supply for his lands on the great 200,000-acre East Mesa of Imperial Valley. Rose was a blocky, heavy-shouldered dirt farmer, roughshod and even crude, but a man with a quick wit, a quicker tongue, and a facility for getting what he wanted. While his property was situated too high for a gravity flow from the Mexican canal, Rose found that it could be watered by a ditch built from the Colorado through the sand hills.

For several years he badgered congressional committees in Washington for an appropriation, emphasizing the enormous amount of government land on the East Mesa awaiting irrigation from the river. To remove the fear of the sand hills, he got a plank road built through them; its success proved that the sand moved in a direction which would not menace a canal. But at the same time the I.I.D. became alarmed at the thought that, even with an All-American Canal, Mark Rose's private company might stand between the valley and the river.

Heading the district's legal affairs at that time was alert and vigorous Phil Swing, a rising young lawyer who had already served as Imperial County's district attorney. Born in San Bernardino, Swing had settled in Imperial in 1907 to begin his first practice in a young and booming frontier territory. With him he brought a dynamic energy and a flare for showmanship that soon made him a forceful leader in valley affairs. As chief counsel for the I.I.D. he had clashed more than once with Harry

Chandler's Mexican interests. But determined as he was to free Imperial from Mexican control, he was equally certain that little relief could be had from a canal in California which was dominated by Mark Rose.

"If an All-American Canal is to be built," Swing told the district directors, "Imperial Valley will have to build and maintain it."

By 1917 he realized that Rose was making dangerous headway in Washington and was soon hurrying East to block him. Swing left the capital armed with an agreement between the Reclamation Bureau and the Imperial Irrigation District to investigate Imperial's need for an All-American Canal. With one stroke he had elbowed Mark Rose out of his own project.

But Rose was a man of cast-iron feelings. He was interested in getting the canal through, regardless of who owned it. Unable to beat the leaders of the I.I.D., he joined them.

"You've knocked me out of this," he told the district directors, "and you're going to build the canal. Now I'm going to get on the board and see that you do."

At the next district election Mark Rose became a director of the I.I.D. by an overwhelming vote. From that time on he and Phil Swing worked together and made an irresistible team in their fight for the All-American Canal.

Their first task was to convince the Reclamation Bureau, and this meant convincing its distinguished chief engineer, Arthur Powell Davis. Swing and Rose found, however, that there was little he did not already know about the Colorado. As a nephew of Major John W. Powell, the famed explorer of the river, Davis had been immersed in its lore from boyhood. He had first glimpsed its meandering channel at a point near Grand Canyon in 1882, while serving as a topographer with the Geological Survey. From the middle nineties until his transfer to the new Reclamation Bureau in 1902 he had measured the river's annual flow in its upper tributaries. With engineer J. B. Lippincott he examined the lower Colorado and in the bureau's first annual report recommended a dam at Boulder Canyon.

Swing and Rose could not help regarding Arthur Davis as the tall and dignified veteran of Western reclamation, the man who most deserved the name of "father of Colorado development." In repeated interviews and conversations his advice was always the same: if the All-American Canal was to bring new lands under irrigation on the East Mesa and elsewhere, the project must have a storage reservoir.

"It just isn't practical," he told Swing, "to reclaim that land with the threat of a drought every five years. We've got to have a dam."

Swing and the I.I.D. were reluctant to complicate their problem with the kind of dam Davis had in mind. Yet they knew that only a great controlling works in the Colorado channel would give them complete relief from recurring floods.

In July 1919 the matter was settled for them. A three-man engineering board had investigated Imperial's water problems, according to the agreement Swing had won between the Reclamation Bureau and the I.I.D., and had rendered a report. It not only recommended an All-American Canal but added that the government "should undertake the early construction of a storage reservoir on the drainage basin of the Colorado River . . ." Now there was no doubt that A. P. Davis and Imperial Valley were on the same side.

At this point the water-conscious states of the Rocky Mountain region took sudden notice. Storage reservoirs meant greater use of water, and greater use meant larger prior rights to the flow of the Colorado. If these states of the river's upper basin were not to find most of their water pre-empted by the time they were ready to use it, they must step wholeheartedly into this Colorado question.

Water discussion between the states, in fact, had already begun by 1919. Preliminary talks among interested groups from several states had been held the year before at Tucson and San Diego. Already the whole state of California had taken up Imperial's cause as its own and had asked the other Colorado River states for a general meeting on the water problem.

On January 18, 1919, a distinguished assemblage of governors, senators, and the foremost engineers in the Southwest gathered at Salt Lake City—and thereupon began the long struggle over Colorado development. California, backed at that time by Arizona, pressed for hurried construction on the lower river to prevent floods at Yuma and Imperial Valley. But the upper states—Colorado, Wyoming, Utah, and New Mexico—opposed such development unless future water rights were protected.

They had ample reason for their fears. In two previous Western projects the Rocky Mountain states had found their irrigation restricted by downstream activity. In 1904 the Reclamation Bureau had filed on the North Platte River in Wyoming and constructed the giant Pathfinder Dam. At its completion, it was feared that there was insufficient water for its full use; Wyoming irrigators on the upper North Platte were "embargoed" by federal statute from making any additional water diversions. Wyoming found its own development hampered for the sake of a project which mainly benefited Nebraska.

Similarly, the great Elephant Butte Dam in New Mexico was begun in 1907 to fulfill an American agreement with Mexico over

171

the waters of the upper Rio Grande. To insure a full water supply for this reservoir—largest in the United States before the Boulder project—the government clamped another embargo on any new upstream irrigation by withholding right-of-way permits across public lands.

Water users on the upper Rio Grande in New Mexico and Colorado were outraged. A Colorado senator voiced the fury of the two states in a powerful speech in Congress, ending with the declaration that "while it is too late to save the waters of the Rio Grande, because the treaty has now been ratified, yet I say this is a warning that it may not happen again on the Colorado."

Such was the sentiment the Californians faced at the Salt Lake conference. It ended with a resolution that Colorado development should start at the headwaters and proceed gradually downstream—a clear first victory for the upper-basin states.

The Californians returned home, however, with one accomplishment. The question of the Colorado had been projected to the national scene, and a new organization had been formed for the river's development among water users throughout the basin— the League of the Southwest.

During the next few years the gathering conflict over the Colorado centered in its stormy meetings. In 1920 at Los Angeles, where the Californians held the advantage of numbers, they overrode the Salt Lake resolution and passed another calling for an investigation of the Boulder Canyon dam site "with a view to prompt construction." At this the northern states courteously invited the League to a third meeting at Denver—the stronghold of upper-basin sentiment. Here in January 1921 they put through a rule for unit voting by states, giving them a 4-3 majority over the three lower-basin states of California, Nevada, and Arizona.

From then on the Denver conference was in the hands of the upper states, and in particular of Colorado and its chief representative, Delph Carpenter. One of the great water attorneys of the West, Carpenter combined the talents of eloquent persuasion and political cunning. He was a product of the cattle country north of Denver—a former cowboy turned lawyer. So great were his tact and agility that he represented both sheep and cattle interests in a region where the two were incompatible. On one occasion he is said to have been riding with a group of cowpunchers who shot up a sheepherder's camp. Unnoticed by the sheepmen, Carpenter rode hurriedly back to his law office in the town of Greeley. He was seated behind his desk, out of breath but smiling, when the outraged sheepmen arrived and had him draw up a complaint against their assailants.

By 1921, Carpenter was no longer a local lawyer of limited practice. Specializing in water law, he represented his state in

172

the two great cases which patterned Western irrigation rights—Kansas vs. Colorado in 1911 and Wyoming vs. Colorado, which was then still pending before the Supreme Court. He became known as the "silver fox of Colorado," and though he championed his own state in conflicts with her neighbors, the entire Rocky Mountain region looked to him for leadership in dealing with the lower Colorado basin.

Carpenter's main contention at the Denver meeting was that before the upper states would agree to Boulder Canyon or any other lower-basin project they must be guaranteed against any interruption in their own development. Rejecting California's proposal that the entire Colorado program be left to the Reclamation Bureau, he insisted that the seven Colorado-basin states should first agree among themselves through an interstate compact.

It was an idea which Carpenter had long fostered as the only way to solve the legal conflicts which kept Western water usage in constant litigation. Within most Western states, water rights rested on the simple rule of prior usage—"first in time, first in right." But priorities between users in two separate states were still in doubt and would remain so until the pending Wyoming vs. Colorado case was decided. If this was settled so as to eliminate state boundaries in water rights, the upper states feared they could never compete with the populous and growing California in a race to appropriate the river's water. Carpenter's own state of Colorado, which supplied sixty-five per cent of the river's flow, did not intend to allow it to pass by unused for the sole benefit of irrigators in the arid Southwest.

A Colorado compact, however, would end any possibility of priorities across state lines and would enable the upper states to preserve their water rights for future use. Carpenter and his upper-basin supporters were able to convince the delegates at the Denver convention. They adjourned with a resolution that the Colorado basin be rapidly developed and that its waters be divided by interstate compact.

After that, events moved rapidly in the direction of a Colorado settlement. Early in 1921 the seven state legislatures passed enabling acts for the framing of a compact. In August, Congress gave its consent. Members of the new Colorado Commission were soon being chosen to represent each state in laying out a basic law of the river.

But if the upper states were making progress with their compact scheme, Imperial Valley was gaining ground for its canal and dam. With the help of A. P. Davis of the Reclamation Service, Mark Rose and Phil Swing were working to get

173

congressional action. In May 1920 they were rewarded with the Kincaid Act—authorizing a full-scale report on an irrigation and storage plan for the lower Colorado. Imperial was asked to share the expense, and it eagerly delivered a huge overpayment just to insure an adequate investigation. Davis took personal charge and in little more than a year had turned out a preliminary version of what came to be known as the Fall-Davis Report, after the Reclamation chief and his superior, Albert B. Fall. At that time the lid was still tight on the scandal of Teapot Dome, and the name of President Harding's Interior Secretary lent distinction to the report. But its own thorough coverage was enough to earn the title of the "Bible of the Colorado River."

When initial copies were passed out in July 1921, the reaction was electric. Davis had recommended not only an All-American Canal and a reservoir "at or near Boulder Canyon" but also the development of hydroelectric power to repay costs of the dam. The Southern California Edison Company lost no time in adding to its other power filings on the Colorado River by posting notices at Boulder Canyon. The Southern Sierras Power Company sent its general manager to Imperial Valley, where he met with the Associated Chambers of Commerce at Calipatria late in July. Southern Sierras and the Edison Company, he announced, would build Boulder Dam free of charge if Imperial Valley would support their power applications.

But down from Los Angeles that night came the Big Three of the Water and Power Department—Bill Mulholland, W. B. Mathews, and E. F. Scattergood, chief of the electrical division. Their unexpected appearance threw consternation into the private power camp.

"It would be monstrous and heinous," Mathews exclaimed to the assemblage, "to place all remaining power potentialities of the Southwest in the hands of a great combination of private industries."

In the face of this broadside from the Los Angeles public power champions the Southern Sierras retired in temporary defeat. It was only the first skirmish, however, in the power battle that was to dog the Boulder Canyon project to its completion.

With this dramatic entrance the Los Angeles Water and Power Department threw itself into Imperial's cause. But while the valley had gained an ally, the association brought new enemies. When the League of the Southwest convened for its fourth meeting early in December at Riverside, California, the upper states delegates were more fearful than ever of California's ambitions. At Denver they had secured agreement for their Colorado compact to guarantee their rights in the river. This

174

time they meant to make it unmistakably plain that the compact must be in full operation before they would tolerate any construction of dams and canals. Without an agreement on the river there was no telling how their own development might be affected by such wholesale water and power rights downstream.

When the Riverside meeting opened on December 8, 1921, it was plain that the California members held a majority and meant to use it to pass a resolution demanding immediate dam construction on the Colorado. Delph Carpenter heatedly reminded them of the precedent set at Denver for unit voting by states.

Still the Californians would not yield the advantage. Delegates from Utah, Colorado, Wyoming, and New Mexico then threatened to walk out and wreck the conference if they did not get the unit rule. Just before the end of the first day's session Arizona and Nevada joined them against California in refusing to participate in any League resolutions. The whole problem of the Colorado was now focused in this tumultuous conference at Riverside.

Next day the case for the upper states was argued by one of their ablest delegates— the powerful L. Ward Bannister of Denver. Known as one of the foremost water lawyers in the nation, Bannister was president of the Colorado River League, an organization of upper-basin cities and corporations which had an interest in developing the river. Together with Delph Carpenter, against whom he often contended for leadership, Bannister made the Colorado state delegation a dynamic factor at any water meeting. He now proceeded to harangue the assembly on the rights of the upper basin. As for Colorado, he warned, she would fight "any and all development on the lower river" till her interests were protected by interstate compact.

In the middle of his tirade Secretary of the Interior Fall strode into the auditorium. Amid a welcoming applause from the California delegates he took his seat on the platform. Having heard part of Bannister's remarks, he now leaned forward in his chair and answered him. The states did not have absolute control over interstate rivers, Fall declared, intimating that the federal government could build Boulder Dam without sectional interference. California's members showered his words with a wild ovation. They now had the whole Interior Department on their side.

On the last day the other six states framed a compromise, but California did not intend to lose an inch of ground already gained. Before the compromise could be presented a Los Angeles man moved to adjourn. The conference broke up in loud and desperate quarreling, during which a Californian shouted the undeserved charge to Delph Carpenter: "I have a graveyard full of better men than you!"

The League of the Southwest, formed to further the development of the Colorado, left Riverside with its organization broken. A fifth meeting was later held at Santa Barbara, but as an effective voice for the Colorado basin the League had already fallen victim to the row between the states.

Besides, the impatient Boulder advocates could not be held down to interstate meetings after the promise of federal dam construction. Two days after the Riverside conference they gathered at San Diego's U. S. Grant Hotel, where Secretary Fall held a hearing on the final version of A. P. Davis' Colorado dam report. There they cheered while Fall repeated his assurance on construction of Boulder Dam. Enthusiasm rose even higher in further fiery words from Mark Rose, Phil Swing, Billy Mathews, and other leaders.

But as the evening session began, a sour note in this happy chorus was voiced by L. Ward Bannister, the same who had clashed with Fall at Riverside. He declared that Colorado would support federal construction in the lower basin only after the water rights were settled by compact. Otherwise, he pointedly warned, "We must meet the men of California upon the floor of Congress and through our senators and representatives oppose absolutely their plans for the development of the lower part of the river. . . ."

Bannister had made no empty threat. In both houses of Congress the irrigation committees were dominated by Rocky Mountain men. Californians knew that without the support of the upper states they could never get a Boulder project passed into law. In spite of California's triumph in winning government support, Bannister and his upper-basin friends still held the aces in the Colorado poker game. It was a matter of no compact, no Boulder Dam.

Californians, in fact, were already resigned to the bargain. Phil Swing was busy in Washington laying a background for the forthcoming negotiations which would further the cause of Boulder Dam. Of necessity the government would have a representative sitting on the compact commission, and Swing was determined to get the most formidable ally possible. "Herbert Hoover," he told A. P. Davis, "would be the man if we can get him."

The Reclamation chief promptly abandoned his own ambitions for the post and seized Swing's idea. More than anything else he wanted Boulder Dam, and no one would be a more

176

powerful advocate than Hoover—former European relief administrator, now Secretary of Commerce, and potentially the most likely successor to President Harding. At Swing's suggestion Davis went to Hoover with the proposition, drew up impressive plans for him to examine, and convinced him of the magnitude of the scheme.

In mid-December Harding appointed Hoover federal representative on the new Colorado River Commission. When delegates of the seven states arrived in Washington for the first meeting on January 26, 1922, they immediately named Hoover chairman. As the tug of war over the Colorado opened, California had won the first advantage.

It was to be her only one. The four upper-basin states— Utah, Wyoming, Colorado, and New Mexico—arrived with a definite plan of attack. Their leader was Delph Carpenter, who had first suggested the compact solution. Carpenter knew water law, and he knew every trick of negotiation and compromise. Together with his three upper-state allies, the "silver fox of Colorado" meant to write a compact that would protect every present and future right of Rocky Mountain water users.

Against this formidable array sat California's representative, Wilbur F. McClure, the state engineer who had investigated the seizure of the Los Angeles Aqueduct gates in Owens Valley. He was, as an associate described him, a "kindly old gentleman" but utterly lacking in an understanding of Southern California's water needs and an ability to drive a bargain. It apparently did not occur to him that in the succeeding meetings California would be fighting for a share of Colorado water on which to base its entire foreseeable development. McClure should have been the forceful leader of the commission; but even the Nevada delegate, representing only a small interest in the Colorado, made a stronger showing.

In this situation the Arizona representative appeared as the tiger of the commission. Like Carpenter, Winfield S. Norviel of Phoenix was an irrigation lawyer—one of the most experienced in Arizona. He was a man of powerful build and unrelenting will; while he fell short of Carpenter in brilliant oratory, he gave way to none in slow and dogged cross-table argument. As state water commissioner he was acutely aware that Arizona's future was now staked on his bargaining ability.

At the first meeting Norviel presented a full draft of a compact, imposing on each state a limit for the number of acres to be put under irrigation in the next twenty years. Carpenter and the upper delegates were aghast at the suggestion. They had come to Washington to secure unlimited protection in return for their support for Boulder Dam, not to submit to restriction.

For the next few days the commissioners wrangled over Arizona's limitation idea. Each state was invited to estimate its total water needs, but when their figures were submitted the total ran far beyond the Colorado's volume. Every estimate except California's was far beyond the official Reclamation figures in the Davis Report. When Hoover asked for a modification of claims, each state in turn refused to yield or made only a token reduction. He began to realize with rising impatience that there could never be a division of water between the seven states. Had they been dividing any other resource, compromise might have followed. But in the arid West water was the foundation of each state's hopes. They would never compromise on it.

The commissioners knew they were at the crossroads as the seventh session opened on the afternoon of January 30. More than one was convinced it would be the last. "I do not believe we are going to progress to a real basis at this meeting," declared the Utah delegate.

Hoover was desperate. He had joined this cause to bring about an agreement that would lead to Boulder Dam. In one last effort he asked the commissioners whether they would not consent to some plan that would merely control the river and save Imperial Valley from devastating floods.

"It would seem a great misfortune," he observed, "if we dissolve this commission without at least agreeing upon so primary a necessity as a control reservoir."

"We are not here to jump in a bandwagon with California," fumed the Wyoming delegate. "We in turn want the lower river to agree with us that our rights in Wyoming are entirely protected."

At last Hoover turned in despair to the final question. So far, he observed, they had not been able to agree on a single idea. "The question arises, is it worth while to have another session? Or shall we make the declaration now that we are so hopelessly far apart that there is no use in proceeding?"

After a pause the Utah representative suggested that they should adjourn and "try again" later in the year. With ruffled feelings smoothed, the commissioners agreed on this one issue. They disbanded to gather data and meet again somewhere in the Southwest. Perhaps time and a fresh approach could bring agreement to the fractious Colorado basin.

When the commission gathered for the first hearing in Phoenix on March 15, it seemed that the whole basin had suddenly come alive to its water interests. Phoenix hotels were jammed with delegations from every basin state. Water men from at least two dozen Southern California organizations

178

caucused ahead of time to present a solid front before the commissioners. A packed gallery of local citizens supported every new demand for Arizona's rights with thundering applause.

By the time the commissioners met at Salt Lake City, where Utah water advocates demanded unlimited rights, Hoover was despairing of any progress. The commission could never reach an agreement, he declared, "so long as each state insists on unrestricted use of the Colorado within its own borders and restricted use in all the other states." Finally at Denver the Colorado people carried on the campaign for unlimited rights.

"I fail to see," shouted one, "why Colorado should join a compact which surrenders one drop of water."

This period of fact-finding, Hoover could see, had done nothing more than stir up state jealousies. During the summer he confided his despair to Carl Hayden, veteran congressman from Arizona, stating that he could get absolutely no harmony between the states. Hayden was an old campaigner whose ten years in Congress had taught him the subtle shortcuts to agreement.

"What you say is due to your political inexperience," he replied and pointed out that a fall election was approaching. Whatever a state official might agree, "his opponent is going to say that he has traded away the heritage of his people." Wait until after the fall election, advised Hayden, and then the commissioners "will write a compact."

The Arizonan's strategy was undeniable. Hoover set the final meetings at Santa Fe, New Mexico, to start November 9, two days after the election. Meanwhile other events occurring through the summer of 1922 played into Hoover's favor. On June 5 the Supreme Court handed down its final decision in the long-awaited Wyoming vs. Colorado case: the rule of prior appropriations in water rights—"first in time, first in right"— applied regardless of state lines. It was a costly setback for the upper states. Their worst fears of being caught in a race for development with California were now confirmed. More than ever they needed a compact for protection against such lower-basin projects as Boulder Dam.

As if to add to the threat, the Boulder Dam bill came up for serious consideration in Congress in the same month. Phil Swing himself had taken his seat in the lower house the year before—elected to represent Imperial's district on a single campaign promise: he would go to Washington and put through Boulder Dam.

The freshman congressman later said that if he had known at the start the long and bitter fight that awaited him he would

179

have hesitated to begin. But Swing was young and confident, with the world before him. Soon after he reached Washington, he descended on the office of California's stern and dynamic Hiram Johnson, who was then nearing the end of his first term in the Senate. Wise in the ways of congressional politics, Johnson waited accommodatingly while Swing eagerly described his Boulder Dam bill. Then with paternal warmth Johnson put his hand over the younger man's shoulder and walked with him to the door.

"You go right ahead," he soothed. "You get it through the House, then send it over here, and I'll get it through the Senate."

If Swing caught the warning in this gentle sarcasm, he did not heed it. For two years he buttonholed legislators on both sides of the Capitol, pouring out his plan for taming the Colorado. While he made little headway with the rest of Congress, he succeeded at least in firing California's own delegation. Even Hiram Johnson, with one ear cocked to the rising sentiment for the project in California, joined Swing in sponsoring his bill and became the rousing champion of Boulder Dam on the Senate side.

Their arguments were roundly supported by news of the Colorado's latest antics. Already it had broken out of its levees again, forcing Imperial's river fighters to fall back to a new line of defense. With Volcano Lake overflowing northward once more, they made a counterattack against the river and by means of a new cut turned it into another delta basin called the Pescadero Depression. But they knew it would be only a matter of years before it filled and placed them once again at the river's mercy.

Then in 1921 the Colorado flung itself against the levees at Yuma, and the entire farm community turned out to fight the rising flood. One hero is said to have discovered a leak several feet wide in an emergency dike and in true Dutch-boy fashion flung himself into the hole and plugged it until his cries brought a rescue crew. Up and down the levees the farmers were able to hold the river that year, though they had nearly run out of the materials for levee building when the water stopped rising scarcely an inch from the top.

In 1922 the Colorado turned its fury on California's Palo Verde Valley, sixty miles above Yuma. Breaking through the levees below Blythe, it rolled into the thriving little valley without warning on May 22. Farm families took flight with no time to salvage their belongings before the water rushed over their lands. Then it swept into the rising young town of Ripley and stood four feet deep in the lobby of its new $100,000 hotel.

While these dreadful tidings were still reaching Washington, hearings began on Swing's bill in the House Irrigation Committee. But it was also a time when the Wyoming vs. Colorado decision was fresh in the minds of the Rocky Mountain congressmen who dominated the group. They were not willing, as an Arizonan later put it, "to let the sheep of flood protection cover up the wolf of power and water greed." The first Swing-Johnson bill died without reaching the floor of either house, but it had made the upper basin more intent than ever on a Colorado compact.

On November 9 the commissioners gathered at the designated meeting place of Bishop's Lodge, a resort situated three bumpy miles from Santa Fe, New Mexico. With them was a virtual horde of water men from the seven interested states. The California contingent, consisting of Billy Mathews, Mark Rose, and seven others, had wired ahead for reservations and arrived on the day before the first meeting. They found Bishop's Lodge loaded to the walls but cheerfully bunked together—four and more in a room.

Hoover looked upon this invasion with dismay. He had no intention of allowing the conference to become a seven-ring circus. Four days later he notified the proprietor of Bishop's Lodge that quarters were congested and provided him with a new rooming arrangement. When this was posted on the morning of the thirteenth, the California group was outraged. Seven of them had been left out altogether, with only Mathews and one other colleague allowed to remain. They appealed to Commissioner McClure, but he only advised them to find rooms in Santa Fe. Three of them did so, taking a taxi every morning over the rutted canyon road to Bishop's Lodge. The other four took the next train for Los Angeles.

McClure was now left with only a fraction of the support he needed to drive a bargain with Delph Carpenter and the men of the upper basin. Only the state attorney general, another northern Californian, was allowed to attend the meetings with him, while most of the other commissioners insisted on being accompanied by the best-informed engineers and lawyers available.

When the real negotiations opened on November 11, Delph Carpenter presented a revolutionary departure from previous compacts—one which divided the river while avoiding the impossible task of allotting water to each of the seven states. A fifty-fifty division would be made between the upper and lower basins, leaving to each one the later job of allotment according to states. It would divide the flow at Lee's Ferry, an arbitrary point between the two basins near the Arizona-Utah border, and

181

give the lower basin 6,264,000 acre-feet. Together with the Gila and other southern tributaries, this was supposed to equal one half the river.

The principle of division by basin was Delph Carpenter's crowning stroke—the compromise that undoubtedly saved the Compact. The upper states, having already been consulted, swung behind it immediately. McClure did not object and soon accepted not only the basin principle but also the fifty-fifty settlement—"as a fair basis for discussion."

But Norviel of Arizona was suspicious: "It isn't, as I conceive it, what we were appointed for. . . . It leaves the two divisions of the basin to work out their own salvation, which does not mean anything." After two days of wrangling he finally relented enough to accept the principle of division by basin. He insisted, however, that the water be apportioned according to the needs of each basin, rather than by "the gambler's chance of fifty-fifty."

With the upper basin standing firm, Hoover made a new approach on the afternoon of November 14. Taking the 16,400,-000 acre-feet average flow estimated in the Davis Report, he sliced it in half and suggested 8,200,000 for each basin. Norviel abruptly retired to consult his Arizona colleagues and came back agreeing to discuss the figure. But Carpenter objected that the upper states could never deliver such a quantity in dry years: "Nature will force us into a violation. . . ."

The commission was still deadlocked. At last Hoover suggested that the two sides retire and frame separate propositions. That night they caucused separately behind closed doors. Next morning the upper states returned with a proposal to guarantee to deliver 6,500,000 acre-feet. McClure then and there agreed, "I am willing to consider the figure named."

Norviel was immovable. Obviously, he said, it was a division of 6,500,000 to the lower basin and 10,000,000 to the upper. "I like to be moderate in my statement, but I think that is certainly an unfair proposition, and feeling that way about it at this time, I certainly must reject it."

The atmosphere in the room was almost explosive. Carpenter and the upper-basin men hotly reminded Norviel that the guaranteeing states needed ample protection against drought. Norviel retorted that he had not asked for a guarantee of delivery—and thereby put his finger on the veiled crux of the issue. Both sides were fighting for water rights, against which they could be free to plan and finance new reclamation projects. Neither side, however, said so. The upper states insisted that a guarantee of delivery was the only practicable method and then

182

asked for special consideration because of the responsibility they assumed. Norviel wanted to talk first about dividing the water in the river before discussing guarantees. He answered the upper-basin proposal by offering to accept Hoover's 8,200,000 acre-feet to each basin.

Hot words flew back and forth while the gap remained at 1,700,000 acre-feet. With tempers almost at the breaking point, the Nevada delegate finally exclaimed that if the upper states would guarantee only 6,500,000 "we might as well abandon the discussion."

"I think we could say the same thing of the lower states," snapped the New Mexico commissioner.

Once again Hoover moved in and suggested a compromise: "I am wondering if the northern states will make it 7,500,000." At this the upper delegates demanded a recess, and for a whole day the two sides conferred among themselves and bargained with their opponents.

When they convened on the morning of the sixteenth, agreement had been reached. Hoover's 7,500,000-acre-foot compromise passed without argument. One by one other sections of the Compact were introduced and unanimously accepted. So far as most of the commissioners were concerned, the main battle was safely past.

But for California something had been left out. The upper states had secured their water rights—enough to give them unlimited use on their own tributaries—but they had not in turn agreed to Boulder Dam. Carpenter had admitted that the lower basin was in desperate need of flood control, yet he would accept no such provision in the Compact.

After the tentative agreement had been drafted, the Nevada delegate turned over a copy to W. B. Mathews, Mark Rose, and the few California water men remaining at Bishop's Lodge. They read it and were appalled. In the whole document there was not a sentence or even a footnote on Boulder Dam—nor on any water storage at all. For the first time California's water interests realized the utter impotence of their state's representation. California had simply come to Santa Fe to quitclaim half the river to the upper basin.

When the meetings were reopened on November 19, Mark Rose led the group before the commissioners and insisted that water storage would have to be included in the Compact, as all the low flow of the river was now being used. Subsequently Hoover suggested a provision for a reservoir of 5,000,000 acre-feet—enough to satisfy existing water needs. Such a capacity, however, was a mere pond compared to the vast reservoir the

Californians had in mind. They told Hoover that no storage clause at all would be better than this. The Secretary believed it was worthwhile, however, and was able to get agreement from the seven commissioners.

But the California men were not through. They wrote a letter to McClure, stating that they could never stomach the Compact he had permitted the commission to frame.

The reaction was immediate. They were invited to a conference at Secretary Hoover's suite in Bishop's Lodge. At the appointed time Mathews, Rose, and three others filed in and took their seats at one end of the parlor. Facing them was Hoover himself, flanked by the California commissioner. After an embarrassing pause the Secretary began.

"Mr. McClure has shown me your letter of protest. It is perfectly outrageous to write such a letter to Mr. McClure. . . . Your criticism of the proposed Compact is unjustified. Unless you withdraw it in writing, I will be forced to end the conference, and the blame for the failure of Colorado development will be on you."

For a moment the California men sat perfectly still. Hoover's declaration had left them dumfounded. Mark Rose was the first to move. He stepped solemnly forward, took his hat, and started across the room toward the door. Behind him filed the rest of the California men while Hoover watched them in silence. As Rose passed the Secretary he paused, leaned over, and growled two words:

"Aw hell."

The California contingent left Hoover's room, Bishop's Lodge, and Santa Fe. The next train for California carried all but one or two. The last chance for the water interests of Southern California to influence the negotiations had passed. There was now no hope that the great storage project they had envisioned could be tied to the Colorado Compact. Instead the upper states had secured their water rights and California had no security for its half of the bargain—Boulder Dam.

Still, the lower basin as a whole had not staged its last fight at Santa Fe. What happened next remains in dispute, as the final minutes of the commission meetings have since been lost. But according to the Arizona version, W. S. Norviel made one last demand. As long as he had compromised on the division of water, Arizona would have to withhold its Gila River out of the bargain.

The fireworks that followed can be reconstructed only from bits of testimony by some of the participants. Norviel's opponents instantly objected. The Gila was as much a part of the river as any tributary. If one state withheld its own contribution to the main stream, then the rest would demand the same right.

Norviel then insisted—still according to Arizona's version—that if the Gila must be included in the Colorado basin as defined by the Compact, then Arizona would have to be given special compensation—1,000,000 acre-feet. To this the upper states raised objections more furiously than ever, but Norviel made it plain that otherwise he would not sign the Compact. Like the stubborn twelfth man on a jury, he finally made the others relent. In Article III of the Compact, which allotted the water, was inserted a paragraph (b) : "In addition to the apportionment in paragraph (a), the Lower Basin is hereby given the right to increase its beneficial consumptive use of such waters by one million acre-feet per annum."

Delph Carpenter, the shrewd Colorado lawyer who had been expected to dominate the commission, had met his match in Norviel of Arizona. There was now little left to recognize in the ready-made Compact he had brought to Santa Fe. The doughty Arizonan had seen to that. His stand had earned him Hoover's admiration as "the best fighter on the commission."

"Arizona should erect a monument to you," he later wrote to Norviel, "and entitle it 'One Million acre feet.' "

This is the water which was for years afterward the nub of the Arizona-California controversy. Arizona claimed that the 1,000,000 acre-feet of "III b water" belonged to her alone and that the only reason the Compact does not say so is that the commissioners wanted to keep it uniform in its division by basins and not by states. At least two men from other states who participated in the negotiations support this claim. There was a gentleman's agreement at the time, according to Arizona, that this water was to be hers.

In 1934, Arizona told this to the United States Supreme Court. California objected, and the case was thrown out on the ground that the Compact was perfectly clear: III b water was for the lower basin, not for Arizona alone.

California's version did not attempt to describe the negotiations leading up to the puzzling paragraph III b, except to say that its purpose was to allow the lower basin an additional use after it had reached the limit of its 7,500,000 acre-feet. California also said that there was no such gentlemen's agreement; that in the negotiations and congressional debate following the Compact agreement no such claim was made; that Arizona's elaborate explanation of III b was concocted at a time when she wanted to accept the Compact; and that both before and after the 1934 case Arizona actually objected to the document on the very ground that it did not define her right to the Gila.

While it might be true that the 1,000,000 acre-feet represented Norviel's triumph, California could feel fortunate that water was not allotted in the Compact according to the zeal of each commissioner. As one of her present-day water men remarked, "Norviel was the best commissioner California had."

On November 24, 1922, the seven delegates reached final agreement on a full draft of the Compact and then drove into Santa Fe for the formal signing. At the historic Governor's Palace they assembled in the *Ben Hur* room, where Governor Lew Wallace had penned his classic novel. Writing on the same lapboard used by Wallace, the commissioners placed their signatures on the document and made an irrevocable division of the Colorado. Herbert Hoover went back to Washington after a personal triumph in bringing harmony out of what had seemed a hopeless impasse. And Norviel went back to Arizona in a state of nervous exhaustion.

The first part of the huge bargain had been made. Colorado and the upper states had gained their security against large-scale water appropriations in the south. It now remained for the state legislatures to ratify the instrument, and for California to achieve its part of the trade—congressional approval of Boulder Dam. The long battle for the waters of the Colorado, begun with the founding of Imperial Valley, was only half finished.

12: TEMPEST IN WASHINGTON

Early in 1923 the state legislatures took up the Compact and ratified it one by one. In California, Mark Rose and some of the water people opposed it, but not strongly enough. Herbert Hoover made speeches in Los Angeles and San Francisco urging its adoption, and finally on February 3 the California legislature assented. By the time Colorado approved it on April 2 six states had ratified the Santa Fe Compact.

In Arizona, however, the agreement struck trouble. The Republican administration which had negotiated the Compact had been defeated in the fall elections, and Democrat George W. P. Hunt had resumed his long reign as governor. Arriving in Arizona as a cowpuncher in its territorial days, Hunt had risen rapidly in local politics to become the first state governor in 1912. By the early twenties his powerful figure, with the familiar bald head and walrus mustache, had become a dominating institution in Arizona politics. Intellectually he was no heavyweight, but he possessed an uncanny political acumen which almost invariably landed him on his feet at election time.

As the Colorado Compact came to Arizona under Republican auspices, Democrat Hunt opposed it on principle when he took office after the 1922 campaign. As the new legislature convened at Phoenix in January 1923, Hunt warned in his opening address against a water agreement which might be giving away Arizona's "greatest natural resource."

"In laying before you the official copy of the compact," he said dramatically, ". . . I place in your hands the future destiny of Arizona."

Thus in one state the very thing happened which the commissioners had feared. The Colorado Compact became a political issue between opposing parties. Its merits were therefore lost in the maelstrom of partisan charges and countercharges.

Yet the force which proved decisive in the Compact fight was Arizona's sudden interest in the resources of the Colorado River. Nothing had brought this transformation more than the pact itself, which made the state doggedly aware of her water necessities. By the end of 1922 an engineering commission was dragging instruments across Arizona deserts, searching out a route for a gravity canal which would bring Colorado water to the fertile lands of the Phoenix plateau.

The man behind this movement was George Maxwell, a Phoenix citizen who had championed Southwestern irrigation projects for twenty-five years. In the 1890s he had formed the National Reclamation Association and helped to lead the fight for federal water projects in general, and for Salt River Valley development in particular. More than any other man, he was responsible for securing the Reclamation Act of 1902 and the construction of Roosevelt Dam which immediately followed.

The first suggestion for the gigantic scheme of irrigating millions of acres in central Arizona by Colorado water was an article by Maxwell in the Los Angeles *Times* as early as 1905. But his project did not crystallize until after World War I, when he settled in Phoenix and pursued the idea with the characteristic zeal that had already carried the reclamation fight.

By the early twenties he had made a rough survey of the route and determined the height of key mountain passes. Then he laid out "a possible plan for reclamation of . . . an area of approximately 2,000,000 acres and over." It required a dam at Bridge Canyon (between Boulder and the Grand Canyon), a tunnel some eighty miles long, and several hundred miles of canal—altogether a project bold enough to make a practical irrigationist's hair stand on end. Bill Mulholland, viewing it with "considerable amusement," dismissed it as "absolutely ridiculous." Phil Swing remarked that Maxwell had "the advantage

187

over engineers because he was not tied down to the facts." When A. P. Davis laughed at his explanations before a congressional committee, Maxwell was furious.

"I never knew of anything that was really big being built," roared the old reclamationist, "that some people did not say it was impossible beforehand."

But Maxwell succeeded in convincing Arizonans that his scheme was more than an irrigationist's dream. Enlarging on his rough plans, an engineering committee took the field and was still working out a report when the legislature began its consideration of the Compact in January 1923. Some of the engineers, called in for consultation by the Irrigation Committee of the upper house, described the possibility of using Colorado water "for generating several millions of horsepower of electrical energy and for reclaiming more than two millions of acres of arid land, all within the state of Arizona."

After that the Compact ratification was doomed. There was enough water in the river for such plans as these, but not in half the river. Almost the entire allocation for the lower basin would be needed for 2,000,000 acres; but at the rate California was appropriating the water, there would be little left by the time Arizona's scheme could be made feasible. Arizona was willing to compete with the entire basin for the use of the river, but she could not afford to be thrown in a match race with California for half of it. For the first time Arizona now realized that the Compact would leave her with the same fate from which it had spared the upper basin. If Arizona ratified the instrument, she would be squeezed between the upper states and California.

Leading the fight against ratification, George Maxwell wrote articles for every anti-pact newspaper in the state and carried his crusade before chambers of commerce and service clubs. In the legislature the Compact battle waged for weeks while the Republicans argued for ratification and the Democrats blocked it. After first accepting the Compact with conditions, then with certain "interpretations," the legislature finally failed to ratify by a tie vote in the House of Representatives on March 8, 1923. The one chance for a water agreement in the Southwest had been killed. As the upper states would allow no river development without a compact, the biggest victim would be the proposed Boulder Dam. California was paying a bitter price for ignoring its water men at Santa Fe.

As soon as Arizona's rejection became known in the other basin states, she encountered a chorus of criticism. Failure to join the other six states in a Colorado agreement made her a virtual outcast. Upper-basin men declared that until the Compact was ratified they would oppose construction anywhere in the lower basin—including Arizona's Gila River. A California newspaper ran a cartoon picturing Arizona as a "dog in the manger" over the Colorado River. One Arizonan answered that the cartoon should have shown California as a "dog running away with the bone."

The simple fact was that the Compact served the interest of the other six states but not of Arizona. Through it the upper basin secured almost unlimited use of Colorado water, California got support for Boulder Dam, and Nevada got the commercial benefits of the dam's construction. Arizona would share in the latter, but it had bigger reclamation plans which were blasted by a fifty-fifty division of the Colorado.

"Santa Fe is not Sinai," insisted one Arizona spokesman. "The Compact is nothing but a contract between interested parties. It is not divine. No other state has shown any altruism in this transaction, but Arizona alone has not posed as being benevolent."

Neither was the state sparing in its self-interest. Since the site for Boulder Dam was too far down the river to permit a gravity canal to the Phoenix area, Arizona had no more use for it than for the Compact. Its main effect, said the Arizonans, would be to regulate the flow of the river, increasing its low-water stage, so that more land could be cultivated in Lower California. If it was true that there was less water in the river than could be used by all the arable land in the basin, the more water Mexico put to use the less would be available for Arizona when its great plans materialized.

Harry Chandler and his Mexican lands, already the foe of Imperial Valley, now became the great bugaboo for Arizona. In Imperial he was said to be fighting Boulder Dam because it made an All-American Canal possible. In Arizona he was said to be the guiding power behind Boulder Dam because it would yield him more irrigating water. It was an ironic demonstration that nothing helps a cause so much as the right enemies.

Nor were Arizona's demands confined to water. The millions of horsepower in hydroelectric energy stored in the Colorado canyon were looked upon by Arizonans as part of their state's natural resources. When California proposed to build Boulder Dam and use some of this potential waterpower, Arizona levied her demand: a royalty on every kilowatt equal to the tax that could be expected from a private corporation. Since Arizona was equally vigorous in fighting the project itself, Californians looked upon this new requirement as a consideration for her acquiescence on Boulder Dam. The irate mayor of San

Diego, John L. Bacon, simply called it "hush money." Arizonans called it a royalty tax for the use of a natural resource.

Meanwhile Boulder Dam itself was vigorously opposed by George Maxwell and his "High-Liners," as the group was called which clamored for a high-line canal from the Colorado to central Arizona. Through articles, speeches, and mass meetings they made Arizona believe she was the intended victim of a California conspiracy. The irrepressible Maxwell made the anti-dam fight the crusade of his National Reclamation Association; up and down Arizona he went on a membership drive, backing his words with a formidable pamphlet against the project.

"Now that means," he would say, shoving the leaflet before a prospective member, "that the construction profit goes to Las Vegas; the franchise goes to Nevada; the power goes to Los Angeles; the water goes to Mexico; and Arizona goes to hell."

The appeal was irresistible, if the facts were not. Except in those sections along the river which would benefit by the dam, Arizona sentiment was formed solidly against it by the end of 1924. Even Republicans who supported the Compact had nothing but hostility for the "California scheme." No candidate for public office could afford to miss a chance for a blast at Boulder.

Across the Colorado, California was equally fired in favor of the dam and all the water and power development it promised. In May 1923 delegates from Imperial and Coachella valleys, Los Angeles and San Diego, and every community which looked to the Colorado for its growth, met at Fullerton and formed the Boulder Dam Association, "to advance by all legitimate means the construction by the Government of the Boulder Dam and All-American Canal. . . ." Led by Mayors John L. Bacon of San Diego and S. C. Evans of Riverside, it became a clearinghouse for publicity and political strategy on the Swing-Johnson bill. Southern Californians were showered with pamphlets and besieged with speeches on the development in store for their section through the great dam. A formidable lobby of the ablest men was maintained in Washington at every session of Congress to support Swing and Johnson in their fight. W. B. Mathews, personal friend and political pillar of Hiram Johnson, became such a familiar figure in the Capitol that he earned the nickname, "California's Third Senator." Providing a background of constant agitation was the Hearst newspaper chain, which was wedded to the project from the beginning by its advocacy of government reclamation, public power, and Hiram Johnson.

Natural enemies of this combination were the Los Angeles *Times* and the electric-power utilities of Southern California. They favored a dam for flood control only on the Colorado

River and objected to the government's building any structure high enough to put it in the power business. Imperial Valley was also aware of opposition to the All-American Canal by the *Times*, whose owner held vast acreages of cotton lands below the border.

A major test of strength between the two factions came in the Los Angeles city elections of 1924, when Boulder Dam was the main political issue. In spite of furious campaigning by the *Times*, nearly every Boulder supporter was swept into office by a rousing majority. The popular sentiment had already been sensed by Dr. John R. Haynes, Southland Republican leader and chairman of the Los Angeles water and power board. He wrote Calvin Coolidge that presidential support for Boulder Dam would be not only "right, just, and proper," but "tactful and politic." When Coolidge's Southern California campaign manager later advised the same thing to help carry the state, the President broke his silence on Boulder Dam.

"I am in favor of a high dam at or near Boulder Canyon," he announced in October 1924, ". . . and I believe that the United States Government is the proper agency to undertake the work."

Undoubtedly the move helped Coolidge to carry California in the campaign of 1924. From that year on Boulder Dam was as much a political bandwagon for California office seekers as it was a political whipping boy for those in Arizona.

Greatest campaigner of all was the drought of the early twenties. If any doubt of the dam's necessity remained in Imperial, it was dispelled when the farmers used the entire Colorado River for seventy-three straight days in the late summer of 1924 and still saw some crops wither of thirst. California cities which depended on Sierra streams for electric power suddenly faced a critical shortage. E. F. Scattergood of the Los Angeles power bureau declared that only Boulder Dam could save the city from a loss of investment and assure its continued growth.

As early as 1923, Los Angeles was looking to the Colorado for more than power. Years of sparse snowfall on the Sierra had made the city's Owens River aqueduct a trickling stream. Shrewd old Bill Mulholland knew the loss of San Fernando Valley crops was only the beginning. If he did not begin to plan now for a new source of water, Los Angeles would find its mushroom growth cut off abruptly.

Through the early twenties a deluge of population was bursting Los Angeles at the seams. The sudden doubling of population after its 1920 census of 576,000 amazed its water men and upset their calculations for the future. Without a new water hole for this Southwestern giant, the next drought might attack not only crops but lives.

In October 1923, Mulholland took a small corps of friends and engineers from the Water Department and boarded the Union Pacific for Las Vegas, Nevada. On the banks of the Colorado they looked down at the brown serpent gliding below.

"Well," observed the Chief, "here's where we get our water."

The prospect was breathtaking. Water would have to be pumped out of the canyon and over several mountain ranges to the coastal plain. Here was no Owens River aqueduct, with its downhill flow all the way to Los Angeles. As an engineering feat it would have few rivals; this would be, as Mulholland realized, "the largest aqueduct the world has ever seen."

Plunging into the river with two boats, the Chief and his companions rode downstream through Boulder Canyon. Below Parker they left the water and headed westward again on the Santa Fe. They had seen enough of this "last water hole" to be convinced that Los Angeles could safely bid for a share.

From then on the city moved quickly, driven by unparalleled drought. High up in the Sierra, where snow should have been packed fifteen to twenty feet deep, there was only a scattering of it in shaded gorges during the winter of 1924.

"This drought is one of the most appalling things that could happen," admitted Mulholland. "We have never even half conceived of such a thing."

In July 1924, Mulholland filed for 1500 second-feet of Colorado water—nearly four times the capacity of the Owens River aqueduct. In acre-feet per year it measured out to more than 1,000,000—just about one eighth of the share allotted the lower basin by the Compact. That same year Phil Swing introduced Mulholland before the House Irrigation Committee in Washington as a new proponent of Boulder Dam.

"I am here in the interest of a domestic water supply for the city of Los Angeles," Mulholland told the congressmen; "and that injects a new phase into this whole matter."

It did indeed. The committee was impressed by his plea for municipal water. Arizona redoubled her opposition to Boulder Dam, which would help California appropriate more of the river. Upper states representatives were more determined than ever to resist the dam until the Colorado Compact became effective by Arizona's ratification. In Southern California the possibility of a Colorado aqueduct brought new water-scarce communities to the Boulder Dam banner. Over a forty-year period the 315 square

192

miles of artesian area around Los Angeles had shrunk to a scant 55 miles through unrestricted pumping. Wells that had yielded strong artesian fountains at the turn of the century now held their water fifty and more feet below the surface. Pasadena, Santa Monica, Long Beach, San Bernardino, and almost every nearby city became enthusiastic members of the Boulder Dam Association.

By 1925 most of them had begun to organize into a Metropolitan Water District, which would undertake to build the great aqueduct from the Colorado. So great was popular feeling for the program that when the California legislature refused to grant the proposed district a charter those members who voted against it were turned out at the next election. In 1927 the legislature was careful to authorize the project, and the following year Los Angeles, Pasadena, and a handful of charter cities founded the Metropolitan Water District. They were prepared to reach four hundred miles across the desert for life-giving water.

Farther down the coast San Diego was also hard hit by drought. Furiously developing all possible sources in its nearby mountains, she turned in final desperation to the Colorado. In April 1926, San Diego filed for 110,000 acre-feet a year of Colorado water and set about discovering a route for an aqueduct. Even in the rural communities—in the San Gabriel and Santa Ana valleys—citrus and vegetable farmers were looking to the Colorado for relief.

Through the twenties Boulder Dam, the All-American Canal, and the Colorado Aqueduct became Southern California's great hope for continued expansion. Every community from the river to the coast rallied behind Johnson and Swing with a continuous barrage of publicity, political pressure, and irresistible enthusiasm.

But in Washington, Phil Swing was finding that Boulder Dam faced formidable competition. No matter how meritorious his project, there were a dozen others already demanding the attention of the nation. Introducing a revised Boulder Canyon bill in December 1923, Swing opened the second round of his campaign before the House Irrigation Committee the following month. In his initial speech he began by comparing Boulder with other national projects, hoping to convince the committee of its prior importance. But to water-minded Westerners, who composed the group, Swing had merely opened a Pandora's box of pet reclamation schemes.

"Mr. Swing," interrupted the congressman from Oregon, "in mentioning these great projects do you not overlook the Umatilla Rapids project?"

"Do not overlook the Great Salt Lake basin project," added the Utah representative. By this time Swing realized his mistake.

"Do not forget that we have a big project in Montana."

"Also the Pit River project in California. I just wanted to get that in."

"And please do not forget the San Carlos project in Arizona."

Swing was offering to let them submit a written list for the record when the Kansas member interrupted:

"I would like to say a word in behalf of the Missouri River."

This was enough to snap Swing's patience.

"Of course," he cut in sweetly, "the Missouri River will live forever, both in song and poetry. Mark Twain made it famous."

Before the Kansan could elaborate, Swing hurried on with his Boulder Dam speech, having learned a lesson in water geography and the ways of congressmen. He knew already that persuasion alone would not carry Boulder Dam through the two-ring congressional circus. After two years of fruitless argument Swing decided on a change of tactics. Henceforth he would become a listener; he would be one of the most sympathetic men in Congress on other states' projects. In the end it proved the key formula in winning friends for Boulder Dam.

It also gave enough alarm to the project's enemies to make them rally in desperate opposition. An association of electric companies set up a headquarters in Washington to fight the passage of Boulder Dam and other government power measures. The Arizona High-Liners pleaded that Boulder Dam was too far down the river to serve their state with a gravity flow and insisted that Congress choose a site farther upstream for the Colorado's first dam. But to this argument A. P. Davis, Herbert Hoover, and other engineers had an undeniable answer: no other large storage site was within practical transmission distance of the power market in Southern California, and no other was far enough downstream to control the heavy silt discharge of the Little Colorado and Virgin tributaries.

Arizona, however, had another formidable point. Engineer E. C. La Rue, who had helped make the the initial survey for the high line, came to the House hearings fresh from a trip down the Colorado with the Geological Survey. Boulder Dam, he said, would equalize the flow of the river, making a bigger volume in the low-water stage. Thus while Arizona was denied a supply by the dam's location, Harry Chandler's Mexican lands would be able to establish new and bigger rights to the river's flow. His studies showed, moreover, that the United

194

States could not afford to do this, as there was not enough water in the river to supply all irrigable lands in the basin.

This statement took the committee by surprise. One member excitedly observed, "So far all the evidence before the committee has been all the other way—that there was enough water on this river."

"I have always understood it that way," agreed another.

"That makes this question very important."

"It does."

But La Rue's story could not be shaken. He later reappeared with statistics to prove that over 900,000 arable acres must go unirrigated somewhere. Phil Swing pointed out that the Imperial Irrigation District could prevent any benefit to Mexico from Boulder Dam by taking the added water into its All-American Canal at the crucial seasons. Arizona, however, would not be talked out of her new and effective slogan: "For every acre put under irrigation in Mexico by Boulder Dam, one acre in America is forever condemned to desert."

Bolstered by this weapon, the Arizona forces redoubled their attack when the Boulder fight shifted to the Senate side. But as hearings began in earnest before the Irrigation Committee in the fall of 1925, they faced the implacable figure of California's Hiram Johnson. Calling upon his early training as a courtroom prosecutor, the veteran lawmaker moved against the Arizona witnesses with relentless cross-examination. When La Rue claimed that Boulder Dam could not be fitted into the best plan for developing the river, Johnson showed him no mercy. Where, he queried, did Mr. La Rue think the first Colorado dam should be built? The witness hedged, stating that the other sites had not been drilled for depth of bedrock.

"So that you cannot say definitely at this time," prodded Johnson, "which dam would first be built under your plan?"

"No, sir."

"Nor where it should be built?"

"No, sir," repeated La Rue, and attempted to explain.

Johnson cut him off, insisting, "As I understand you, you are not able at the present time, with the data at your command, to suggest a definite substitute. Now is that statement correct?"

"Well, unfortunately it is correct," croaked the harassed La Rue. "And that is the reason why we should not have a dam built on that river until we have the information."

"I think 'unfortunately it is correct,'" mocked Johnson, clinching his argument. "I think we now understand the situation."

195

The triumph was the beginning of the end of La Rue's impressive testimony. Bombarded with technical questions from other committee members, he protested that he could not carry all the figures in his head. Finally he exploded bitterly that he had worked months on his calculations, "and if you can figure out mistakes in these, or suggest a better plan in a few minutes in this room, it would seem to me to be nothing short of a miracle."

His cause scarcely advanced by this outburst, La Rue next found his technical claims challenged by Frank Weymouth, a distinguished Reclamation Bureau engineer who had completed a ponderous report favoring Boulder Dam the year before. He testified that La Rue's plan for developing the river, which left out Boulder completely, would waste more water and generate less power than the Reclamation Bureau plan.

But despite this setback the Arizonans continued to champion La Rue and his river report. They now had engineering data of their own with which to attack Boulder Dam. Against its witnesses they turned with the same ferocity that Johnson displayed against their own. At length Arizona's tall and fiery champion, Senator Henry Ashurst, loosed a memorable threat:

"Arizona asks that this dam be placed high enough up the river so that we may irrigate our uplands. The Colorado River is Arizona's jugular vein; sever our jugular vein and we die. We have asked you in polite language and we now ask in vehement language to build the dam far enough up the river."

The stalemate over the Colorado continued on every front in 1925. In Congress the Swing-Johnson bill was shunted aside by being referred to an engineering committee "for further study." Negotiations between Arizona and California on a lower-basin agreement were deadlocked. Arizonans were insisting they would never ratify the Colorado Compact without such a lower states pact; Colorado and the upper states were equally determined to oppose Boulder Dam until Arizona's ratification made the Compact effective.

There still seemed hope of unlocking this log jam when the Arizona legislature convened in 1925. Irreconcilable old George Hunt had been re-elected governor on an anti-Compact, anti-Boulder, anti-California campaign. But the pro-Compact faction had captured the chairmanship in both legislative houses. The Interior Department, two congressional committees, and six states now waited in the hope that Arizona would ratify.

A tremendous fight developed in both chambers that had the Phoenix capitol fairly trembling by the second week in March. On the eleventh a crowd of "anti-pactists" gathered in the capitol's first-floor corridor, heard speeches from George Maxwell and other High-Liners, and made their presence known by the angry noise that drifted to the legislative chambers upstairs. After a stormy debate the House of Representatives ratified the instrument with heavy reservations, including a stipulation that the Gila River be reserved for Arizona outside the Compact's allotment.

But when it was proposed that Governor Hunt's approval was necessary for final ratification, taut nerves snapped and the chamber almost exploded. Republicans and Democrats shouted each other down while the chairman pounded for order. One member challenged another to meet him outside; three excited speakers had to be forced to their seats by the sergeant at arms. At last the amendment for the governor's approval was defeated in a close vote.

On the other side of the capitol an aroused Senate first rejected the Compact, then reversed itself and ratified. Seven copies of the final joint resolution, laden with reservations, were handed over to the Secretary of State for transmission to the other basin states and the federal government. But he simply turned about and faithfully delivered them to Governor Hunt, who declared the ratification "void, worthless, and of no effect." Though his outraged opponents charged that he had no right to veto a ratification, Hunt made his action stick.

"I'll be damned," he bellowed at the next election, "if California ever will have any water from the Colorado River as long as I am governor of Arizona."

In spite of pugnacious "George V," as his enemies called him, there was still hope that Arizona and California water men might be able to agree on a lower-basin compact. On August 17, 1925, representatives of the two states, together with those of Nevada, gathered around a conference table in Phoenix and began the first of a series of bargaining sessions that were to last for a generation. The meeting was almost doomed from the start. Governor Hunt opened it with a partisan speech that cast doubts on Boulder Dam and almost sounded like an ultimatum on Arizona's river rights. The California delegation was furious.

"I would like to ask," its leader demanded of the Arizona group, "whether or not the address of Governor Hunt expresses the sentiment of the committee."

A heated exchange followed that lasted through the rest of the session. California and Nevada insisted that Arizona agree to Boulder Dam before discussing a lower-basin compact. Arizona countered that she would have to know the details of the dam's operation before she could even consider agreeing. Behind their maneuvering was some hard strategy; undoubtedly Arizona wanted to use her approval of Boulder Dam as a trump card in the negotiations, while California and Nevada wanted the card played first to reduce Arizona's bargaining power. At length it was obvious that neither side would relent.

"I think that it is a waste of time to attempt to negotiate any further," concluded the California chairman.

"You want us to sign on the dotted line, do you?" retorted an Arizonan.

"No, I don't want you to sign anything."

It was a fair description of the situation. That first conference broke up with little will to agree in either camp. To a large extent Arizonans thought that by obstructing the Colorado Compact they could block Boulder Dam. At the same time other events were stirring in the Colorado basin that made Californians believe they could get Boulder Dam regardless of Arizona.

It was the resourceful Delph Carpenter of Colorado who first presented an alternate plan. Since Arizona would not ratify the seven-state Compact, he argued, why not a six-state compact? So long as California could be pinned down to a water division, the upper basin might take its chances with Arizona. After getting the approval of other leaders in the Rocky Mountain states, Carpenter took his proposition to California. He found its water men agreeable enough; a six-state compact would require new ratification by the legislature, and they would have a chance to attach a proviso for construction of a high dam at Boulder. At last they could make certain that the Compact would work for California's cause.

The new six-state Compact was submitted to the upper-basin legislatures in February 1925. Utah, Colorado, and New Mexico promptly ratified it, as did Nevada of the lower basin. In Wyoming the legislature killed the new pact on the last night of its session; but Governor Frank Emerson, who had helped to frame the Compact at Santa Fe, held the lawmakers in continuous session until they decided to ratify.

California's legislature took up the six-state Compact late in February 1925. Attached to it, in what became known as the Finney Resolution, was the proviso that ratification by California would take place whenever Congress authorized a 20,000,000-acre-foot reservoir "at or below Boulder Canyon."

Implications in the move raised immediate protests. Such huge storage meant a high dam, and a high dam meant hydroelectric power. California's utility companies did not intend to let the Los Angeles Bureau of Water and Power write such a rider into the Compact. Their agents in Sacramento quickly organized against the bill. The Los Angeles Chamber of Commerce and Harry Chandler's *Times* joined the opposition.

At the same time the governors of upper-basin states served notice that they would not countenance such a reservation in the Compact. Herbert Hoover sent a hurried telegram to the California governor; if the legislature made any reservations, he warned, "the whole Compact will need to be abandoned and we will have another setback for five years in the development of the river."

But at the same time the Los Angeles water men, the Imperial Irrigation District, the Boulder Dam Association, and Hiram Johnson's political forces in California all swung behind the Finney Resolution. After heated debate in both houses it passed by large majorities on April 5, 1925, and was signed into law. Mark Rose and the I.I.D. immediately sent their congratulations to the legislature for "having stood stanchly by the people against the corporate interests. . . ." But the Los Angeles *Times* berated the act next day under the headline, "Colorado Compact Killed."

At first the reactions among the upper states bore out the fear that the Finney Resolution was a dangerous expedient. While Californians insisted that it merely established a date for ratification, upper states representatives called it a reservation which threw a new wrench into the Compact machinery. California, they insisted, was obstructing Colorado development as much as Arizona. When the Senate Irrigation Committee resumed consideration of the Boulder Dam bill in December 1925, Delph Carpenter was on hand to block it.

"Had California adopted the six-state Compact as the other states did," he angrily told the committee, "the Compact would be before you now and the whole question could now be settled."

Senators from the Rocky Mountain states joined Carpenter in claiming that California had killed the six-state Compact. Hiram Johnson was forcibly denying the charge when William H. King of Utah interrupted him.

"Some of us think contrary, Senator," he shouted, "and feel that California did destroy the Compact. We feel that no action can be taken by Congress until California withdraws her reservations."

There the matter stood in a deadlock that resembled a vicious circle. California would not ratify the Compact until Boulder Dam was assured. The upper states would not allow Boulder Dam until California ratified unconditionally. Behind the stalemate was California's fear of the private power interest. Her

199

public water and power boosters believed the upper states were motivated by the utility companies in the opposition to Boulder. California would therefore take no chances on dividing the water without being certain that the upper states would actually fulfill their bargain and support the dam.

For more than a year the determination of upper-basin congressmen blocked any progress on the Swing-Johnson bill. In October 1926 the California governor, hoping to break the interstate deadlock, called the legislature into special session to withdraw the Finney Resolution. But the Boulder Dam advocates, rising in protest, beat down the proposal for repeal.

The upper states, having waited for the outcome of the vote, now realized that California's stand was irrevocable. Their water men met in Denver and drafted some twenty amendments to the Swing-Johnson bill for protection of their water rights. Ward Bannister took them to Washington and told the House Irrigation Committee that if they were accepted the upper basin would support Boulder Dam. Phil Swing and Hiram Johnson were prompt in accepting them, and it seemed that the interstate row had been patched at last.

But Utah was irreconcilable. When California's legislature failed to withdraw its storage proviso, the Utah governor deplored the act in a heated letter.

"Apparently California is in no hurry to have the Swing-Johnson bill passed," he told California's governor. "Neither is Utah."

Early in December, when the Swing-Johnson bill came out of both committees with a "do pass" recommendation, Congressman E. O. Leatherwood of Utah wrote his governor that California was making dangerous headway. Utah, he said, could block her by withdrawing from the six-state Compact, thus leaving the basin once again without a water agreement. Early in January 1927 a bill was introduced in the Utah legislature to repeal its ratification.

At the same time the powerful House Rules Committee, through which all bills must be cleared for floor debate, agreed to consider Swing's application for a right-of-way on Thursday, January 20. Utah's congressional delegation then offered an amendment to the Boulder Dam bill, which was supposedly rejected, though Swing claimed he had never heard of it. All four of the Utah members of Congress—two senators, two congressmen—thereupon sent their state legislature a peremptory wire:

"California's representatives refuse to consider amendment to protect Utah's interest in Boulder Dam bill. . . . Utah legislature should take whatever action it deems proper at once, but not later than January 19."

Obviously the "proper action" was the repeal of the six-state Compact, to cut the ground from under the Swing-Johnson bill. But the president of Utah's state Senate had little imagination. He wired back for an explanation. The exasperated congressmen dropped their courtesy.

"All we want is repeal of the six-state Compact," shot back Utah's veteran Senator Reed Smoot. ". . . Pass bill Monday."

The order has since become famous. Utah's legislature obediently repealed its Compact ratification on Monday, January 17. The six-state Compact, which would have gone into effect with the passage of the Swing-Johnson bill, was now smashed. The entire upper basin would have to oppose Boulder Dam. It would now be a near-miracle if Swing got his bill past the House Rules Committee.

Meanwhile the Los Angeles *Times* had leaped with gusto into this rising climax to the Boulder Dam fight. Still opposing any government power development, Harry Chandler threw his weight behind a simple flood control dam at Needles. In an effort to stampede this proposal through Congress he rushed correspondents to Imperial Valley to build up a case for flood menace.

In December 1926, Chandler's paper began to blossom with stories on the Colorado's threat to Imperial, complete with photos of former flood damage and inadequate levees. The entire valley was pictured as living in fear of the record snowpack on the far-off Rockies, source of the Colorado's runoff. This would not bring floods until spring, but in the meantime every winter freshet of the Gila tributary was seized upon as a threatening flood. Phil Swing, realizing Chandler's strategy, wrote Imperial leaders to pay no attention to the clamor for flood control. Mark Rose excitedly called it "the most treasonable conspiracy of a generation." Both men knew Chandler was now in deadly earnest and were witnessing the full, irresistible force of a *Times* editorial campaign.

Five days before adjournment on March 4 the *Times* flood control drive reached a clattering din. But Swing and Johnson were able to hold their supporters in line; they had not worked five years for the Boulder Dam bill to have it shattered by an emergency dam at Needles. The *Times* retired in defeat, charging that the fate of Imperial Valley now rested on their heads. But if the flood control scheme had failed, Swing's own bill had also died in the Rules Committee.

Over in the Senate, Hiram Johnson was making better headway. The Boulder Dam bill reached the floor, but there it rested through the unyielding opposition of Arizona. There was no doubt that Johnson had enough support for his measure, but his problem was to maneuver it to a vote. Senators Ashurst and Cameron of Arizona had warned that as soon as the bill came up for debate they would talk it to death.

On February 21 the Senate took up Boulder Dam in earnest. After Johnson's opening speech Henry Ashurst jumped up and secured the floor. Within a few minutes the chamber knew that the filibuster was on.

Ashurst first talked of the mighty Colorado, its length and its tributaries; then he launched into his favorite subject—Arizona. The Petrified Forest, Grand Canyon, and other scenic wonders droned from his lips. After several hours he was relieved by Senator Cameron, who still held the floor when the Senate adjourned for the day.

On the twenty-second, with Cameron still controlling the debate, Hiram Johnson launched his own strategy. As floor manager of the bill, he was able to insist that the Senate remain in continuous session through the night. If Arizona wanted a showdown, she would now have it.

Cameron was still talking when Ashurst relieved him just before midnight. Most of the senators had gone home to bed, but it was up to Johnson to keep a quorum on hand. When some of the members refused to answer the summons, the sergeant at arms was authorized to get warrants for their arrest. By 2:40 a.m. a quorum of sleepy-eyed senators filled the chamber. At this hour of the morning they cared little for Boulder Dam, even less for Senator Ashurst.

But the Arizonan talked on. By three o'clock he began over again on his opening speech, reciting the Colorado's tributaries, Arizona's scenery, the Petrified Forest, the Grand Canyon. His listeners sank deeper in their chairs. Near five some of his weary colleagues were trying to help him get a recess. But Ashurst refused, fearing that he would lose the floor in yielding to anyone for such a purpose.

"This is going to be a savage fight," he admonished them hoarsely. "Do not beguile yourselves with the belief that this is going to be a soft-glove affair. This is a fight to the finish. . . ."

His audience had faded once more, but by the full light of morning the sergeant at arms had secured another quorum. Shortly afterward Lawrence Phipps of Colorado, practically an open representative of private power, came to the Arizonan's rescue and took the floor.

Johnson's famous all-night session was over. Ashurst had met the challenge and had passed the torch to another. But now the entire nation, made aware of the spectacle by newspaper headlines, was aroused to the drama of Hiram Johnson's battle.

While the filibusterers droned on, Americans from coast to coast waited for the outcome.

Hiram Johnson knew he dared not hold the Senate in another continuous session. One more sleepless night would not leave his colleagues favorably disposed toward Boulder Dam. But a final weapon remained. Johnson himself had opposed cloture—the limiting of debate by a two-thirds vote—but he now turned to it in desperation.

Next day, while Henry Ashurst held the floor and read the senators an unending succession of documents, the Californian passed from desk to desk with his cloture petition. Ashurst saw what he was doing and, with reddening face, talked on more determinedly than ever. At last Johnson strode resolutely down the aisle to the rostrum and demanded that he be allowed to introduce his petition.

Vice-President Charles Dawes was out of the chamber, and a senator was substituting in the chair. He hesitated while Ashurst loudly denied Johnson's right to present the cloture motion. Just as loudly Johnson insisted that he be heard. Amid the babel he impatiently tossed the petition on the desk.

Cameron of Arizona then leaped up and doubled Arizona's noise; for a time all three senators were shouting at once. Vice-President Dawes hurried into the room and irritatedly took the gavel from his substitute, who retired in obvious relief. After a vigorous pounding on the rostrum Dawes silenced the pandemonium. Quietly he ordered that Johnson could introduce his resolution limiting debate.

Ashurst saw his defense crumbling. Angrily he appealed the ruling but was voted down. Then the Arizonan exploded. In a frenzied voice he charged that Johnson was trying to smother Arizona and called him a "bifurcated, peripatetic volcano, in perpetual eruption, belching fire and smoke. . . ." With outstretched hands, his face flushed, his words quavering, he shouted that Arizona was being strangled.

"Senators, if you vote for this cloture motion you may drown the voice of Arizona, but there will ever afterwards be in your bosom an unstilled voice from which you cannot escape . . . your conscience."

The admonition was enough. The cloture lost its necessary two-thirds majority. Johnson had been beaten twice in his attempts to stop the filibuster and now found himself out of weapons. The Boulder Dam bill died when the Californian agreed to take up other urgent legislation before the March 4 congressional deadline. Arizona had won the first round in the Senate arena. Boulder Dam was now dead in both houses.

There was nothing to do now but wait till the next session of Congress in December 1927. But Johnson's spectacular fight in the Senate had brought the issue before the entire country and had captured the imagination of a public which appreciated a good scrap. Through the summer and fall the California water men and the Hearst newspapers worked to keep this interest alive. Led by Mayor Sam C. Evans of Riverside, the Boulder Dam Association kept up its publicity, sending speakers and pamphlets across the country. When Swing and Johnson introduced their new bills early in December, they had a nationwide organization behind them. Letters and telegrams were soon pouring in on Congress, urging early debate. The House Rules Committee sent the bill to the floor on May 15.

It was now thoroughly amended to meet the arguments of its enemies. Charges that the government was entering the power business were answered by a provision that it would build the dam but not the generating stations, selling nothing more than falling water to local Southwestern power users. Even Arizona was placated with a royalty tax on every kilowatt of power generated at the dam—a privilege which was to be shared by Nevada.

But Swing found that Arizona still opposed the dam on the water issue. She was joined by Utah, whose legislature had withdrawn its approval of the Compact. Her senior representative, Elmer O. Leatherwood, stood ready to continue his fight against Swing's bill. Though ill from overwork, the old warrior appeared on the chamber floor when debate opened on May 22 and harangued his colleagues for an hour in bitter opposition. Not many days later the Utah lawmaker died from complications brought on by fatigue. It was said that he was a victim of the Boulder Dam fight.

The day after Leatherwood's speech the opposition was taken up by young Lewis Douglas of Arizona, who had succeeded Carl Hayden as his state's sole representative when the latter rose to the Senate. At thirty-three Douglas was "the baby of the House"; it was the first appearance on the national scene of the man who was to become Director of the Budget and later ambassador to England.

After delivering his maiden speech against the Swing-Johnson bill, Douglas was left with the task of fighting single-handedly a measure which the entire country and most of his colleagues were determined to pass. Debate was limited in the House, and a filibuster was impossible. His only chance was to smother the bill with amendments. But when Boulder Dam came up for final vote on May 25, 1928, Phil Swing met Douglas in the House

204

corridor and warned him that he could limit debate to five minutes on each amendment if he chose.

"I don't want to cut you off on any serious amendment," he explained. "But I understand you have about a hundred of them, and I'll not allow you to drag this bill to death."

Douglas knew Swing could make good his threat. Arizona's only chance was to make the bill as acceptable as possible with some earnest amendments. Lewis Douglas promised he would introduce no more than twelve.

Swing now went into the chamber with a majority of votes promised and House passage assured. This was to be the final fruit of eight years of strategy. The help he had invested in other sectional bills now came back with interest. John Garner of Texas, Democratic floor leader, had once come to him with a bill to create a commission for dealing with Mexico on the division of the Rio Grande and Colorado rivers. Swing had consulted with Hiram Johnson, and the two had earned Garner's gratitude by helping him pass the measure.

With the flood problems of the Mississippi region Phil Swing had been particularly sympathetic. In his second term he had gained a seat on the House Flood Control Committee and during the great deluge of 1927 had boated down the Mississippi with the committee inspecting the fearful damage. When the Mississippi Flood Control bill came before Congress, he fought mightily for it, securing the friendship of the Southern congressmen. Once his Boulder Dam measure came to a vote, they promised him, there would not be a voice against it from the Mississippi Valley. It is said that one reluctant member, who opposed Swing's bill, was ushered into the corridor by his colleagues just before the roll call began. Those Southern congressmen took a promise seriously.

All this accumulated strength was at Swing's command when Lewis Douglas unleashed his amendments on the House floor. As fast as they were introduced and explained by the lone Arizonan, the House voted them down.

But as Douglas dragged the session into the afternoon, Swing feared a break in his line of support. The New York City Democrats, under the dominance of Tammany Hall, had promised their votes for that great national enterprise, Boulder Dam. Still, this was a Friday afternoon, and they were determined to head home for the weekend. Swing was reminded that they would have to catch the New York train that afternoon. As time wore on one New Yorker after another slipped over to Swing's desk and asked when the measure would come to a vote. At last Swing went to the chief of the Tammany delegation and offered to limit debate if it was necessary to insure the Tammany vote.

"Mr. Swing," boomed the New Yorker, pounding his desk, "I assure you, when the vote comes, they'll be here!"

It was not long in coming. Douglas' last desperate chance came in a motion to send the bill back to committee. When it lost by a vote of 219-139, Douglas knew he was beaten. By three o'clock Swing's forces had regained the floor, and a few minutes later the roll call began. Jack Garner and his Texas colleagues contributed their votes. The entire Mississippi Valley delegation went for the measure without a dissenting voice. Tammany came through with its votes and headed for the railroad station. Boulder Dam passed the House by a safe majority.

When the news of Swing's victory reached Imperial Valley, its communities virtually erupted with joy. The streets of El Centro were jammed with hysterical celebrants. While bells clanged and whistles tooted, a hilarious automobile parade was hastily formed with mufflers open and horns blaring. That night a more organized but equally uproarious jubilee was held in Brawley. It was the biggest excitement in Imperial since the Armistice.

Hiram Johnson, however, was still fighting an uphill contest on the Senate side of the Capitol. The second Arizona filibuster began in earnest on May 26, bringing the bitter warning from Johnson that he would force "a test of physical endurance." This time Ashurst had a young and virile partner in obstruction, Carl Hayden. Together they kept debate dragging on Boulder Dam, supported at intervals by Utah Senators Reed Smoot and William King.

At the same time Johnson was hampered by the old-guard leadership of his own party. Adjournment of the session was already overdue; and on May 27, Charles Curtis, Republican majority leader, moved for adjournment—a step which would mean success for the filibuster and defeat for Boulder Dam. But Johnson was able to muster enough votes to tie up the motion 40-40, whereupon Vice-President Dawes cast the deciding vote against it.

Debate was on once more, and Johnson increased the pressure by invoking his "endurance" test. The Senate was placed in continuous session once again—another sleepless night for the harassed senators. Through the early morning hours of the twenty-eighth they were routed out of bed for quorum calls, while Ashurst went through his old speech on Arizona's scenery, including the Petrified Forest and "the equally petrified speeches of some of my colleagues." Arizona was still battling late in the morning when a final blow felled Johnson's hopes once more. Senator Curtis had been picking up votes during the nightlong session and now tossed out his adjournment motion again. By a close count the Senate voted to end its business with that day's session. Johnson knew it was the end; Ashurst and Hayden could easily hold out through the afternoon and prevent a vote. With supreme resignation he capitulated and moved to consider other bills.

"Yes, I am whipped," he told his colleagues, "but, by heaven, another day is coming and then someone else will be whipped."

He referred to the second session of the same Congress, due in December 1928. The Boulder Dam bill that had passed the House and reached the Senate floor would have to be given first consideration then. But Ashurst of Arizona warned that he and Hayden would be on hand to fight a vote "to the last drop of our blood. . . ."

During that summer the California men made political progress. Senators King and Smoot of Utah had supported the Arizonans in their fight, but Phil Swing now moved to cut off that source of help. When the Union Pacific Railroad opened its new hotel on the north rim of the Grand Canyon, he was on hand to witness the celebration—merely as a representative Californian. But as the busses left the railroad at Cedar City for the drive to the canyon, Swing was somehow seated in the first car alongside the head of Utah's Mormon Church, Heber J. Grant. While the coach rolled over the Utah countryside, Swing leaned over and opened the conversation. Soon he was well into his stock Boulder Dam speech, raving on about "liquid gold" and "white coal." Heber J. Grant, tumbling to his purpose, interrupted.

"Mr. Swing," he explained, "I'm only the spiritual head of the Church. President Ivins is in charge of business affairs."

Swing was not dismayed. "Where is he?"

"In the bus behind us."

"Stop the bus!" cried Swing. "I'm in the wrong place."

At the next stopping place he was ushered to the other coach, where he was introduced to Anthony W. Ivins, a leading counselor in the Church and a powerful figure in Mormon politics. By the time the caravan was rolling again Swing was launched once more on his Boulder Dam speech. When he had finished, Ivins smiled and gave his answer.

"Mr. Swing, you know Senator Smoot is a stubborn man. I can't promise you his vote, but I'll promise you Senator King's support. And I will try to get Senator Smoot not to vote against you."

Swing was elated. He had not hoped for such a response. For him the rest of the Grand Canyon tour was superfluous; he had accomplished his mission in getting the Mormon Church behind Boulder Dam.

207

As soon as the Senate took up the Swing-Johnson bill in December 1928, William King of Utah sought out Swing and proposed some amendments. The Californian knew this was the first fruit of his Utah excursion. Together King and the California group worked out six amendments satisfactory to both. While King introduced them on the Senate floor and Johnson "reluctantly" accepted them, Reed Smoot sat glowering at his desk. Swing, watching from the gallery, marveled at his own handiwork.

But if Utah was now out of the way, Arizona was not. Hayden and Ashurst opened their third filibuster on December 5, apparently determined to talk through the entire session if necessary. It was a hopeless stand; even their former allies in the upper-basin states were now clamoring for a vote.

For a week, while debate raged on the floor, negotiations were going on in the corridors and cloakrooms. The bitter deadlock between California and Arizona over water rights was now to be broken by writing into the bill a limitation on California's share. The amendment gave California a certain part of the 7,500,000 acre-feet apportioned to the lower basin by the Compact, plus half the extra 1,000,000 acre-feet of III b water and half of any added surplus.

But before this division could be voted on an unfortunate thing happened. On December 10, Senator Phipps of Colorado introduced a substitute amendment which made no specific mention of the extra 1,000,000 acre-feet. In addition to her share of apportioned water California was simply allowed one half the surplus. Here was the crux of the long feud between California and Arizona over III b water. Arizonans later said that everybody knew the 1,000,000 was reserved exclusively for their state. Californians were equally insistent that everybody understood the surplus water included that 1,000,000. They argued that in six days of exhaustive debate there was no mention—by Ashurst, Hayden, or anybody else—of Arizona's having sole right to III b water.

At any rate the Phipps amendment was adopted over Arizona's opposition on December 12, giving California 4,400,000 acre-feet of "apportioned" water and one half the surplus. But in its failure to define III b water were the seeds of continued conflict. For if California limited herself to 4,400,000 acre-feet of "apportioned" water, then it made a lot of difference whether III b was "apportioned" or "surplus." Arizona said it was part of the lower basin's "apportioned" water, to which California had a definite limitation. California said it was part of the "surplus" water, of which she was entitled to one half.

Nevertheless, that restricting amendment on December 12, 1928, was the real end of the Boulder Dam battle. On the same day a motion was made to limit further debate—thus spiking Arizona's last chance to filibuster. To Hiram Johnson's surprise, Hayden and Ashurst calmly kept their seats. They had been forewarned of the move and were resigned at last to defeat.

Boulder Dam came to a vote two days later. From his gallery seat Phil Swing watched the roll call—a monotonous ending to a dramatic nine-year fight. He saw Senator King of Utah vote for the bill, as Anthony Ivins had predicted. The Mormon leader had not promised Senator Smoot's vote, but he had agreed to ask the "stubborn man" not to vote against it. Still, if Smoot backed down now on his pet annoyance, he would look extremely foolish. As the roll call neared his name, Smoot's face reddened. Just before his name was called he sat up, complained of a headache, and hurried out of the chamber without voting. Smoot's honor had been saved and Utah's promise had been kept to the end. Boulder Dam passed, 63-11.

The House quickly agreed to the Senate amendments, and on December 21, Swing and Johnson were on hand to watch Calvin Coolidge sign their bill into law. Also watching was W. B. Mathews of Los Angeles, who had helped to bring about this historic day. From Washington to California some hundred other legislators, lobbyists, and publicists had reason to rejoice. The news reached the Southwest as the glorious Christmas present of 1928. Imperial, San Diego, Los Angeles, Yuma, Las Vegas, and scores of other communities suddenly exploded with delirious celebrations.

Within a few weeks—on March 4, 1929—California's legislature restricted its use of Colorado water in a Limitation Act, so as to comply with the Boulder Canyon law. Two days later the Utah legislature, urged by pressure from Anthony Ivins, renewed its ratification of the six-state Compact. Now every condition had been met. President Herbert Hoover, who had played his part in the long drama, was able to announce on June 25 that the Boulder Canyon Project Act was in full operation.

It was the end of the first great battle for the Southwest's last water hole. The conflicting interests had been satisfied, or nearly so. "For the American people as a whole," concluded the New York *Times*, "it removes all obligation to try to understand what the Boulder Dam business is all about." But for the citizens of the Southwest it was a beginning. There remained the technical task of damming the Colorado and bringing the water to the land and the people.

13: A DAY FOR THE ENGINEERS

The United States opened work on Boulder Dam with an enthusiastic team of Californians in charge—Elwood Mead of the Reclamation Bureau, formerly professor of engineering at the University of California; Secretary of the Interior Ray Lyman Wilbur, later president of Stanford University; and Herbert Hoover himself. Together they took a proprietary interest in launching this project which would remake the face of the great Southwest. As soon as Congress appropriated the first $10,000,-000 in July 1930, Wilbur sent an historic message to Mead which set the national machinery in motion:

"You are directed to commence construction on Boulder Dam today."

Immediately the Reclamation Bureau hastened to draw up its specifications; the depression of the thirties had struck the nation, and the giant Southwestern project could be a desperately needed source of employment. In less than six months the government had surveyed Black Canyon—chosen as a more promising site than nearby Boulder Canyon—and had calculated its cost data. Then it announced a call for contract bids on the greatest construction job ever undertaken by man.

No single engineering firm was big enough to tackle it. But three combinations of them submitted bids before the deadline of March 4, 1931. The contract went to an organization of some of the most experienced builders in the West—Six Companies, Inc., whose low bid of $48,890,995.50 turned out to be just $24,-000 over the Reclamation Service estimates.

Quickly the member firms completed their organization. As chairman of the board they chose financier Henry J. Kaiser of Oakland, whose dynamic energy was able to hold the group together without serious dissension. The actual task of field construction fell to Frank T. Crowe, a lanky, hardheaded engineer in his early fifties who had built and helped to build some of the biggest dams in the West. Crowe was a congenial friend but a hard-driving boss; he was the kind of field engineer who liked to boast, "I never bellied up to a desk in my life." While serving with the Reclamation Bureau in 1919, he had helped to make the first rough surveys between the Colorado's towering walls. Now the responsibility of fulfilling them was his.

Then before Frank Crowe could begin his assault on the Colorado, the state of Arizona made good her threat to fight Boulder Dam in the courts. In October 1930, Arizona sought an injunction against construction from the Supreme Court, claiming that the Project Act was unconstitutional. Arizona's lawyers claimed it not only took away her control of dam and reservoir sites but enforced the Colorado Compact against her when she had not approved it. California, the Interior Department, and the other basin states promptly argued that the suit be dismissed for failure to show any real damage to Arizona. In an 8-1 decision the Supreme Court threw out the case in May 1931. Arizona's last attempt to block Boulder Dam had failed.

It was mid-March, 1931, when Frank Crowe, armed with charts and blueprints, reached the site of construction in the desolate heart of the great Southwestern basin and looked down upon his opponent. Silently the brown Colorado wound its tortuous way along the bottom of sheer walls 1500 feet deep. His first task was to divert it through giant side tunnels around the dam site, so as to clear the ground for his army of men and machines. Then the canyon bottom must be excavated over 100 feet down to bedrock, a monolithic block of concrete raised 727 feet between the walls, and the biggest power tunnels and stations in the world constructed—all within seven years' time.

According to contract, Six Companies would have to forfeit $3000 for every day its work continued beyond the deadline of April 11, 1938. The government was making every effort to see that the long years of delay by debate were not matched by delay in construction while the Colorado increased its threat to Imperial Valley. It now remained for Frank Crowe to discover how the sullen river would react to this invasion by man.

The Interior Department was already completing the first step in the conquest. From a point near Las Vegas, Nevada, a thirty-one-mile branch of the Union Pacific Railroad was built into the depths of Black Canyon and promptly began hauling material and equipment across the desert for the monumental work ahead. One other requisite had already been supplied by Interior Secretary Wilbur, who a few months before had sent official notification to Mead of the Reclamation Bureau: "The dam which is to be built in the Colorado River at Black Canyon is to be called Hoover Dam."

As for the army of several thousand men needed to fight the river, Frank Crowe found it at hand before he ever saw the Colorado. All the way from Las Vegas to the dam site the desert road was dotted with temporary shanties. Here were hundreds of indigent families, caught in America's worst depression, who had come from every corner of the Union in the desperate hope of finding work at Boulder. Upstream from Black Canyon there sprang a "Ragtown" of flimsy shelters, housing some thousand people without means of subsistence. By the time Crowe arrived many families were near the brink of starvation.

The situation forced Six Companies to begin large-scale operations immediately. After a hurried conference with his

211

engineers, Crowe decided to hire as many men as possible by working three shifts a day, round the clock. Skilled crews were rushed from other Western construction jobs to hasten the assault on Black Canyon. Roads were blasted along mountainsides, telephone and power lines installed, work houses and mess halls erected. In the barren desert a few miles away Six Companies built Boulder City, complete with schools, hospitals, lawn sprinklers, and air conditioning—everything possible to make life bearable in the merciless heat of Nevada summers. By the end of the year Frank Crowe had over 2700 men on the payroll, and the ugly crisis was over. Six Companies had met its first emergency and now was ready to tackle the river itself.

Into the shadows of Black Canyon in early May went Frank Crowe with his men, trucks, and drilling machines. On Crowe's drawing boards were two giant diversion tunnels for each side of the canyon—all of them to be fifty feet in diameter after the concrete linings were laid. Only one other bore in the world—the Rove Tunnel in France—had a greater diameter.

First blast on the tunnels was fired May 12, 1931. From that time on the canyon was alive with metal-hatted men and their jackhammers, with dust-raising trucks hustling along mountain roads, with loads of materials swinging out between the giant walls on cables suspended across the chasm. Out of the sides of Black Canyon came incessant rumblings as the tunnel faces gave way to blasts of dynamite. Then the "muck" would be scooped up by monster power shovels working inside the tunnels and dumped into trucks for disposal.

Crowe and his engineers knew there was no time for delay; they planned to make the big diversion of the Colorado in the fall of 1932—at a time when the river would be in low stage, with little chance of flash floods from the Virgin or Little Colorado tributaries. If the tunnels were not driven and lined by that time, Six Companies would have to wait another year; there was no grappling with the mighty Colorado except in its most docile moment.

As the yawning tunnels were driven farther into the sides of Black Canyon, new methods and machines were contrived to hasten the work. The hugeness of the bore made the drilling of the "shot" holes the most tedious part of the job. But one of Crowe's engineers devised a mammoth framework of platforms mounted on a truck, from which up to thirty drillers could attack the face simultaneously. By the use of these "jumbos," as they were soon called, Crowe's tunnelers drove with renewed speed through the sides of Black Canyon. Before the first tube was holed through in January 1932 some of the crews were completing three rounds of drilling, firing, and mucking every twenty-four hours, advancing the work as much as forty-five feet a day. Frank Crowe calculated that they would all be finished and lined with time to spare before the deadline at the end of the year.

But the Colorado could not help noticing this persistent human activity along its banks and suspecting the plot being laid to tame it. Early in February 1932 it reared in anger. Over the mountain country to the north a heavy rain fell, melting winter snows and sending a gathering flood down the arms of the Virgin. On the afternoon of February 9 it hurtled into Black Canyon without warning.

Instantly Crowe's hive of activity was turned into pandemonium. Tunnel work was dropped and crews were rushed to the surface to fight the river. While the water rose foot by foot, men worked feverishly, raising sandbag embankments to protect the tunnel openings. By midnight the trestle bridge supplying the works on the Arizona side was staggering under the furious battering of torrent and debris. Machine shops and power engines were flooded, but Crowe's battlers kept the river out of the tunnels. When the Colorado began to subside next morning, it had taken out the bridge and wrecked some equipment but left Six Companies holding the field.

Then the Colorado tried a flank attack. The same storm that had flooded the Virgin passed over Arizona and filled the Little Colorado two hundred miles to the east. This time Crowe's army received the alarm hours in advance. But there was still no time to rebuild the trestle bridge swept out by the first flood, and the Arizona tunnels were almost isolated from help. Men were sent hurrying across a small suspension bridge to retrieve vital equipment and fortify the dikes in front of the tunnel mouths.

They were still piling sandbags when, on February 12, the Colorado's second flood came rampaging into Black Canyon, 50,000 second-feet strong. Like an enraged lion, it swept out the Arizona banks and poured headlong into the tunnels. Before this onslaught Crowe's men were powerless to do anything but protect the other tunnels on the Nevada side.

Next day the Colorado's fury was spent. The waters receded and the river passed on, but in the bottoms of the Arizona tunnels the crews found everything a dripping confusion. Intricate electrical equipment was standing in brown liquid that was "too thin to shovel and too thick to pump." Wearily they turned to the task of cleaning out the great dungeons and restoring the machinery. Meanwhile other crews rebuilt the trestle bridge, and within a few days trucks were rumbling over it once more with new rock blasted from the diversion tunnels.

213

A month later the crews began lining the tunnels with concrete. Filling the bottom sections was easy enough, but for the sides and top they rolled giant steel frameworks—like modern Trojan horses—into the depths of the tunnel for use as concrete forms. At the same time the openings were fortified against the long summer flood of the Colorado; if its water swirled in on this fresh concrete, weeks of tedious work might be undone in an instant. Fortunately 1932 was a dry year, and the river's flow never reached higher than 100,000 second-feet.

Late in August, when the water level was on its way downward and the engineers thought the worst was past, the Colorado made its last desperate stand. On the thirty-first it unexpectedly raised a flash flood of 60,000 second-feet and caught the Black Canyon crews off guard. Before they could stop it, water penetrated the barriers, flooded the tunnel pumps, shorted out electric motors, and poured over considerable fresh concrete. Then the diabolical river subsided, leaving the hard-bitten Six Companies workmen a week's work of cleanup and more recementing.

By October the lining of the Arizona tunnels was nearly finished, and Frank Crowe was ready to turn the river. Through hard driving and the use of labor-saving machines, his men had met the schedule for the great diversion in the fall of 1932. All Frank Crowe had to do was to lift the Colorado River ten feet in its channel, blow out the barriers in front of the tunnel mouths, and then heave the river into them. The only way to do this was to use the trick Harry Cory had perfected in the battle for Imperial Valley twenty-six years before. At the trestle bridge just downstream from the openings they must dump rock faster than the river could wash it away.

On the evening of November 12, Frank Crowe had a hundred loaded dump trucks lined up along the canyon road with engines idling. In the canyon bottom the Colorado swirled silently through the pilings of the trestle bridge, apparently unaware that this was to be its final battle. At a signal the trucks swung into gear and rumbled toward the bridge. One after another they dumped their rock into the water and roared back for reloads. For fifteen hours they bombarded the river at the rate of a truckload every fifteen seconds. All night long the Colorado rose steadily, pouring through the bridge pilings and over the top of the mounting wall of rocks. By eleven-thirty next morning it had been lifted ten feet and was cascading down the lower side of the barrier. At the right moment a blast of dynamite ripped open the levee in front of the outside Arizona tunnel, leaving a beckoning path for the beleaguered river. From the mouth of the bore came a jubilant shout:

214

"She's taking it, boys; she's taking it!"

Into the smooth round maw of the tunnel flowed the docile Colorado. A few hours later it was also pouring into the companion tunnel on the Arizona side. After laboring eighteen months to set a trap for the wary river, Crowe had diverted its entire flow out of the canyon in a single day's battle.

A third of a mile downstream another barrier was thrown across the canyon, just above the point where the tunnels emptied the Colorado back into its channel. The corridor between was then pumped dry—and the great working space for the construction of Hoover Dam was laid bare for the first time in the river's geologic history.

"Now all we gotta do," exclaimed one of the water boys, "is go down to bedrock and back."

Yet, where the tempestuous Colorado was concerned, anything could happen as long as these slim rock barriers were all that stood between it and the power-shovel crews who promptly began digging their way down to bedrock. If the first flash floods of the winter did not overturn those obstacles, the Colorado's spring rise would surely do so.

Six Companies was well aware that dams were necessary to build dams. Two staunch earth-fill cofferdams, with great sloping sides like pyramids, were built to wall off the site at each end. The upstream structure, ninety feet high, was finished in March 1933—none too soon to ward off the spring rise of the river. By then the two diversion tubes on the Nevada side had also been finished, and together the four tunnels were able to carry 200,000 second-feet—the highest recorded floods of the Colorado.

Down at Needles, however, Santa Fe Railroad engineers had found watermarks on the canyon walls indicating a past flood of some 384,000 second-feet. If another such deluge came hurtling down on the infant works in Black Canyon, raw nature would turn one of man's greatest engineering efforts into catastrophe.

Frank Crowe knew there was no room for delay in driving ahead on the dam itself. Six Companies was already over a year ahead of the Reclamation Bureau's timetable, but the unpredictable Colorado knew no schedules. Southward in the delta country it was still building up its bed at almost a foot a year, bringing closer the day when it would spill over into Imperial Valley. Settlers and engineers alike knew they could never stop another break like that of 1906. Their hopes rested on the determined progress of Frank Crowe's legions in the depths of Black Canyon.

215

Through the winter and spring of 1933 his shovel and dynamite crews were stripping away more than a hundred feet of silt and debris from the bed of the channel. Meanwhile he was making preparations for the biggest concrete-pouring job the world had ever seen—bigger than the aggregate of dams built under the Reclamation Service since its inception. Two giant cement plants were assembled in the canyon; one of them, perched high on the Nevada side of the gorge, was the largest in the world. From these two plants railroad cars would carry mammoth buckets, each holding sixteen tons of concrete mix, down to the dam site. Huge sky hooks from overhead cableways would then snatch them up and swing them out over the canyon to be poured.

Greatest single problem would be the cooling and setting of the dam's 5,000,000 tons of concrete. Enormous temperatures would be created deep inside it, and unless special devices were used it would take some hundred and twenty-five years to cool. In the process it would be hopelessly cracked by the shifting expansions and contractions. Therefore the dam would be built with over two hundred individual forms, each big enough for an ordinary house, which would be advanced upward as the dam progressed. Supplementing these would be a network of water pipes, and a maze of shafts and corridors through which every corner of the structure could be inspected by Six Companies engineers. There was to be no room for chance in a dam backing up a lake a hundred and twenty-five miles long.

By June 1933 the bedrock floor of the canyon had been laid bare, and on the sixth the first form was in place. Out of the sky came the first bucketful of concrete. Over two years had been spent in preparing Black Canyon for this epochal event—beginning of construction on the dam itself.

Month after month that skyward traffic of buckets continued from five separate cableways. An operator situated high on the cliff above would lower a bucket into the chasm like a spider on the end of its thread. Directed by signals from below, he would place it over the designated form and then trip the cable on the bucket gate. Out of the bottom dropped sixteen tons of lavalike mix, to be attacked by a concreting gang and tamped with shovels and the stomping of rubber boots. As the dam reared upward, bucket operator and form crews became a well-coordinated team; by March 1934 ten times as much concrete was being laid as in the first month of construction. Buckets were soaring through the air at a rate of nearly one a minute, hour after hour.

With this kind of furious activity in the narrow breadth of Black Canyon, accidents were inevitable. More than once a bucket cable snapped, sending men scurrying out of the way as wet concrete, bucket and all, hurtled downward and crashed into the checkered surface of the dam. One evening early in 1934 a bucket of mix was swinging into place above a concreting gang when the line broke. The steel behemoth plummeted across the form below, taking two men with it. Next moment it was clattering across the smooth surface of the mammoth dam. Then it bounced off the cliff and flung itself and its cement cargo into the bottom of the canyon.

In a minute men were scurrying over the great structure, looking for the victims. One was found dead on a catwalk below the top. Parties were searching for the other at the foot of the dam when a light was noticed halfway up the bold front. The second man was found on another catwalk, bruised and covered with wet concrete, but otherwise very much alive. He had struck a match to find out where he was.

Ordinarily, however, the relentless campaign in Black Canyon went on with smooth precision. By March 23, 1935, the last bucketful of mix had been poured and all forms were standing at crest level, 727 feet above bedrock. Then pure cement mixture was forced into the remaining spaces between the forms, and in every other crevice left open in the construction work. Frank Crowe and an army of 4000 metal-hatted men had finished Hoover Dam four years almost to the day after they had first descended into Black Canyon.

At the same time they had also completed the final conquest of the river. The two inner diversion tunnels had already been plugged with concrete, and a set of gate valves placed in the outer tunnel on the Nevada side to give a controlled flow for irrigation downstream. Then on February 1, 1935, a 1500-ton steel gate was lowered over the mouth of the outer Arizona tunnel. The waters that had rushed into the earth a moment before now lapped peacefully against the bulkhead. There was nothing for the river to do but rise against Hoover Dam.

This was the end of the Colorado's freedom; in low water or flood, it was now bridled to man's purposes. From that February 1—three years ahead of schedule—Imperial farmers ceased to have the river on their backs. No more would it threaten their valley with inundation at every summer flood; they could now leave their levees without strengthening them each year against a rising river bed, for the irrigating water that now passed below Boulder Dam was regulated and almost clear of silt. Until now total disaster had been relentlessly approaching; possibly the three years by which Six Companies had beaten its schedule had been the crucial three for Imperial Valley.

On September 30, 1935, Black Canyon played host to some 12,000 spectators when President Franklin D. Roosevelt, flanked by cabinet members and governors of six states, officially dedicated the dam. Most of the stalwarts who had fought for years to get it authorized were there—all except Arthur Powell Davis, former chief of the Reclamation Bureau, who had first proposed the project in 1903 and had pressed its adoption for twenty-five years. He had died in August 1933, two years before this climactic event which his efforts had largely produced.

Even at the time of its dedication the dam had formed a reservoir of nearly 4,000,000 acre-feet, enough to make it one of the largest artificial lakes in the world. But this was merely a beginning. Eventually it would reach the size of 30,000,000 acre-feet—not only the biggest man-made body in existence but one large enough to make permanent changes in the climate of its immediate region in the Southwest and to cause local earthquakes by its weight. Early in 1936 it was named Mead Lake, after the Reclamation commissioner who had overseen its creation through Hoover Dam.

To the cities of the Southern California coast the Boulder Canyon Project now yielded a seemingly unending supply of hydroelectric power. From the huge generating plants at the foot of Hoover Dam a brigade of giant steel towers marched three hundred miles over desert and mountains to bring the electric energy that afforded Los Angeles and its neighbors their industrial growth through the 1940s.

One other benefit the Southern California cities were to receive from the Colorado—1,000,000 acre-feet of municipal water. Toward this goal they were already driving in a gigantic project of their own. Los Angeles and eleven other cities, grouped together since 1928 in a Metropolitan Water District, were building a 240-mile ditch across the California desert.

Surveys of the route had been finished before Hoover Dam was started, but one obstacle after another had delayed construction. Of first consideration was the tangled question of water rights. A definite amount had been allotted to the lower basin in a compact to which Arizona had not agreed, and this contradictory situation made a definition of rights necessary before the cities could even begin to finance their project. Government contracts for delivery of water provided the answer, but this in turn necessitated an agreement among all water interests on a division of California's share.

Negotiators from Imperial and other agricultural districts thereupon sat down with others representing municipal users and after months of wrangling turned out the Seven Party

Agreement of August 18, 1931. It allowed priorities of use for existing water rights totaling 5,362,000 acre-feet a year—just under the U. S. Interior Department's figure on the amount to which California had restricted herself in her Limitation Act.

On this basis government water contracts were immediately executed. Arizona later disputed their validity, but California pointed out that they grew out of a proposal being pressed in negotiations at that time by Arizona herself.

At any rate the contracts were made, and on the strength of them the Metropolitan Water District launched into a $220,000,000 investment to bring Colorado River water to city faucets. The bond election to raise this sum was set for September 29, and the Southland swung into one of its rousing water campaigns. Nearly every newspaper fought for the bonds, while city water departments published pamphlets and mailed them to customers with their bills. Prominent leaders formed themselves into a Citizens Colorado River Committee which took active charge of the campaign. By early September it was turning out its own newspaper, *Water News*; at the same time service clubs were provided with speakers, radio listeners were besieged with water programs, audiences were shown sound movies entitled "Thirst," and even auto windshields blossomed with aqueduct stickers. On the morning before election housewives all over the metropolitan area found their milk bottles decorated with a printed reminder: "One more day until September 29, 1931." Southern Californians, already made water-conscious by their environment, were convinced. They went to the polls on the twenty-ninth and voted in the $220,000,000 bond issue by a ratio of five to one.

Legal obstacles and the depressed financial conditions blocked sale of the bonds for over a year and a half. But late in January 1933 the eager Metropolitan District engineers were able to break ground. A reservoir site had already been chosen just above Parker, Arizona, a hundred and fifty-five miles south of Hoover Dam. From here the conduit would strike westward across some of the wildest country in the arid Southwest.

All of the experience of the Los Angeles Water Department in building the Owens Valley aqueduct would now come into play. But whereas Mulholland's army had gone into the desert without modern refrigeration or gasoline trucks, this second generation of aqueduct makers would be armed with the latest advances in engineering.

While the Colorado builders were no pioneers, they were to fight under their own disadvantages. No railroad traversed the greater part of their route; they would have to start from the empty desert in building supply roads, telephone and power lines, and in developing a water supply for the work itself. And this was no gravity conduit, sloping by careful gradients from source to city. Aqueduct water would have to be pumped out of the Colorado canyon, then over intervening mountain ranges to the coastal plain—a total rise of some 1600 feet.

Here were problems unknown on Mulholland's Owens River ditch. While the two aqueducts were almost exactly the same in distance—over two hundred and forty miles from river to distributing reservoir—the Colorado conduit would cost nearly ten times more than its noted parent.

Mulholland's modern counterpart was staunch, white-haired Frank Weymouth, former chief engineer of the Reclamation Bureau, whose expert testimony had helped steer the Boulder Canyon Act through congressional committees. Among his triumphs in twenty-two years of government service was the giant Arrowrock Dam of southern Idaho, highest in the world until Hoover Dam was built. Since 1929, Weymouth had been chief engineer for the Metropolitan Water District; at the age of fifty-eight he was now embarking on the crowning achievement of his career—the biggest municipal aqueduct on the face of the earth.

Geography necessarily divided the task before him into two distinct sections. The first extended from the Colorado a hundred and twenty-five miles uphill to Hayfield Reservoir, the halfway point east of Coachella Valley. Through this rugged desert country the aqueduct wound its way in alternating tunnels, siphons, and open canals; and it was here that all the pumping stations were located. But from Hayfield pump lift westward the water would run downhill at a slope of three and a half feet to the mile, through an entirely closed conduit of tunnels, siphons and concrete pipe. Its 117-mile course paralleled Coachella Valley, headed into San Gorgonio Pass, swung below Banning through the San Jacinto Tunnel, and ended finally at Lake Mathews, south of Riverside. From here a distributing system would carry water to the cities of the Metropolitan District as far as Santa Monica on the coast, nearly four hundred miles from the Colorado.

Early in 1933 a ceremony for the opening of construction was held at Banning, and standing at Weymouth's side was another veteran engineer who watched the proceedings with satisfaction. At length old Bill Mulholland was called upon to speak. The seventy-seven-year-old patriarch shuffled forward, hands in pockets, and immediately gave the occasion an informal spirit.

"Well," he began, "anything I might say would be pretty old stuff. I've tramped these hills since '77 . . . and I'm getting

220

along. I am glad to be of service to you and to this community—now—and forever!"

It was to be his last public statement. Two years later, while aqueduct work was in full progress, Mulholland's robust health faltered. During his illness the old man fought valiantly for life, telling those at his bedside, "The Irish never give up." But on July 22, 1935, Bill Mulholland succumbed—and all of Los Angeles joined in mourning. The city's flags were flown at half-mast while every newspaper carried stirring eulogies on the engineer whose water adventures had laid a foundation for Los Angeles. During his funeral, which was attended by thousands, Frank Weymouth ordered work stopped all along the Colorado aqueduct for one minute of silence. Southern California was paying final tribute to the man who had fulfilled his own prophecy: "Whoever brings the water will bring the people."

By January 25, 1933, Frank Weymouth's crews had broken ground on the first of the aqueduct's forty-two tunnels, which made up a third of the entire route. On their construction, and especially on the thirteen-mile bore under Mount San Jacinto in the Coast Range, depended the estimated building time of six years for the whole aqueduct. Over half of them were driven by contracting firms, while district forces attacked the forty miles of almost continuous tunnels where the conduit paralleled Coachella Valley along the slope of the San Bernardino mountains.

Experience gained in the construction of the Hoover Dam diversion tunnels was now available to push this monumental work. Soon discarded was the old "heading-and-bench" method, whereby the upper part of a tunnel was excavated a few hundred feet ahead of the lower, and the new "full face" system was substituted. Jumbo carriages mounting up to eleven power drills assaulted the heading from ceiling to floor, while hard-hatted crewmen drove the powder holes. Then they were backed out of range while the dynamite was tamped and blasted. Powerful blowers at the tunnel mouths promptly sucked out the noxious gases of the explosion, turned in fresh air, and allowed the mucking crews to take over with their excavating machines and clear the loosened rock for the next advance. By this quick-moving system the tunnel crews drove forward over seven feet with every "round," or an average of twenty-one feet a day.

By the fall of 1934 more contracting firms were invading the desolate country east of Hayfield Reservoir to carve sixty-three miles of open canal across the desert sands. It was a job for giant mechanical machines. Along each canal section came chugging bulldozers to break ground and prepare the way. Then huge dragline cranes attacked the route and did the main work of excavation. To complete the shape of the fifty-five-foot-wide ditch, one construction company invented the "canal trimmer"— a mammoth framework of moving machinery shaped to fit the outline of the canal and cut it to precise shape. Drawn along tracks on each bank, it crept forward at the rate of a foot a minute—like some prehistoric behemoth crawling over the face of the Colorado Desert. Behind it, after reinforcing rods were fastened in place, came another monster—obviously a relative of the first. It was a "canal paver," which spread the concrete lining and tamped it into place in a single operation. Nowhere had such weird machines been used before, and nowhere, because of their size, could they be used again.

Within a year, as new sections were opened, men and machines swarmed over a hundred miles of desert west of the Colorado. A dozen temporary towns, complete with air-conditioned barracks and ice plants, had been built along the route to shelter an army which had grown to nearly 11,000 by the peak year of 1936. In the midst of depression they were braving merciless summer heat in the most forbidding part of the Southwestern desert to hold jobs on the aqueduct. By early 1936, under the energetic direction of Frank Weymouth, the builders were halfway through their job of delivering Colorado water to the thirsty cities of Southern California.

But over on the river itself trouble had suddenly arisen at the canal's starting point a few miles north of Parker. Reclamation Bureau men had arrived at the dam site early in 1934 to begin diamond drilling and determine the depth of bedrock. Thereupon the state of Arizona rallied her forces for another round. As long as her own water rights in the Colorado were still undetermined, she would not stand by while California began building a dam to divert her water—especially as that dam would be partially founded on Arizona soil.

Implacable old George W. P. Hunt was no longer Arizona's governor, but in his place now sat a man of equal showmanship and nerve—Governor B. B. Moeur. He lost no time in notifying the California governor that Arizona would oppose any activity on her own side of the river.

California, the Metropolitan Water District, and the Reclamation Bureau ignored the warning. Late in February 1934 their forces at the Parker site began drilling operations from barges in midstream. In order to hold them in place, they swung heavy cables across the Colorado and anchored them on the Arizona side.

222

When Governor Moeur heard about the cables, he moved swiftly in the best Arizona tradition. On March 3, 1934, a squad of militia was ordered to the dam site with instructions to "protect the rights of the State and report at once any encroachment on the Arizona side of the river."

Immediately the Southwest prepared for some frontier excitement. Phoenix was in a flurry as its troops gathered equipment, checked their ammunition, and prepared to strike out for "the front." The Los Angeles *Times* rushed a "war correspondent" to Parker, where he joined the natives in waiting for the arrival of the Arizona guard; he passed the time by writing with tongue in cheek of the "impending movement of State troops into this theater of war to protect the State of Arizona from invasion by all or part of the State of California. . . ."

It was agreed by the old-timers that Governor Moeur would have to send a squad of mountain goats if there was to be any approach to the dam by land. Only a dim and ancient wagon road, crossing sharp ravines and fording the Bill Williams River a dozen times, approached the spot on the Arizona side of the Colorado. An oiled supply road served it in California, but this was ruled out as enemy territory.

Meanwhile the federal workmen continued to drill in the bed of the Colorado as though nothing was amiss. The Metropolitan Water District's engineer in charge was simply instructed to "inform anyone who might want to remove the cables that we are not through with them."

On the afternoon of March 5 the spearhead of the Arizona forces descended on Parker in a whirl of dust after the long trip from Phoenix. While the town population gathered, two men emerged from the dust-caked station wagon. One was the governor's secretary; the other was Major F. I. Pomeroy of the 158th Infantry Regiment, Arizona National Guard. Together they made cautious inquiries, reconnoitered the terrain, and decided that the old-timers were right. The only way to reach the scene of operations several miles up the river was by water.

At this point appeared Nellie and Joe Bush, leading citizens of Parker. Mrs. Bush was, in fact, a member of the Arizona legislature and was proud to be of service in this crucial hour. From Parker to the town of Earp, on the California side, they had long operated a pair of ferryboats, the *Julia B.* and *Nellie T.* These they placed at the instant disposal of the state of Arizona.

Early next morning the long-heralded military advance began. The *Julia B.*, flying the Arizona flag, left the Parker dock and chugged northward through the brown current. Some distance upstream Nellie and Joe picked up the two-man Arizona military force and pressed onward. The *Times* reporter, also on board, was quick to label the whole expedition with the magnificent title of "Arizona Navy." The appellation was a happy stroke of genius; its incongruity immediately captured the nation's sense of humor. Across the country uproarious headlines described the antics of the Arizona Navy. A group of enthusiastic Arizonans wired their representative in Congress, urging that the battleship *Arizona* be sent at once to the scene of action at Parker.

Up the river stalked the staunch little craft, doing its best to fulfill the title. Drawing eighteen inches of water, it sported an engine room and pilothouse aft, with a flat forward deck big enough for a single auto. Manning the wheel on the voyage was officer Nellie; Joe Bush acted as admiral. Through the willow-lined canyon walls it plowed, while isolated settlers stood on the banks gazing in wonderment at this strange invasion.

Early in the afternoon the brave craft reached the dam site. Water District men watched from their barges and, according to an eyewitness, were "somewhat embarrassed as to proper naval procedure." Knowing that some kind of a salute was required "when a foreign vessel comes into port carrying dignitaries," they are said to have produced a shotgun and sounded off properly. When the *Julia B.* finally reached the bank on the Arizona side, the Californians waved their hats and sent up a resounding chorus of halloos.

Unruffled, Major Pomeroy busied himself inspecting the cables anchored on the Arizona shore. He then decided to inspect the mouth of the Bill Williams River as a possible camp site for his troops, but when the *Julia B.* turned to continue upstream, the low-hanging cables barred the way.

Here, indeed, was a crisis. But seeing the distress of the Arizonans, the California engineer obligingly sent a small motorboat across the river. This time the embarrassment was Arizona's. While the *Julia B.* sulked disappointedly at her mooring, the California vessel carried the major upstream to complete his mission. It was a crowning stroke in the Arizona-California hostilities.

That evening the proud *Julia B.* churned homeward, having fulfilled her destiny as flagship of the Arizona Navy. Next day she was back at the odious task of hauling autos back and forth from Parker to Earp, on the California shore.

Major Pomeroy returned to Phoenix and three days later burst into the town of Parker again with his expeditionary force —three vehicles and five soldiers. Shunning the ignominy of

224

naval transportation, they struck determinedly across the Arizona desert next morning in a station wagon. By noon, after a back-breaking ride across the fordings of the Bill Williams, they reached the Colorado a half mile above the dam site. There the troops encamped to observe the movements of the enemy and "report any encroachment." Through the scorching heat of an Arizona summer they remained at their isolated outpost—the vanguard of resistance for the sovereign state of Arizona.

After nine months' time they suddenly sent an emergency report to Governor Moeur. Construction had begun on Parker Dam. Six Companies, the firm that had built Hoover Dam, had taken the contract and was now laying a trestle bridge across the river toward the Arizona shore. Survey parties had already set foot on Arizona soil.

Governor Moeur acted immediately. On November 10, 1934, he declared martial law over the territory embracing the Arizona side of the Parker site. The National Guard was ordered to take possession of the area, eject trespassers, prevent construction of the bridge, and "repel the threatened invasion of the sovereignty and territory of the State of Arizona. . . ." To Secretary of the Interior Harold Ickes he sent a message explaining his stand. To the press he summed up Arizona's determination with a fiery comment:

"We may get licked in the affair, but we will go down fighting."

Over on the Colorado the Metropolitan Water District was equally adamant. Six Companies kept operating its pile driver as usual, pounding closer to the Arizona side. The workmen themselves were resolved to push ahead, even if it meant a clash. They had sought this work too long in the midst of a national depression to give it up now without a struggle. The Reclamation Bureau engineer backed up their defiance.

"My survey parties," he announced solemnly, "will cross the river tomorrow and go on with work as usual."

Downstream at Parker the citizens came alive in anticipation of hostilities. Miners, cowboys, and even Indians came to town from the surrounding country to witness the "big showdown." Newspaper correspondents, photographers, and newsreel cameramen swarmed into Parker, ready to record another sortie of the Arizona Navy for an expectant nation. Joe Bush ordered the *Julia B.* recommissioned for another advance up the Colorado.

"We're ready to move troops up the river any day," he announced dramatically. Scouts sent upstream, however, returned to report that the water level during the Colorado's fall stage was too low to float the Arizona Navy. Joe Bush was undismayed. "She'll go anywhere," he proudly insisted.

"When are you going to shove off?" somebody asked him.

"Oh," he countered slyly, "you don't think we're giving out military information, do you?"

On November 12 the Six Companies pile driver at the dam site had almost reached the Arizona bank; plans were made to begin work on diversion tunnels on the Arizona side. Out of Phoenix on the same day rumbled a caravan of eighteen army trucks, carrying over a hundred armed troops, several machinegunners, and a hospital unit. There seemed no way of preventing the long water feud between California and Arizona from ending in a pitched battle on the banks of the Colorado River.

Next day Interior Secretary Harold Ickes stepped in. From the Denver headquarters of the Reclamation Bureau came orders to stop work on Parker Dam. Six Companies laid off its crews at noon and called some two hundred additional men off the projected job on the Arizona tunnels. To Governor Moeur came a telegram from Ickes that work had been shut down; until the question was settled, he declared, "there will be no invasion of Arizona's rights."

State troops whirled into Parker in fighting trim that afternoon, only to be stopped from further advance by a message from the governor. Dejectedly they camped that night on the edge of town, while all of Parker gathered its frayed nerves. The drama of the Colorado water war had ended in ignoble frustration.

Next day the whole militia was called back to Phoenix, including the six-man squad which had guarded Arizona soil for nine months near the dam site. Their departure was accompanied by the homeward trek of another squad of disappointed newspapermen, who had waited for days with poised typewriters, newsreel cameras, and sound equipment for the battle that never happened. As for the noble *Julia B.*, she bravely carried on in her mundane task of ferrying autos across the Colorado, as though she had never been the flagship of the mighty Arizona Navy.

The military phase of the Colorado controversy was over, and the fight was now transferred to the courts. In mid-January 1935 the government brought action in the Supreme Court to enjoin Arizona from interfering with construction of Parker Dam. After granting a temporary injunction, the Court threw out the case on April 29. Arizona was held to be within its rights in halting work, as the dam had no authorization from Congress.

But Arizona's victory was short-lived; four months later Congress specifically authorized Parker Dam, and Arizona was

226

left with nothing to do but permit the resumption of work in the Colorado channel. Six Companies immediately began boring the diversion tunnels on the Arizona side and by October 1936 had started excavating in the dry riverbed to reach bedrock 240 feet below—a distance that makes Parker the "deepest" dam in the world.

Meanwhile Frank Weymouth's aqueduct builders were encountering far greater obstacles than political obstruction. In the depths of San Jacinto Mountain the contractors who were driving the aqueduct's longest tunnel were stalled by heavy flows of water. Like the famed Elizabeth Tunnel on the Owens River aqueduct, this thirteen-mile bore was being blocked by the very element it was being built to convey.

When excavation had first started in May 1933, two shafts were sunk down to grade level—one three miles in from the west portal, and the other less than two miles from the east portal. The eight-mile distance between these two points ran under the heart of Mount San Jacinto, second highest peak in Southern California. This was the crucial distance which determined the length of construction time not only for the tunnel itself but for the entire aqueduct. In less than a year the crews had reached grade level in the two shafts and were working on four headings deep in the interior of "old San Jack."

But in July 1934 the miners in the eastbound heading of the west shaft suddenly struck a fault. From the sides and top of the tunnel a shower of water rushed in upon them. They were scarcely able to remove equipment before the tunnel was flooded completely.

The water had risen almost to the top of the 800-foot shaft before the contractors could install pumps to fight the overflow. They had nearly cleared the shaft when an accident occurred which disabled two of the three pumps and gave way to the flood once more. When the works were finally pumped out in November 1934, a third flood promptly filled them again. Finally the crews were able to resume work by the end of the year but could still make little headway against a constant flow of water.

By this time Frank Weymouth and his Water District engineers feared that delay in San Jacinto would hold up the entire aqueduct—a result which would cause a high loss of interest payments on the bonds. Little more than two miles had been driven in over a year and a half—a rate which would bring completion in nearly ten years instead of the estimated six. Early in 1935, Weymouth decided to cancel the contract and push the work directly. Metropolitan Water District engineers took over on February 12 and, with a more powerful set of pumps and heavier excavating machines installed in each shaft, drove ahead three more miles in a year's time.

Frank Weymouth knew, however, that even this pace could not make up for the time lost. In March 1936 he called his engineers together for a council of war. More than three years, he reminded them, had been consumed in driving only two miles in the key central section of the tunnel. Surface exploration indicated that several more water-laden faults lay ahead. Clearly a whole new strategy was needed for the assault on indomitable old San Jack.

Out of that meeting was born a new line of attack. A mile-long shaft—the "Lawrence Adit"—was begun from a canyon paralleling the tunnel on the north, four miles from the town of Banning. Striking the central tunnel section roughly in the middle, this new access would provide two more headings from which Weymouth's hardy miners could carry on the assault. The alignment of the tunnel itself was swung northward to meet the new shaft—a device which added over a thousand feet of length but hastened the shaft connection. Weymouth calculated this entire strategem would cut a year off the construction time.

Through this and other expedients his tunnelers drove through the mountain at a still faster pace, fighting off floods that sometimes poured out over 15,000 gallons a minute at a single heading. By December 1937, when the mile-long Lawrence shaft reached the tunnel line, it was clear that the final three miles would be finished within the six-year limit.

As the last barrier was pierced on November 19, 1938, the event was witnessed by hundreds of miners and a crowd of Metropolitan District officials. Even the nation itself shared their triumph, for a CBS microphone was on hand to record the final explosion which left an unbroken thirteen-mile hole through the heart of old San Jack. After the muckers cleared the heading, they found the historic connection was exactly true for lateral alignment and a tenth of an inch off for elevation. Frank Weymouth's team of surveyors, engineers, and drillers had not sacrificed accuracy in winning their battle against time.

Within less than a year the concrete crews lined the tunnel, and the last link in the conduit was completed. Then the ponderous machinery of the world's greatest domestic aqueduct shifted into motion. Power transmitted southward from Hoover Dam began lifting water from Parker Reservoir and over the mountains of the Colorado Desert. In November 1939 it was turned into the terminal reservoir, which was soon dedicated Lake Mathews, in honor of the Los Angeles water lawyer whose indefatigable efforts up till his death a few years before had largely made this aqueduct possible.

228

Another year and a half was consumed in finishing the distribution system to member cities of the Metropolitan Water District. On June 17, 1941, the first Colorado water was delivered to Pasadena, and in rapid succession to Santa Monica, Long Beach, and other cities.

It was the welcome end of a long ordeal; ten years had passed since these cities had first voted the aqueduct bonds, and eighteen years since Mulholland had journeyed to the Colorado to consider it as a source of municipal water. To those who had scoffed that the project was fantastic, Frank Weymouth and his hard-hatted army had written an imperishable answer across four hundred miles of California desert.

Colorado water came none too soon for the Southern California community. The wet cycle of the late 1930s ended with the winter of 1941, and in the years that followed many cities would have found their reservoirs dropping dangerously low without the new supply. For Santa Monica, Long Beach, and several others it soon became a main source of drinking water.

But Los Angeles, with its own gravity supply from Inyo and Mono counties, was slow to make use of pumped water from the Colorado. During the first full year of operations only 114,000 acre-feet came through the aqueduct—just about one tenth of the ultimate capacity. In an effort to put the project on a paying basis, district officials encouraged new communities to join; and several, including Inglewood and Anaheim, were quick to accept.

But other cities declined, believing their local supplies were enough, and thereupon made a drastic civic mistake. Later some of those same communities tried in vain to gain the membership they once shunned. The Metropolitan Water District became the one stable source of water in Southern California; membership in this exclusive club meant the difference between a prosperous future and tragic stagnation.

As the giant projects of the Colorado unfolded during the early 1930s, the one that had fathered them all still remained to be launched. Out of Imperial Valley's project for the All-American Canal, conceived by her water seekers before World War I, had grown the whole Boulder Canyon Project. It was, as Phil Swing had put it, "the tail that wagged the dog."

Like the Colorado Aqueduct, the canal was not begun until Hoover Dam was well advanced, because its diversion dam in the river could best be built after the parent structure had controlled the flow. Yet by 1933 the metropolitan aqueduct project was under way, and the All-American Canal was still on the drawing boards.

Phil Swing was then in Washington representing the Imperial Irrigation District after the end of his twelve-year congressional career. Neither he nor Imperial had forgotten the canal that was to free their water supply from Mexican control. As long as it remained unbuilt, Swing knew the nine-year battle he had waged in Congress was still unfinished. With his fighting spirit aroused, he invaded the Reclamation Bureau and found the cause of the delay. Although the Boulder Canyon Act had appropriated funds for its construction, the government was reluctant to begin work while other states were clamoring for irrigation expenditures.

Phil Swing then went to Harold Ickes, the blustery head of the Interior Department. Imperial Valley, he told him, could not afford to have the canal postponed. Ickes took him to a wall map near his desk.

"All these other states have water projects pending," he explained. "You'll just have to wait."

"I can't wait," replied Swing.

If the Interior Department would not grant his plea, he would find a higher authority. Swing secured a fifteen-minute appointment with President Roosevelt and then with his usual showmanship succeeded in gathering a number of Colorado basin congressmen to appear with him. The Californian even approached his old friend and enemy, Senator Carl Hayden of Arizona, appealing to him on the ground that if Hoover Dam was finished without an All-American Canal there would be no way to prevent Mexico from irrigating more land by the increased low flow of the river. Swing had nudged Hayden in a vulnerable spot. The Mexican menace to Colorado water had long been a bugbear in Arizona, and Carl Hayden agreed to support the All-American Canal.

On the afternoon of October 23, Phil Swing took his impressive troupe to the White House. Already on Roosevelt's desk were telegrams from John Garner of Texas and Ward Bannister of Colorado urging the All-American Canal. Swing had set the stage well.

After the introductions he launched into a ten-minute speech on the canal project, finishing almost out of breath.

"Well, Mr. Swing," Roosevelt responded amiably, "you've made a good statement and you've brought a good crowd with you." Then, with a sly smile: "When you've brought Senator Hayden, I almost think you're right to begin with."

The President concluded by asking the views of the others and told Swing he would send word of his decision. The group

230

had no sooner filed out than Roosevelt called Senator Hiram Johnson, who had jumped Republican traces to support him in the presidential campaign the year before. Here again Phil Swing had laid his groundwork. Forewarned of a possible call, Johnson gave stout approval of the All-American Canal.

Next day Swing was in his Washington quarters when a Public Works Administration official telephoned. Would he come over and help to write up the resolution allotting $6,000,000 to begin the All-American Canal?

"What resolution?" blurted out Swing.

"You ought to know," returned the voice. "You put it through."

"I'll be right over."

That day Phil Swing was able to send a long-awaited telegram to the jubilant directors of the Imperial Irrigation District: "Glad advise canal approved and six million allotted start work." By a final application of his bulldog spirit and astute showmanship, the veteran water fighter was making the tail do some wagging of its own.

Surveys and contracts immediately followed, and by August 8, 1934, three hundred Imperial settlers journeyed to the Colorado to watch the first excavation on the All-American Canal. While the crowd assembled on a nearby point under a blazing midsummer sun, a huge power shovel ambled into place on the east slope of Pilot Knob. Sitting at the levers was blocky Mark Rose. As the long-standing "pioneer" of the project, he had been given the honor of releasing the first bucketful of rock from the eighty-mile ditch. With his Imperial friends cheering him on, the doughty farmer raised the first scoopful of earth and dropped it into a waiting truck. So far as Mark Rose was concerned, this completed his twenty-two-year efforts for the All-American Canal; the rest of the work he left to the engineers.

Straight through the barren border country went the giant machines, fulfilling on the ground a plan that had been on drafting tables for a generation. Within a few months the route was swarming with dragline cranes and power shovels—and a suntanned army of two thousand men. By 1935 they encountered the valley of the shifting sand hills, the barrier that had forced Rockwood and Chaffey southward into Mexico with their original Imperial Canal. Through this forbidding land of sterile white sand dunes the modern builders met their greatest test. Opponents of the canal had scoffed that it could never be pierced; engineers had reported that even if the ditch was built it could not be kept clear of the relentless encroachment of moving sand.

231

Against these walking hills the canal makers brought in an equally formidable weapon—a mammoth dragline crane of 650 tons. It was so huge that twenty boxcars were needed to carry its parts to the nearest Southern Pacific siding and so heavy that no wheels could support it in those yielding sands. Instead it was fashioned with two mechanical "feet," each weighing twenty-one tons. Mounted eccentrically on an axle, they actually "walked"—seven feet at a step.

So against the walking hills was pitted a giant walking crane. Laboring around the clock, with floodlights attached to its booms by night, it scooped up seven tons of sand at a mouthful and built a great embankment against the shifting sand dunes. As fast as the hills were effectively stopped, the canal itself was gouged out to precise form. Then the workmen applied oil or vegetation to the canal banks, to provide a more lasting control of the elusive sand. Thus the obstacle that had been publicized for years from Imperial Valley to Washington was wiped away by applied ingenuity in a few months' time. Whatever sand found its way into the ditch would be carried off by the irrigating water.

By 1936 work had been started on Imperial Dam, a few miles above the Yuma diversion works on the Colorado River. Here the canal water would be impounded, then turned into a great "desilting" plant, the first such device on any irrigating works in the world. It included four settling basins from which fifty thousand tons of silt could be removed every day by mechanical plows and sent back into the river below the dam. No longer would Imperial farmers be harassed by water so muddy that it filled their irrigation ditches and clogged the furrows in their fields.

After six years of steady construction, the canal's engineering phase was over. From the Colorado to Imperial Valley stretched an unlined canal, complete with flumes and siphons to carry the water through intervening canyons. On October 13, 1940, the first water was delivered to Imperial Irrigation District; from that time on the quantity was increased as the last miles of the canal were finished. By March 1942 the valley had completely abandoned its Mexican lifeline and was taking its entire supply through the All-American Canal. The project that had suffered innumerable delays over the previous thirty years had barely escaped another interruption in the coming of World War II.

Less fortunate was the Coachella Valley branch of the canal, which was begun in 1938 from a point fourteen miles west of Pilot Knob. Its course first traversed the upper edge of the famed East Mesa, providing a final water supply for Mark Rose's rich farming acreage. Then it pushed on along the prehistoric shore line of Imperial Valley, passed the Salton Sea, and circled around the upper limits of Coachella Valley. Beginning in 1942, the work was interrupted for four years by the war while Coachella farmers found their water levels sinking to alarming depths, owing to an accompanying drought. By the end of 1948 the 119-mile branch was driven into Coachella Valley, and in the following spring the first Colorado water began to run through furrows in the thirsty land. An empire of 18,000 people and some of the most famous date palms and grapefruit groves in the world were rescued by a project first conceived thirty-seven years before.

Redoubtable old Mark Rose did not live to see the fulfillment of his dream, having died during the construction period of the 1930s. But Phil Swing and other crusaders who took up his fight were on hand and could say that, while the first was last among the giant Boulder projects, they had not rested until their entire program was finished. Imperial Valley, saved by Hoover Dam from threatened annihilation, had likewise been freed from the foreign control fastened on its lifeline for forty years. California had completed the monumental task, against the opposition of both man and nature, of harnessing the mighty lower Colorado.

14: THE MEXICAN MORTGAGE

The completion of the All-American Canal in 1941 set in motion a chain of events which ripped open the dormant Colorado controversy. Its first effect was to rearrange the entire irrigation picture in the lower basin. No longer was Imperial Valley dependent on Mexico for its water supply. Instead the water users below the border found themselves at the physical mercy of the Americans. The old Imperial Canal south of the line had been abandoned, and the thirty-seven-year concession which had reserved half of its flow for Mexican farmers was now useless. Irrigators south of the line would have to maintain and operate the ditch themselves—a task which would cut deeply into their margin of earnings.

But most of all, Imperial Valley now virtually controlled the lower river with its All-American Canal. At its will enough Colorado water could be drawn off above the border to ruin every crop on the delta. Phil Swing had warned that this very device could be used if Mexico sought to benefit by Hoover Dam's regulation of the river.

"While you could not turn all the surplus into Salton Sea," he had told fellow congressmen, "you could do that at intervals and over sufficient lengths of time to prevent the increase of additional area . . . in Mexico."

There was, after all, not enough water in the river to allow American improvements to benefit Mexico. So far as the Colorado's natural flow was concerned, Lower California had reached the limit of its crop expansion before Hoover Dam was built. The whole low stage of the river had been appropriated by water users on both sides of the line, and any additional supply would have to come from reservoir storage. Geography, however, had been unkind to Mexico. There were no reservoir sites on the flat delta lands, and the only possible location for a Mexican dam lay in the twenty-mile stretch where the Colorado formed the border between Mexico and Arizona. Without United States permission Mexico could not count on more than 750,000 acre-feet a year out of the Colorado.

Hoover Dam, of course, had changed this situation. Arizonans who had fought the Boulder project in Congress during the twenties had argued that the increased low flow caused by the dam would benefit Mexican irrigators. By helping them to use and claim more water, it would be condemning that much more American land to desert.

In the end Arizona had won her point. An amendment by Senator Carl Hayden of Arizona had been inserted in the Boulder Canyon bill warning Mexico that water was being stored for use "exclusively within the United States." As soon as the Boulder Act took effect in 1929, moreover, this country moved to pin down Mexico's water use by treaty. Dr. Elwood Mead, chief of the Reclamation Bureau, had met with Mexican agents and offered 750,000 acre-feet—the most that Mexico had been able to use in any one year. But the Mexicans demanded 3,600,000. The Mead offer was rejected and the negotiations collapsed. Mexico was counting on the increased low flow that would take place with construction of Hoover Dam.

Using Phil Swing's method, the United States would still have been able to halt such added use if the All-American Canal had been finished at the same time as Hoover Dam. But its delay had justified every fear of the Arizonans. Out of the regulated flow of the Colorado, beginning with the completion of the dam in 1935, Mexico built a bigger agricultural empire than ever before on the Colorado delta.

Harry Chandler's Mexican holdings, however, were benefiting little from the Lower California boom. In 1938 the Mexican government expropriated some 287,000 acres of the property—

234

including practically all of the cultivated area—and dealt the Chandler company a fatal blow. But there were other Mexican owners who were prospering by the increased water supply, putting more land under irrigation every year in a race to develop as far as possible before the All-American Canal was completed to give the United States the advantage.

By the late thirties American water users took sudden alarm. If Mexico secured a right to this increased use through a treaty with the United States, their own established water rights would be endangered. In July 1938, American water interests—from California to the Rocky Mountains—met at Phoenix to organize against the Mexican menace. There they formed the Committee of Fourteen, with two members from each of the basin states, to advise the government on Colorado matters and especially on the Mexican question. When sitting with representatives of the Hoover Dam power contractors, it became the Committee of Sixteen. Without delay the organization asked the Secretary of State to notify Mexico that she could gain no right to water stored in the United States. The suggestion, however, was not followed.

By 1941, Mexico was diverting nearly twice as much water out of the Colorado as she had been able to use from the unregulated river. But as the All-American Canal neared its completion that year, Mexico's period of grace was over. Knowing that Imperial Valley would soon gain control over her water usage, Mexico indicated that she was ready for a treaty. The move was scarcely unexpected. Having built up her water claims as high as possible, Mexico was now willing to negotiate.

Out of this situation was born a new struggle for the long-contested waters of the Colorado. By this time there were two divergent opinions on Mexico's rights: The American view that she should receive only the most she had been able to use before construction of Hoover Dam, and the Mexican idea that she should also have all the use she had developed since then. The difference between the two would put such a burden on the Colorado that American developments would be threatened.

Of the seven Colorado states, California stood first in jeopardy. She had contracted to receive 5,362,000 acre-feet a year from Hoover Dam storage, but nearly 1,000,000 was classed as "surplus"—outside the 7,500,000 apportioned to the lower basin by the Colorado Compact. According to that document, any Mexican draft would first be satisfied out of unapportioned surplus; California knew that Mexico's claim would consume so much of this that part of her own water contracts would be invaded. It simply meant that her Colorado Aqueduct and All-American

235

Canal would never receive the capacities for which they had been built and that she would have to turn elsewhere for a new water supply much sooner than expected. And beyond the Colorado the water holes were slim indeed.

As soon as the U. S. State Department realized that Mexico would negotiate, the Colorado basin states were called upon for advice. In 1941 a subcommittee of the Committee of Fourteen recommended unanimously that Mexico be given no more water than she had been able to use before Hoover Dam—750,000 acre-feet a year. When this was discarded by the State Department as too low an offer, the committee made a token concession. In June 1942 it unanimously approved a water delivery formula, giving Mexico 800,000 acre-feet during years of normal flow below Hoover Dam and ranging more or less as that flow varied.

Once again the State Department balked. Already larger considerations were crowding in to influence its approach to the Mexican question. For years previously the United States had also sought a treaty with Mexico on the waters of the lower Rio Grande, where the Colorado situation was reversed. Most of its flow rises in Mexican tributaries, but the rough terrain had made it impossible for Mexico to use any large amount. Texas, on the other hand, had rich citrus areas in the river's lower valley and stood to be the beneficiary in any treaty negotiations. Thus Mexico had everything to offer on the Rio Grande and everything to ask on the Colorado.

The implications in this picture were not ignored by Mexican officials. Years before, they had made it plain that they would not negotiate on the Rio Grande without also considering the Colorado. So it was that the International Boundary Commission, which handled the negotiations, took up both rivers when serious talks began at El Paso in 1943. Whatever advantage the United States had as the contributor of Colorado water was neutralized by simultaneous discussion of the Rio Grande.

Once the Mexican-American talks had started, the pressures of international diplomacy took hold. For years President Roosevelt, through Secretary of State Cordell Hull, had cultivated a long-needed good-neighbor policy toward Latin America. Military necessity during World War II had made American prestige below the border even more imperative. By the time the Mexican treaty negotiation was well advanced, the State Department believed it was being regarded in Latin America as a crucial test of United States sincerity in its good-will program. Being the "underdog" nation, Mexico could not be dealt a hard bargain without jeopardizing years of careful American diplomacy.

By early 1943 the American negotiators had given up any attempt to press the Committee of Fourteen's formula of 800,000 acre-feet or any plan based on Mexico's use before Hoover Dam. Instead they began thinking in terms of her water usage built up since that time. In the spring of 1943 the government called another conference of the committee, meeting with its members in mid-April at Santa Fe, New Mexico.

From California came a formidable delegation of experts— a second generation of water fighters in the tradition of Billy Mathews and Mark Rose. Chief among them was lean, hard-bitten Arvin Shaw, assistant attorney general of California, who brought with him more than twenty years of experience in Western water law. Suave in manner but unrelenting in debate, Shaw had a dramatic way of speaking that was alternately deliberate and explosive. With them also was another veteran of the Boulder Canyon fight—redoubtable Phil Swing, now chief counsel for the San Diego County Water Authority. Together they were resolved to hold Mexico's allotment to her pre-Hoover Dam use.

They were not prepared, however, for the awakening in store for them at Santa Fe. As the conference opened in the swank La Fonda Hotel, a government negotiator presented a proposed treaty which amounted to a guarantee of 1,500,000 acre-feet to Mexico—double her usage before Hoover Dam. Immediately the Californians launched a volley of questions, only to find themselves the lone objectors among the seven state delegations. Finally Phil Swing demanded whether the federal officials intended to give away part of the water in California's contracts. The government men would not commit themselves.

California's delegates stormed out in a fury at the end of the first session. Next day they requested a delay until they could find how far their water rights would be invaded. When this was rejected by the other states, California asked to discuss the question without the presence of government officials. The upper states and Arizona blocked this move as well and pressed for a vote on the treaty.

At that point the irate Californians concluded that they were victims of conspiracy. E. F. Scattergood of Los Angeles, representing the power contractors, charged that if the committee wanted to act without any more discussion "there must have been a great deal of discussion somewhere," unknown to the Californians.

"Now we are not permitted," he raged, "even an opportunity to discuss it with our engineers, and among ourselves; that doesn't seem to be wanted."

The Californians were able to delay action for another day, but it was a hopeless fight. Next morning the proposed treaty passed overwhelmingly, with the California men as the sole objectors and Nevada abstaining. Another resolution was quickly offered, lauding the State Department in its work, and passed by the same vote. Before the Californians could recover, a third resolution was proposed, urging that the government take over all Imperial Valley diversion works, including the All-American Canal, for the delivery of water to Mexico under the treaty. To the outraged Californians this was final proof that the other states were playing the State Department's game. Phil Swing, who had devoted his life to acquiring those facilities for Imperial, erupted with anger.

"This is the final humiliation," he roared, "and adds to the indignity already done to California and its communities." Charging that the committee was invading their constitutional rights of ownership, he shamed the other states for the "steam-roller methods . . . with which you have rolled toward your predetermined goal."

Chairman of the meeting was Judge Clifford H. Stone of Denver, one of the best-known irrigation lawyers in the West and a leading figure in the upper-state delegation. With coolness and determination he replied that the conflict was merely a difference of opinion. "I want to say some of us fully appreciate the position California is in. . . . We think we know there are some reasons why you cannot join in some action and yet that should not deter the best judgment of the other members. . . ." To Californians this was the same as saying that as long as the other states believed they were protected by the treaty California could rot.

"Is there any comment?" asked Stone, preparing for the vote on the final motion.

"There is no use arguing the obvious," Arvin Shaw concluded bitterly.

Thereupon the committee passed a last motion to strip California of its border irrigation works. Even Nevada voted with Arizona and the upper states. Then the Santa Fe meeting adjourned, and the crisis in the Mexican question was over. Until that time California had been secure in the support of the upper basin and Arizona for a Mexican burden which would not harm her contracts.

But to her representatives it was now obvious that government negotiators had somehow drawn away the other states. Undoubtedly their main argument had been that 1,500,000 acre-feet was the least that Mexico would take and that if an agreement was not reached now she could later appeal to the Inter-American Arbitration Court for a settlement. By that time the Mexican irrigators would have built up an even greater use of Colorado water, and the United States might lose much more than

238

1,500,000 acre-feet. The irrigating canals on both sides of the border, however, were now controlled by Americans. Without their consent Mexico could not increase her water use or even maintain the use she had built up since Hoover Dam.

In the end the upper delegates adopted the State Department's proposal because they were determined to pin down Mexico's use by some treaty and because they believed this particular treaty would do so without invading their own water rights. Arizona's reasons were more obscure. She claimed to share with California the river's unapportioned surplus, but this proposed treaty practically wiped that out.

Even during the negotiations with Mexico the Californians were unable to fight the proposed treaty. The affair had been treated as a military secret, and the government had repeatedly cautioned the committee against discussing the subject. While it would have been uncomfortable if the talks with Mexico had taken place against a background of California publicity, this gag rule forced Californians to sit helplessly by while the treaty was concluded in the fall of 1943.

In December the document—giving 1,500,000 acre-feet a year to Mexico—was submitted to the Colorado basin states. All approved except California. As for Texas, her consent was not delayed on a document which gave her a third of lower Rio Grande water with a guaranteed minimum of 350,000 acre-feet—enough to assure healthy development of key agricultural areas.

From the time the Mexican treaty was signed and announced on February 3, 1944, California roared its opposition. The secret was now out, and the state threw off its gag and pitched in with arms flailing. Since ratification by the United States Senate was needed to put the instrument into effect, California marshaled her weapons for a showdown in Washington.

The Metropolitan Water District promptly got out an elaborate brochure damning the agreement; on its back cover were photographs of Southern California city and farm scenes—all being covered up by a grasping hand labeled "Mexican Treaty." Leading newspapers thundered that California had been "sold down the river," that precious Colorado water had been bargained off to get Rio Grande benefits for Texas, that Arizona and the upper states had deliberately knifed California.

Whether true or not, the charges were effective. A tremendous weight of California public opinion was whipped up against the treaty. Los Angeles, warned that every added acre-foot for Mexico meant a loss of five persons for the city's ultimate population, was pinched in a vulnerable spot; she promptly became the headquarters of opposition. Senators Hiram Johnson and

Sheridan Downey pledged an unyielding fight when the document came before the upper house. Even the state of Nevada, whose stake of 300,000 acre-feet in the river was comparatively safe, joined California in denouncing the Mexican settlement.

With the treaty thus becoming a political hot potato, the Senate viewed it with a cautious eye and evidently decided to postpone action until after the 1944 elections. For several months the battle of words raged on. By midsummer the treaty advocates had become alarmed at the California clamor and organized for the campaign. Meeting in Santa Fe, the states of Texas, Arizona, and the upper basin struck back with a resolution against "the aggressive and unrestrained activities of those whose opposition to the treaty appears to result from a selfish and misguided local interest."

California was soon facing more formidable odds than a handful of Western states. By early 1945 public sentiment in the East largely favored the Mexican treaty as a necessary earnest of American good-neighborliness. California was regarded as a selfish child which would not subordinate its wishes to the welfare of the family.

"If Senator Johnson got the necessary votes to kill off the treaty," said the New York *Post*, "it would be a famous victory for California citrus growers, but it would be a stunning blow to United States-Mexican amity."

"It is not quite clear," agreed the Baltimore *Sun*, "how California would deny Mexico's claim other than by brandishing the might of the United States over Mexico's head."

Here was the chief weakness in California's stand: her campaign for defeat of the Mexican treaty carried no practical alternative. To reopen negotiations with Mexico toward a water reduction could only make America appear to be "beating down" its weaker neighbor. Most opinion seemed to agree with the news commentator who declared that the treaty "would merit favorable action by the Senate even if it means a real sacrifice on our part." California, however, failed to see the justice in sacrificing water from the one section of the nation which needed it most.

On January 22, 1945, hearings began before the Senate Foreign Relations Committee, with resolute Tom Connally of Texas holding the strategic position of chairman. For a full month the proceedings were mainly a duel between him and a parade of California witnesses. During most of the sessions the only other member of the huge committee present was venerable Hiram Johnson of California; his sharp-witted colleague, Senator Sheridan Downey, called it one of the most "distinguished and intelligent" but also "the most absent" body he had ever addressed.

240

The room was filled, however, with other interested senators and water men from Colorado states, including the spokesman for the upper basin, the resourceful Senator Eugene Millikin of Colorado.

With the treaty's proponents, glowering old Senator Johnson was unrelenting. A fervid American patriot, he could not understand how United States officials could voluntarily give American water to Mexico. His course of attack in questioning the government witnesses never departed from two basic points: 1. "Do you feel you are representing Mexico or the United States?" 2. "Are you seeking to destroy Boulder Dam?" But those who recalled the powerful figure of the 1920s who had rocked the Senate with his Boulder Canyon battle could see that the old tigerlike agility at cross-examination had faded.

Late in February 1945 the entire Foreign Relations Committee assembled long enough to vote an overwhelming approval of the Mexican treaty. Connally and Millikin had won their first round and now guided it onto the Senate floor for debate. There the Californians, backed by the Nevada senators, launched a furious opposition. Leading them was Sheridan Downey, a Democrat bold enough to oppose the Administration on Western water matters. Realizing early in April that the treaty was destined for passage, Downey and Hiram Johnson offered twenty-nine reservations—enough to change the whole complexion of the document. They were quickly attacked by Connally and Millikin, who told the Senate that the Californians were simply trying to smother the treaty with amendments.

But through many days of floor debate one argument of Downey's received no adequate answer. Provision had not been made in the treaty, he pointed out, concerning the quality of the water delivered. State Department officials had assured Colorado basin states that no American projects would ever suffer from the Mexican burden, as their "return flow" (the water seeping back into the river) would always be enough to satisfy the 1,500,000 acre-feet. But return water, insisted Downey, becomes increasingly loaded with alkali from the soil and would almost certainly be worthless for irrigation in Mexico. Could she not, he demanded, ask that the United States send down enough fresh water to dilute the return flow and make it usable? State Department officials had largely evaded the question in committee hearings, except to say that Mexico understood the provisions of the treaty, which were framed to protect the United States from any responsibility for the quality of water.

Here was a vulnerable point, and Downey attacked it unmercifully. On April 12, Arizona's tall and rugged Senator Ernest W.

McFarland was making his chief pro-treaty speech. The Californian interrupted to inquire whether he believed "that the pending treaty means that Mexico must take water regardless of quality . . . ?"

"Yes, I think so," returned McFarland.

In order to prevent misunderstanding, pressed Downey, would he not support a provision that Mexico's water "shall be taken regardless of quality?"

The Arizonan knew that such a provision would almost certainly kill the treaty in the Mexican Senate. "Let us not," he countered, "put into the treaty something which will lead Mexico to believe we intend to put something over on her. . . . Why should we be so concerned about her welfare all of a sudden?"

Downey then made another thrust. Applying the same reasoning to Arizona, he asked McFarland whether his state would never ask the upper basin for any extra fresh water to dilute her allotment. Now the shoe was reversed. McFarland answered that he hoped it could be assured. "I will take all the water for Arizona I can get."

The Californian's proddings brought a quick and unexpected reaction. Immediately one of Utah's senators rose and thundered a warning on behalf of the upper Colorado states.

"I want to serve notice now . . . on Arizona, California, and Nevada that, so far as the quality of the water that arrives at Lee's Ferry is concerned, that is not the responsibility of the upper-basin states; if it is not good water, it is your funeral and not ours."

If Downey had meant to stir up some hidden Colorado River skeletons, he was succeeding too well. The sudden exchange left basin water men a trifle stunned. They could see all their careful calculations on future water use threatened by a new factor. If the lower basin was not willing to make provision for diluting Mexico's return-flow water, it might not in turn expect to demand any quality standards in its own water from the upper basin.

California was alarmed enough to send one of its water lawyers down to Mexico to discover her understanding of the treaty. After searching records in Mexico City, he returned with dark news. Mexican negotiators had told their Senate that the water, according to the treaty, must be usable.

But it was too late to affect matters in the U. S. Senate. On April 17 the lawmakers began voting on California's reservations, discarding them one by one. Finally they considered a last crucial amendment, which would have reduced Mexico's share of water proportionately in any year of below-average drought.

242

At this point Hiram Johnson gained the floor for his only speech on the Mexican treaty, and one of the last he would make before his death in the summer of 1945.

"There is no difference," he began, "between the taking of land, as we all know it, and the taking of water. . . ." Then, charging that the Mexican treaty would take water from California, the venerable warrior called for compassion on the farmers, with their families and their "little homes" in Imperial Valley. "I implore the Senate, I beg the Senate to give them a square deal, rather than reach over into Mexico and give Mexico a square deal."

It was as good a summary of the situation as any. There was not enough water to give everybody a "square deal." Southwestern United States was called upon to make a sacrifice in the interests of international good will. It might as well have been land itself as water, for in that semiarid country it is water that gives value to the land.

A few minutes after Johnson's speech the Senate voted down the amendment he championed. Next day it ratified the treaty, 76-10. Mexico approved it in September, and before the end of 1945 the agreement was declared to be in effect. At last California had lost a major fight in the struggle over Colorado River water.

Still undecided was the question raised by the Californians: What will happen when the use of Colorado water is complete and Mexico receives nothing but return flow? Would this not be too saline for irrigating crops? And would not the United States have to dilute the 1,500,000 acre feet per year with virgin water to make it acceptable—thus imposing a further draft against the river?

For sixteen years this issue slumbered. Then it was forced into the open by another salinity problem in the farms of the Wellton-Mohawk Valley along Arizona's lower Gila River. For years the farmers there had fought against ground salinity, and in 1961 the Bureau of Reclamation finished a fifty-mile canal to drain the mineral-charged water from the Wellton-Mohawk ground. But the mouth of the channel emptied into the Colorado River.

As the river's low stage approached in the fall of 1961, there was not enough usable water to dilute the Wellton-Mohawk discharge. By December the Colorado water reaching Morelos Dam in Mexico was nearly three-and-a-half times saltier than normal. It was unfit for use on the crops below the border, and the Mexicans allowed it to flow on down to the Gulf of California. More that 100,000 acres of crops were lost, according to the Mexicans.

The old water fight between the two countries broke out anew.

At first the United States resisted Mexican complaints. While Mexico claimed it was supposed to get usable water under the treaty, the United States restated its contention that it had promised nothing about the quality of the water.

At this, Baja California farmers fairly howled with outrage. Shouting the old slogans against "Yanqui imperialists," radical agitators made alarming headway among the Lower Californians. Concern in Mexico City was transmitted to Washington, D. C.

Still holding to its no-quality principle, the United States nevertheless opened negotiations with Mexico on an expedient solution. On March 22, 1965, the two countries reached an agreement by which the United States would build a thirteen-mile canal to carry the Wellton-Mohawk discharge around Morelos Dam and send it harmlessly down to the Gulf of California.

Completed by November, it relieved the immediate problem but only complicated the longer-range issue of Colorado River quality. Still disavowing any quality responsibility, the United States had built the canal at a cost of $2,500,000 as a gesture of neighborly goodwill. But in this very act it was demonstrating U. S. involvement in Mexican water needs beyond the bare provision of the 1944 treaty.

In 1973, technology suddenly arrived to solve the dilemma. The United States agreed to deliver water at Morelos Dam of a quality satisfactory to Mexico. In the near future it intended to do so by diluting "bad" water with "good" water. But by 1978 it planned to meet the pledge with the world's largest desalting plant on the Arizona side of the Colorado River.

This and other measures were estimated to cost the United States $115,000,000. Added to this would be the continuing expense of operating the huge plant at cost levels which were not limited by the water's market value.

Again the United States was sacrificing in the interests of international good will, but this time the price was being paid by all American taxpayers rather than by the Southwestern water users. And the resort to technology seemed to foreshadow how the Southwest's larger water struggle might be resolved in the future.

15:    A DAY FOR ARIZONA

Starting in the 1940s the new Mexican burden on the river had one immediate effect: it stirred up the old Colorado controversy north of the border. As soon as Arizona realized that a Mexican settlement was approaching, she hurried to perfect her own water claims. For twenty years she had held aloof from the Colorado Compact, even refusing to accept a proffered government water contract for a share of the river. Now the probability of a heavy Mexican claim forced her to take refuge in the same American water agreements she had shunned. Arizona could not afford to be caught at the end of the line in the last division of the Colorado.

Besides, Arizona had a new governor who was determined to build up his state's water empire, and to do it by accepting the Compact and contract rather than fighting them.

Sidney P. Osborn was an irrepressible product of Arizona. He typified his state in his robust ambition, his down-to-earth style, his stubborn individuality. He was the one governor in the United States who never attended a governors' conference. During the war, while the rest of the nation ran on daylight saving time, Arizona was an hour behind on "Osborn time."

His yearning for the governor's chair took root in boyhood; there is still a school book in existence marked with the cryptic declaration: "Sidney P. Osborn, Governor of Arizona." In 1912 he became Arizona's first secretary of state and six years later ran unsuccessfully for governor. He was to have two more defeats before he was swept overwhelmingly into office in 1940.

Together with Arizona's leading irrigation men, Osborn laid immediate plans for the water future of the state. For two decades she had been able to avoid the Colorado Compact without harm, as her own geography made early use of the main-stream water nearly impossible. While California and the upper states had gained federal financing for Colorado projects, Arizona relied on the belief that continued progress in engineering technique would someday make her own reclamation schemes feasible.

By the time Governor Osborn took office water adversities in Arizona had forced her to turn to these main-stream projects, regardless of expense. Osborn knew that the only way Arizona could seek outside help was to abandon her isolationism, join the Compact, and make the most of it. Accordingly in March 1943 the Arizona legislature announced it would ratify the Compact, provided the government would grant a satisfactory contract for her claim to water from the Colorado's main stream. This, of course, was the issue that had divided the lower basin for years. The Boulder Canyon Act had suggested 2,800,000 acre-feet as Arizona's rightful share of the Colorado but failed to make it clear whether this was all main-stream water or included the Gila tributary.

245

The answer to the riddle was crucial. Arizona was willing to accept such a share, with the understanding that it was to come entirely from the main stream. California claimed such a figure included the Gila, on which Arizonans were said to be using some 2,300,000 acre-feet—leaving only 500,000 from the main Colorado.

On this basis California opposed Arizona's contract in hearings before the Interior Department beginning in May 1943. It was right after the stormy Santa Fe meeting on the Mexican issue, in which Arizona had joined the upper states in approving the government's proposed treaty. When those upper states now supported Arizona's contract claim, Californians declared they knew at last why Arizona had backed the treaty. Arizona argued, however, that this was the same settlement which the government had offered years before.

Finally California conceded that she would not oppose such a contract, provided it constituted no settlement of the controversy and was subject to the prior California and Nevada contracts. Despite these conditions the Arizona legislature accepted the contract on February 24, 1944. On the same day, after the longest continuous session ever held by the legislature, it ratified the Colorado Compact and joined the other six basin states after twenty-two years. It was, cried one bitter opponent, "the blackest day in the history of the state."

But to Governor Osborn and the state's water planners it was another step toward the realization of Arizona's water needs. For on that same decisive day the legislature passed still another measure—an appropriation of $200,000 for surveys on a mammoth canal to bring Colorado water to the Phoenix plateau. This was old George Maxwell's dream of the 1920s— the famed "High-Line" project which Arizonans had cherished for a generation as their state's salvation. Osborn's victory on contract and Compact was now calculated to provide enough water for it, despite Arizona's continued feud with California. All at once the Southwest tumbled to Arizona's strategy, and the battle for the lower Colorado was on once more.

The bold move had come none too soon for Arizona's water users. Drought years and dropping water levels had intensified their interest in the Colorado main stream, regardless of formidable expense. The 1944 water contract came at a critical time, if Arizona's share in the Colorado was to give her any comfort at all.

Since the early 1930s Arizona's water resources had been slipping relentlessly backward. Until then her agriculture had been expanding through construction of great storage reservoirs.

246

Roosevelt Dam, completed on the Salt River in 1911, was the keystone in the rising economy of the Phoenix area. Farther to the Southeast, Coolidge Dam had been finished in 1928 to bring a more abundant supply to Indian and American farmers on the upper Gila. Such projects, together with a wet cycle in the 1920s, had enabled Arizona's cultivated acreage to spread by thirty per cent in the eight years preceding 1930.

With her farmlands thus overextended, Arizona was abruptly caught in the drought of the thirties. In four years her irrigated land dropped by one tenth. The new Coolidge Reservoir on the Gila was never filled to capacity. By 1935 a system of wells had to be installed throughout its project lands to supplement the stored supply with groundwater.

The return of wetter years in the late 1930s only encouraged new crop increases, and sinking underground levels had no chance to recover. With the coming of World War II, Arizona joined the rest of the nation in a furious agricultural boom. In the region served by Coolidge Dam the number of irrigated acres nearly doubled. From 1940 to 1945 Arizona's income from crops soared from $27,000,000 to $90,000,000. The state was beginning to experience some of the lush prosperity which truck and citrus farming had already helped to provide for California.

Arizona's expansion was placed on borrowed water, however, with the beginning of another dry cycle after 1941. Despite the use of her storage reservoirs, there was scarcely an acre in the state that did not depend on pumped water for at least part of its supply. During the war years Arizona's farmers annually withdrew nearly 500,000 acre-feet more water from the ground than nature replaced, sending levels downward at the rate of five feet a year. In some areas they reached depths of more than two hundred feet, forcing a pumping expense which ate heavily into farm profits. Other vast acreages lacked the necessary fresh water to hold down the dangerous accumulation of salt in the soil.

By the war's end water was being pumped out of the land twice as fast as it was being replenished. In 1945, with water standing low behind Coolidge Dam, farmers in the San Carlos area were rationed two acre-feet for every acre—little more than half the amount needed to raise a full crop. In 1946 the ration dropped to one per acre, then to a fraction in 1947—allowing only a fourth of the region's irrigable land to be planted. By spring of that year Coolidge Reservoir was desert-dry, and the farmers subsisted on the slim supply from local wells.

Through most of the state's farm country, the people were competing desperately for fast-disappearing water levels. The race intensified when it was known that the state legislature would soon pass a groundwater code to restrict excess pumping. Faced with emergency, the legislature hastened to pass the code in March 1948, prohibiting any new wells in critical areas.

But this merely assured that Arizona's retreat would be orderly. Unless her failing water sources could be replenished, warned her leading water men, the state had nowhere to go but backward. Some 175,000 acres must be abandoned to desert and several hundred thousand citizens must depart to more fortunate localities.

Here, indeed, was the climactic moment toward which all Arizona's water history had pointed. The ambitious High-Line scheme conceived by George Maxwell a generation before must perform its noble mission for Arizona. No longer was it a matter of watering 2,000,000 acres of desert lands, as Maxwell had envisioned, but of rescuing those already cultivated by Arizona's own streams. Sidney Osborn and the state's water experts had won a favorable water contract; now they meant to make this giant project feasible.

Arizona had already appropriated $200,000 in survey funds, and in August 1944 the U. S. Reclamation Bureau sent its engineers into the desert to locate a canal route to the Granite Reef Dam, in the Phoenix area. They found two possible plans for diverting Colorado water by gravity. One was a diversion at Marble Canyon, near the Utah-Arizona border, involving a tunnel no less than 143 miles long. The other called for diversion of the water at Bridge Canyon, west of Grand Canyon, through a more moderate tunnel—only 77 miles long. The first of these plans, estimated to cost nearly $1,000,000,000, was crossed off with superb conservatism in the bureau's preliminary report of September 1945.

There was a third plan, requiring few engineering difficulties, no long tunnels, and a smaller construction expense. But it meant pumping water nearly a thousand feet high out of Parker Reservoir, where California's Metropolitan Water District diverted its water. As this was an operational expense which any farmer knew was prohibitive, it was suggested that government power for the pumping could be provided by a dam at Bridge Canyon, which was a promising power site anyway. Then, in years hence when the long Bridge Canyon tunnel became feasible, it could be built to take the place of the pumped water from Parker. Moreover, since Bridge Canyon's small reservoir capacity would be quickly filled with sediment, another dam would later have to be constructed upstream at Glen Canyon to desilt the water.

248

The scheme required, of course, a great deal of arithmetic. Repayment of the cost would load the farmer with a burden of $6.50 for every acre-foot of water delivered. Since he could stand only $4.50 and still make a profit, the extra $2.00 would be subsidized by power revenues from Bridge Canyon. Only one third of its potential energy would be needed for the Parker pump lift, and the other two thirds could be sold on the market. And the two per cent interest on the government's investment could be written off and applied to the farmer's burden.

But even with the gift of interest, amounting to something more than $1,000,000,000 eventually, the government still could not get back its investment in the fifty years required by reclamation law. That provision would have to be changed to eighty years.

Arizonans were not awed by these obstacles. In mid-February 1946 their state officials and members of Congress met with Reclamation Bureau engineers for a final strategy conference in Washington. Out of that meeting came a plan of action for what was to be known as the Central Arizona Project. The bureau would make a report on the feasibility of the Bridge Canyon route. The congressmen would introduce a bill extending the time of reclamation project repayments to eighty years. Then the way would be cleared for a bill authorizing the Central Arizona Project itself.

On June 17, 1946, the Reclamation Bureau released its comprehensive report on the Colorado basin, including in it an outline of Arizona's Bridge Canyon scheme. Next day Ernest McFarland, Arizona's lanky junior senator, introduced the bill liberalizing the reclamation law. Immediately California's water men saw the danger. Hurrying across the continent, they descended on Washington like a Western windstorm.

The House Irrigation Subcommittee was then hearing a bill for another Arizona project—a plan for reclaiming some 110,000 acres around the mouth of the Gila River with main-stream water from Imperial Dam. In charge of the meetings was none other than Congressman John R. Murdock of Arizona, chairman of the subcommittee. California had been concerned previously over the amount of water the project might use; now her water men invaded those hearings in genuine alarm late in June 1946. There might be water enough in the Colorado for that Gila plan, but not for both it and this gigantic new Bridge Canyon project.

They found the Arizona men ready for them with legal and engineering data to prove that enough water existed for the two projects. California, they explained, had restricted herself to 4,400,000 acre-feet of apportioned water in her Limitation Act and the Boulder Canyon Act. The Compact, they said, apportioned 7,500,000 acre-feet to the lower basin in paragraph III a and another 1,000,000 in III b—a total of 8,500,000. Subtracting California's 4,400,000 and the accepted figure of 300,000 for Nevada, there remained 3,800,000 for Arizona. Of this, something like 1,100,000 was Gila River water—the natural flow it had emptied into the main stream before Arizona farmers had applied it all to their lands. That left some 2,700,000 for Arizona from the main stream—enough to supply both projects. It was a matter of simple mathematics.

Then the Californians launched their attack. The 7,500,000 acre-feet in paragraph III a, they agreed, were "apportioned," but the 1,000,000 in III b were not. The lower basin had merely been permitted to "increase its use" of the unapportioned "surplus" by that amount. It was surplus water, not apportioned, and according to the Limitation Act, California was entitled to one half. This left 3,300,000 for Arizona. As for the Gila, Arizona's real consumption—measured upstream at the points of usage—was some 2,300,000. Subtracting this from the 3,300,000 left only 1,000,000 of main-stream water. Arizona's long-standing Yuma project took enough of that to make the Gila plan doubtful and the Bridge Canyon scheme impossible. Now, concluded James Howard of the Metropolitan District, if Arizona would abide by these simple facts of life, "I will take the first plane out of here."

Arizona had no such intention. Her chief water attorney, Charles A. Carson, was prepared to argue the water issues with the Californians point by point. A leading Phoenix lawyer since the 1920s, the quick-witted Carson had represented his state in water matters from the time of her Supreme Court fights with California in the early thirties. He now shot back at the Californians a stern observation: Arizona's only demand was that they live up to the provisions of California's Limitation Act and the Boulder Canyon Act.

All at once the old California-Arizona controversy had flared again—this time higher than ever. The drought cycle of the 1930s had not only made both sides more water-conscious, it had also depressed their estimates of the average flow of the river. Then much of the remaining "surplus" water had been snatched away by the Mexican treaty. There was now even less water in a river which had never been adequate for all demands. As an Arizonan had remarked years before, when the Compact had left the lower basin with half the river, "It has always been my observation that the less water in sight, the harder the fight."

Arizona's response was to get her Gila project through Congress and to introduce her bill for the Central Arizona Project, with a pump lift at Parker and a power dam at Bridge Canyon. Placed on top of the Gila project, the new Bridge Canyon project immediately imperiled California's Colorado claims to the extent of some 1,200,000 acre-feet.

For her part, California pressed for a Supreme Court settlement of the water controversy.

At first the Arizonans resisted. They had already been to the Supreme Court three times in the 1930s, and California had blocked settlement then. In fact, in one of those cases—that in 1934 concerning the Gila River—the Court had supported Arizona's current interpretation that III b water was "apportioned." Therefore there was nothing to interpret and no controversy.

California's answer was to do everything in her power to block the Central Arizona Project in Congress. Besides challenging Arizona's title to the water needed for the project, Californians launched a fierce campaign throughout the country against the excessive cost of the project to be borne by American taxpayers. At a time when farmers elsewhere were being paid to keep acreage out of production, Californians asked why the nation should pay three quarters of a billion dollars to create still more farmland.

In the end the disputed title was the crucial argument. Despite the power of Arizonans in key committee chairmanships in both houses, other congressmen served notice that the project would have to wait until its water title was settled.

At this Arizona suddenly looked with new eyes on the Supreme Court. By 1953 California was using more than the 4,400,-000 acre-feet per year of "apportioned" water to which she had limited herself in her 1929 Limitation Act. Arizona believed she was now being "injured" in a legal sense. She therefore had a case, and she took it to the Supreme Court.

It was the beginning of another long chapter in the already exhaustive Colorado River war. The case did not come to trial until June 1956, and then it was not before the Supreme Court but before a Special Master, Simon Rifkind, designated by the Court to determine the facts in this highly technical case. More than two years and 100 witnesses later, Mr. Rifkind concluded the sessions and sat down to draft his report. Submitted in May 1960, it was the basis for a five to three Supreme Court decision on June 3, 1963.

That decision supported Arizona's claim that she should be charged only with the Gila's virgin discharge, not with the

251

actual use upstream. It agreed with California that III b water was not apportioned but surplus, to which Arizona was entitled to only one half. But the surplus became academic, because the Court also ruled that California could only draw firm water backed by federal contracts from the 7,500,000 acre-feet delivered past Lee's Ferry, and it was limited to 4,400,000 acre-feet per year of such water. Arizona, on the other hand, was given 2,800,000 acre-feet of this main-stream apportioned water, on the strength of her contracts with the government, regardless of actual use.

Thus, so far as the Colorado River was concerned, the old law of prior appropriation was overturned, and the impact of this revolution on all Western water law is still undetermined. In place of the old miner's rule of "first in time, first in right," there was substituted the discretion of the Secretary of the Interior as the giver of contracts. In fact, in dry years when there was too little flow to meet even the basic "apportioned" volume, the Secretary could allocate it as he saw fit, regardless of priority rights. So in the field of water use, at least, a government of men was substituted for the long-cherished American concept of a government of law.

Arizona had therefore lost the battle over III b water but had won the Colorado River war. Much of the 2,800,000 acre-feet she now secured was already appropriated for the Yuma, Gila, and Wellton-Mohawk projects, as well as for Indian operations. But there were more than 1,000,000 acre-feet remaining, and this was enough to make the Central Arizona Project feasible—at least from the standpoint of available water.

The jubilation in Phoenix was now complete. With its title clear at last, Arizona again shifted its sights to Congress. As for California, she had lost some 800,000 acre-feet of water, but she still had a second line of defense. Her congressional delegation had a deal to offer Arizona. They would support the Central Arizona Project if they could get a firm guarantee for the 4,400,000 acre-feet, in wet years and dry. That is, California's share defined by her Limitation Act would have a prior draft on the river over all other lower basin claims. California was at least building a fence around what she had left. Arizona agreed to the deal.

When the Central Arizona Project came up in Congress again it was opposed, not by California water men, but by California conservationists. The Bridge Canyon Dam, claimed the Sierra Club, would back water into the Grand Canyon! Actually, it would back water into Grand Canyon National Monument and along one edge of Grand Canyon National Park, without reaching

252

what the world had come to call the Grand Canyon itself. But the scare words were enough to kill the bill in 1966.

Arizonans might have had reason to believe they had been double-crossed by the Californians, but the next year they were able to satisfy enough conservationists by some careful amendments to take the steam out of the opposition. When the vote came, California's delegation came through as faithfully as those which Swing and Johnson had lined up for the Boulder Canyon Act forty years before.

The Central Arizona Project passed Congress in September 1968, and the delighted Arizonans turned to make the dirt fly. Yet it is one thing for Congress to approve a project and another thing to appropriate the money. The wherewithal has been slow in coming, and five years after the Act, it is still a long distance to the actuality. The ghost of ebullient old George Maxwell might not be disheartened, but it would be powerfully tired.

In California there had been much hand-wringing at this second big defeat on the Colorado. But it would still be years before Arizona could use the new water it had won. There was still enough flow in the Colorado to supply California's major users for the time being. Meanwhile, her veteran water seekers were not caught without alternatives. As usual, in the tradition of Bill Mulholland, they have one crew hoisting water from the well, another crew digging a new well, and still a third crew scouting new ground.

16: TOO MUCH WATER

During the drought of the 1950s, frantic California farmers pumped well water at unprecedented rates and drove the water table down to unprecedented depths. On the west side of San Joaquin Valley, one sizable town hauled in every drop of its drinking water by tank car. One day a leather-faced farmer was filling his water cans at the town faucet when a stranger struck up a conversation.

"How far do you have to take that water?"

The man at the faucet straightened up and pointed a lean finger to a farmhouse on the far horizon. The stranger's mouth dropped.

"That's a long way to haul water!" he gasped. "Why don't you dig a well?"

"Hell," snorted the farmer, heaving a can onto his truck. "It's the same distance either way."

The incident symbolized California's water plight—chronic maldistribution, both in time and place. Alternating between flood and drought, it either had too much water or too little. The great bulk of its water was in the mountainous regions, where there were neither the people nor the farm crops to use it. In creating a State Water Resources Board in 1945, Governor Earl Warren made the point that California had plenty of water; what was needed was a plan and a program to develop and use it.

It happened that the stranger who had learned something from the San Joaquin Valley farmer was a member of the state legislature—one of many who felt the same way as Governor Warren. As the Water Board began proposing a solution with reports in 1951 and 1955, the water seekers began gathering their forces for another water battle—this time under the capitol dome in Sacramento.

Leading them was the Metropolitan Water District of Southern California, which had become the spearhead of water ambitions for Los Angeles and its sister cities during the long Colorado fight. Indeed, the threat to California's share of Colorado water posed by the rival claims of Arizona caused the water seekers to turn with hungry (or thirsty) eyes to the bountiful rivers of Northern California.

In 1957 the State Department of Water Resources—which had replaced the Water Resources Board—issued its California Water Plan. It was, in the words of one observer, "comparable to the Book of Genesis in its scope." The keystone of its proposal was to correct the state's enormous mismatch between man and nature—that is, two thirds of the population was in the southern third of the state, while two thirds of the water was in the northern half.

Some of those in the north might have been willing to correct this sobering imbalance by bringing the people northward. But what the Department of Water Resources and the Metropolitan Water District had in mind was bringing the water southward.

Actually, the project to do this job would have to carry water half again as far, and pump it twice as high, as the Colorado Aqueduct. Delivered south of the Tehachapis, the water would probably cost three times the Colorado water. It would be the biggest water project ever undertaken on the face of the globe. Later it would be observed that this man-made works would be one of only three in the world that would be visible from an orbiting spacecraft—the other two being the Great Wall of China and the Panama Canal.

254

But despite its staggering size, it had a priceless advantage to the water seekers. It could be an intrastate project—avoiding the federal involvement with which Californians had such bitter experience in the Central Valley Project to develop the east side of the San Joaquin. And it would eliminate the interstate jealousies and feuding in Washington that had marked the Colorado project.

In addition, the Southern Californians had allies for this new plan in other parts of California. It had something for almost every major section. There was a branch canal to serve San Francisco Bay and a promise of irrigation water for the west side of San Joaquin Valley, where the farmer had hauled his tank water to the horizon. There was a diversion canal to the Santa Barbara-Ventura region, another promise of water for the parched but ambitious Mojave Desert region of Los Angeles and San Bernardino counties, and finally a delivery of water as far south as California's third largest city, San Diego.

It looked as though, for once, the politicians might be able to deliver as much water as the engineers.

They had not reckoned with the native shrewdness of the northerners. As outlined in the California Water Plan, the main source of the water was the Feather River, the principal tributary of California's biggest waterway, the Sacramento. In that northernmost reach of the old "Mother Lode" gold country, a huge dam—the nation's highest—would be built near the town of Oroville. Since the Gold Rush had subsided a century before, that part of California had become a backwater to the booming coastal centers. But its people were not resigned to such backwater status forever. In true Western fashion, when somebody cast covetous eyes on *their* water, they looked to the dryness of their powder.

When California had become a state in 1850, the center of its population was in the gold country, and most of the counties created at that time were concentrated there. Through subsequent decades—even when the population had shifted decisively—this continued to stack the upper house of the legislature in favor of the so-called "cow counties." And in the same manner that the Solid South had protected its interests by returning its congressmen to Washington term after term to gain potent committee chairmanships, the people of the cow counties had won even more than their representative share of power in Sacramento.

So when the Feather River Project began to get the attention of Californians in the 1950s, those in the Sacramento watershed had considerable muscle to match the water seekers

255

from the south. Maybe they weren't using the Feather River water yet, they argued; but who could say when the tide of population might turn to the north, with all its scenic attractions? They said some water rights belonged to what they called the "counties of origin." And the counties of origin were not about to quitclaim the Feather to the southern counties simply for the asking.

Yet the nature that had endowed them with such a generous supply of water also proved a dubious ally. In 1955 record floods rolled over California communities. The Feather swept down upon the twin cities of Marysville and Yuba City, took a terrible toll in lives and homeless families, and reminded the northerners of previous water disasters. Flood control became one of the key objectives in the California Water Plan of 1957, and the regulatory function of the Oroville Dam became a new issue in the state-wide battle. The same year the legislature voted the first $25 million to start preliminary work on the Feather River Project.

But the counties of origin were not subdued. They refused to submit to the diversion of the river without some guarantees. They wanted assurance that if and when they ever needed the "excess" water they could get it back. In the end the south agreed to a compromise plan for allocating the water in emergency dry years, believing that such an extremity would never come. In 1959 the legislature voted to put a $1.75 billion bond issue on the ballot to finance the Feather River Project.

In the election campaign that followed, new opponents challenged the need for the project on economic grounds. The bond issue was the largest ever undertaken in the United States, and even this would not cover the eventual cost of some $2.8 billion. How could we be sure, it was asked, that California would continue to grow at its current rate? Would not other means of winning new water, such as waste or saline purification, be more economical by the 1970s, when the California Aqueduct was scheduled for completion?

For their part, the water seekers relied on the familiar argument that the growing population would need the water— that without it there would be some thirsty throats some time in 1980, or 1990.

It was Bill Mulholland's old adage all over again, with no one questioning whether bringing more people was still a good idea.

In Los Angeles the smog of too many automobiles had been blighting the sunny skies for a decade and a half. The congestion of too many people had made traffic unbearable, even on

256

the freeways that were saving the city from utter immobility. Land developers uncontrolled by any consideration save profit were imposing on the city the most frightful case of urban sprawl, unbroken by parklands or greenbelts. Angelenos were crowded in upon themselves with no place to go, breathing their own waste, yet unaware that they were ruining the very values that had enticed them to California. Still they believed in the growth ethic, like some ritual chant that had lost its meaning. On November 8, 1960, the Californians voted the bonds to build the Feather River Project.

Yet the superlative magnitude of the undertaking—typical of California daring—commands admiration. When Governor Edmund G. "Pat" Brown set off the first blast for construction of Oroville Dam, he said: "We are going to build a river 500 miles long. We are going to build it to correct an accident of people and geography."

When that dam was finished in 1967, it was 770 feet high— tallest in the United States. When that "river" was finished in 1971, it was capable of delivering more water a longer distance than any conduit in history. When the state made water contracts with the Metropolitan Water District and other Southern California agencies, it agreed to bring them an eventual 2.5 million acre-feet a year—twice as much as they had coming from the Colorado Aqueduct. And as it turned to finance more distribution systems for the water, the Metropolitan Water District told its potential bond buyers that the Feather River Project "is the largest such undertaking in the history of water development."

As though inspired by the approach of this triumph, the water seekers were already looking at more imaginative sources. A former planning engineer for California's Department of Water Resources proposed tapping the Columbia River at the Dalles Dam in Oregon, pumping nearly 13 million acre-feet a year some 5,000 feet high through nuclear power and sending it 1200 miles to Lake Mead on the Colorado.

Another proposal envisioned a pooling of the central continent's water resources through a North American Water and Power Alliance. The key to its success was the vast water potential of Canada, and the beneficiaries would include some 36 states of the U. S. and Mexico. The idea was, naturally enough, conceived in the offices of a Los Angeles engineering firm.

Still others proposed bringing water from the mouth of the Columbia River or from Alaska's Yukon River down to Southern California by underwater pipeline, or by tank ship. Recognizing the infinite potential of the polar ice cap, others

257

suggested towing icebergs down the Pacific to Los Angeles. Mulholland's "bring the water" motto had become an absolute imperative, paling all other considerations.

In 1963 Samuel B. Nelson, general manager of the Los Angeles Department of Water and Power, made a proposal of near-comparable magnitude which had to be taken seriously. It involved nothing less than diverting water from the Columbia's largest tributary, the Snake River, carrying it across southern Idaho and Nevada, and dumping it in the Colorado. Expanding on his suggestion, California's Feather River Project Association proposed bringing five million acre-feet per year a distance of 1000 miles from the Snake to the Colorado at a cost of $4 billion.

Quickly the idea was hailed as a cure-all for the ailing Colorado basin. It would solve the salinity problem with Mexico. It would assure plenty of Colorado water for both California and Arizona. It could thus relieve the upper basin states of any water shortage they might otherwise suffer in fulfilling their obligation to deliver Compact water to the south. And it would insure against shortages in all the basin states and Mexico during severe natural droughts.

From the Rockies to the California coast, water seekers now looked to the Columbia. It was, they said, more than 10 times bigger than the Colorado. In fact, as California's Colorado River Association pointed out, the Colorado's flow into the ocean had been reduced by heavy usage to an average of only 170,000 acre-feet a year, while the Columbia's average ocean discharge was more than 1000 times greater. "Wasting 180 million acre-feet into the Pacific" became the Southwest's accusation against the Columbia basin. And bills to study the diversion of Columbia water to the Colorado were dropped into the hoppers on Capitol Hill.

All at once the Northwesterners responded to the threat in true frontier style. This last water hole may have been a huge one, but it was *their* water hole. Idaho's legislature passed a law prohibiting the diversion of water across its boundaries. The supervisor of Washington's Division of Water Resources announced, "We would fight attempts to export water from our state." And in Congress, Senator Henry Jackson of Washington led the Northwest delegation in blocking even a study of such Columbia basin diversion.

The issue came to a head with debate on the Colorado River Basin Project bill which authorized the Central Arizona Project. To get it passed, Colorado's Wayne Aspinall, chairman of the House Interior Committee, had something in it for everybody.

258

Five new projects were included for the upper Colorado basin states. California's fears of a shortage created by the Central Arizona Project were at least mitigated by the bill's recognition of the need to "augment" the river's flow. But on the insistence of the Northwest, the bill prohibited for the next ten years any study on importing water into the Colorado basin.

When the Act passed in 1968, this last provision was a defeat for California's water seekers—comparable in magnitude to the Mexican treaty in 1945 and the U. S. Supreme Court's Colorado River decision of 1963. To many, the ten-year moratorium was a death warrant to the whole diversion concept. By the time studies could begin in 1978, the Northwest would have its own master water plan ready as a weapon against invasion. Rising labor costs would dwarf the original estimates on the diversion project. Technical progress would make other types of water recovery, such as sewage and saline purification, economically competitive. And the voice of the wilderness preservationists would continue to rise in the current ecological climate, giving the Northwesterners potent political support.

By 1971 Ray Hebert, the Los Angeles *Times'* crack water writer, was reporting: "Most of California's water leaders have either abandoned proposals to tap the Columbia River or recognize that the chances are getting slimmer every day."

Still the heirs of Bill Mulholland had not run out of alternatives. Up in California's Northwest corner the Klamath, the Trinity and the Eel Rivers were dumping almost 30 million acrefeet per year into the ocean. This was California's famed Redwood Coast, where the world's tallest trees created forest glades that gave visitors the awesome feeling of standing in God's cathedral.

In 1967 the U. S. Army Corps of Engineers proposed damming the Middle Fork of the Eel and sending 700,000 acre-feet per year through a 21-mile tunnel into the Sacramento watershed, where it would supplement the Feather River supply for all of California. The state's own water seekers jumped in with support, and California itself was slated to finance the diversion tunnel.

Quite naturally the county of origin—Mendocino—objected. It was joined by wilderness preservationists led by the Sierra Club. In 1969 Governor Ronald Reagan canceled the state's participation in the project, and that made it infeasible for the Army Corps of Engineers.

Once more the water seekers had lost. Once again, what was technically feasible was not politically feasible.

Already the water seekers were looking in other directions free from political traps. From going across county and state lines to get water, they turned instead to the sea. Here was a source of truly inexhaustible proportion, though handicapped with the problem expressed in the "Rhyme of the Ancient Mariner," "Water, water everywhere, nor any drop to drink."

From ancient times man had known how to extract drinking water from the sea by distilling salt water, catching and condensing the vapor. In the twentieth century the method was used by the U.S. Navy and by a growing number of small islands around the world where the need for water was so great that the cost was no object. New methods, including chemical and freezing processes, brought the cost closer to that of conventional water sources, and the young state of Israel led the way in purifying saline water on a large scale.

By the 1950s it was clear that the best hope of economic saline recovery was in combination with nuclear generating plants, which needed vast quantities of water. A nuclear "fast breeder" plant taking in sea water and freshening it in the process of generating electricity might provide both power and water at competitive prices.

At first efforts to establish such plants in the United States ran into the very political opposition that the water seekers had tried to avoid. Local populations were fearful of radiation hazard or an unforeseen accident. The Los Angeles Department of Water and Power tried to establish a nuclear generating plant (without a water-making capability) near Malibu Beach but ran into such opposition.

But in the end the real hurdle was economic. In November 1967 a Nuclear Power and Desalting Project was launched jointly by the Los Angeles Department of Water and Power, the Metropolitan Water District, and the Southern California Edison Company, under the direction of the U. S. Atomic Energy Commission and the U. S. Department of Interior. On the man-made Bolsa Island off Huntington Beach, the largest such plant in the world was planned to produce 1.8 million kilowatts of electricity and 1.5 million gallons of fresh water per day, at a cost of $444 million. But by July 1968 the participants realized that the actual cost would be closer to $765 million. Meeting in Washington, they agreed to suspend the project until further technical progress would make it economically feasible.

The ocean, world's biggest water source, continued to defy the water seekers, just as it defied the Danish king who commanded the waves to stop.

Meanwhile, the engineers were looking within their own systems for more water. After all, considering the tremendous

260

effort they had made in bringing water across mountains and deserts, it seemed an economic shame to flush it all out to sea. In the sewage draining into the Pacific the water seekers saw a magic source to which they had previously been blind. Treatment of it could recover at least fifty per cent for reuse and probably more cheaply than the original cost. There was only one drawback—people might feel a little squeamish about the idea.

Before World War II the Los Angeles water commissioners called in their superintendent, H. A. Van Norman, and asked him to build a pilot plant for purifying waste water. Some of them insisted that popular resistance to the idea was ridiculous. If it was technically possible and economically sound, it ought to be adopted. So Van Norman went about his assignment and a few months later appeared again before the commissioners. According to custom, drinking glasses and a pitcher of water were on the table for use of the board members.

"Well," asked the chairman, pouring himself another tumblerful, "is your pilot plant a success?"

"Gentlemen," answered Van Norman, eyes twinkling, "how do you like the water you've been drinking?"

Coughing heartily, the chairman gripped the table.

"What are you trying to do," he gasped, "poison us?"

Although the water was pure enough, Los Angeles abandoned the project.

Thus the political factor—this time in the form of public attitudes—was still dogging the water seekers. Yet the reuse of "renovated" or "reclaimed" water is a matter of degree. At varying levels of purification, it is used today by more than 200 agencies in California—usually to irrigate crops, replenish underground water tables, or to refresh recreation lakes.

Nowhere does it run directly through anyone's taps. However, in Orange County the Water District has started building a "water factory" with state and federal help to use waste water and sea water in providing 30 million gallons a day of fresh water. This will be injected into the ground basin to halt the intrusion of sea water and renew the ground water supply. That supply, in turn, provides seventy per cent of the county's water needs, including domestic. So water reuse, however indirect, will be a fact in Orange County.

Certainly this source, though resisted in the past, should expand. The task is not for engineering or financing or politics, but for public relations. And the ultimate resort of turning such water directly into the plumbing system will almost certainly come in water-short areas where the alternative is to go thirsty.

Since the turn of the century, water seekers of many Southwest communities have turned for water in still another direction—skyward. The most famous rainmaker in California was Charles M. Hatfield, who for a generation made a living as a cloud-coaxer for California communities.

On at least one occasion Hatfield's magic got completely out of hand. During a prolonged dry period early in 1916 he undertook to fill a reservoir for the city of San Diego. As usual, he picked a favorable spot for operations and brought in his outlandish equipment—consisting mainly of huge vats and their foul-smelling brew. He had no sooner removed the lids and released the fumes than the Heavens opened up with the greatest flood in San Diego's history. It not only filled the reservoir but washed out another dam farther downstream and deluged the lower outskirts of San Diego. The City Council was so outraged that it refused to pay his $10,000 fee and successfully defended the action in court.

"We told you merely to fill the reservoir," Hatfield was told, "not to flood the community."

But Californians were never quite sure whether such demonstrations were wholly the work of Hatfield the Rainmaker. In the same period as this San Diego deluge, for example, floods also occurred as far away as Los Angeles and the Colorado River.

Still, the rainmaker's art was on the way to becoming a science. In 1930 a Dutchman named August W. Veraart dropped dry ice particles into the tops of clouds from an airplane near Amsterdam. Ten minutes later a rainstorm began which lasted two days.

Then in the late 1940s Dr. Irving Langmuir of General Electric induced rain by dropping dry ice pellets from airplanes in Massachusetts and by sending silver iodide crystals skyward from ground installations in New Mexico. Here was an unexpected retort to the famed observation attributed to Mark Twain: "Everybody talks about the weather, but nobody does anything about it."

After that, rainmakers blossomed all over the Southwest. The California Electric Power Company hired some pilots and began increasing the runoff into its reservoirs on the east slope of the Sierra Nevada. In 1948 Dr. Irving Krick, a Pasadena weather forecaster, induced rain in Arizona's Salt River Valley and has since become one of the nation's leading rainmakers. "Making" rain is not really the truth, as Krick was the first to point out. "You can't make rain if it isn't going to rain anyway," he has explained. What the rainmakers do is to induce more rain than would fall naturally. Conservative observers put this additional increment at from ten to twenty per cent, but others say it can be as high as several hundred per cent.

Very early the battling states of the Colorado River saw the potential for increasing the river's flow simply by seeding the clouds over the Rockies and adding to the snowpack. Not until 1971, however, did the U. S. Bureau of Reclamation start such a project. After exploratory work for more than two years in the San Juan Mountains of southwestern Colorado, Bureau officials were saying that a full-dress program could increase the Colorado basin supply by up to two million acre-feet a year. This in itself could go far toward solving the Mexican salinity problem and the looming shortage when the Central Arizona Project is built.

Yet there were plenty of storm clouds in the way. Some people in the high Rockies weren't sure they wanted all that snow. Mrs. Joyce Jorgensen, owner-editor of a newspaper in Ouray, Colorado, was one.

"When you've seen 40 to 50 of your friends out with probes trying to find a body in a snowslide, you get darned mad when you find the government is going to put more snow on you."

The issue emphasized what had been the biggest stumbling block to rainmaking since the beginning. Rain that is a godsend to farmers may be a curse to resort operations. When the drought of the late 1940s caused New York City to try rainmaking, upstate resortkeepers threatened to sue and the chief rainmaker publicly denied that he had a hand in bringing on any storms.

So once again the problem was political. With fifty-eight counties, hundreds of municipalities and tens of thousands of private entrepreneurs, each with a different stake in the weather, California was a poor place to tinker with the clouds unless you enjoyed being in court.

There was one final direction to seek added water—straight into the ground. This seemed unrealistic in a state where the dropping water table was chronic. But the art of deep-well digging was advancing along with the science of sea distillation and rainmaking. In 1953 Californians became aware of a new type of water seeker—Stephan Reiss of Simi Valley. He had a theory that you didn't have to limit your water quest to the groundwater that was part of the precipitation cycle. If you dig deeper wells—and know where to dig them—you could tap water manufactured in the earth's processes—"primary" or "juvenile" water which had never surfaced before. To prove it, Reiss had brought in seventy-one successful California wells—

many of them in rocks and on mountainsides where no ordinary water expert would think of looking for a subsoil reservoir.

Other water scientists were skeptical, but even if one didn't agree with Reiss' theory, deep digging into conventional underground deposits still held promise. In other thirsty countries of the world, a hydraulic engineer named Harold T. "Deep-Well" Smith has brought in water from as far down as 6,000 feet. And at Cerro Prieto in Mexico, thirty-five miles south of the California border, the Mexican government has drilled wells deep into the ancient deposits of the Colorado River—the same that had been laid down by overflows into Imperial Valley in ages past. Locked between such layers are vast quantities of steam—the result of previous Salton Seas buried alive by Colorado silt.

American hydrologists believe the same steam pool extends under much of Imperial Valley, and the amount of water in it has been estimated up to ten billion acre-feet. To test it as an American source of water, the Bureau of Reclamation is drilling a 6,000-foot well at Holtville, fifteen miles above the border in Imperial Valley, and the Office of Saline Water will build a desalination plant to produce drinking water.

All of which could—if present hopes come true—provide a vast source of water for Southern California. And it would have the advantage of being drawn from a direction—straight down —in which there are no known political opponents.

Thus on balance it appears that the water quest Mulholland set in motion a century ago is taking a new turn. Politically, the water users are frustrated in getting any more water from other communities. Before they could muster the strength to do so in the future, more economical water may come from the sea, the sky or the earth.

And in effect, the pressure is eased, since according to the new and reduced estimates of Southern California growth, existing sources including the Feather River will be sufficient until the year 2020. In the Los Angeles Department of Water and Power, the Metropolitan Water District, and the State Department of Water Resources, planners have not forgotten the Eel, the Snake, or the Columbia. But the heat of battle has subsided, and the long war for California water has come to a ceasefire, if not a peace. No more will embattled farmers shoot off dynamite and the Arizona Navy patrol the Colorado.

And in the final analysis the water seekers will have to abandon their quest because its justification is gone. They have been defeated by their own success. They brought in so much water for so many people that few cared anymore whether Los Angeles grew at all. No longer can the "water for growth" argument have the old magic effect at the polls. Hardly again can the Los Angeles Department of Water and Power justify advertising for more companies to relocate in Los Angeles so that it can have more customers for its water.

Indeed, one might say that, unlike the less successful water seekers of other localities, they have brought too much water. For if California now has enough water to more than double in population, then much of California is doomed to become insufferable.

Sadly, when that happens, Bill Mulholland and his water seekers will no longer be the heroes they deserve to be. In a later era which will put more value on the quality of life than the quantity of life, there will be little patience with those who bring more people by bringing more water.

BIBLIOGRAPHY AND ACKNOWLEDGMENTS

The following sources, listed informally, have been the most helpful in the quest of information for this book. For the sake of brevity, little mention is made of those standard works, engineering reports, and magazine articles which are readily found through most library catalogues and reader's guides. It should be remembered that, since participants on both sides of controversies have been consulted, no one of them is accountable for observations or conclusions.

Details on William Mulholland and early Los Angeles water history were gleaned from an article on Mulholland by J. B. Lippincott in *Civil Engineering* (February and March 1941); *Irrigation in Southern California*, William H. Hall (Sacramento, 1888), which is part of a water resources report of the state engineer; and interviews with Thomas Brooks, a Los Angeles water official for over fifty years (Los Angeles, December 6, 1948); S. B. Robinson, identified with the Water Department's legal affairs since 1906 (Los Angeles, February 24, 1949); Burt Heinley, Mulholland's secretary from 1907 to 1919 (Los Angeles, May 31, 1949); and Miss Rose Mulholland, daughter of William Mulholland, who also allowed the use of a scrapbook on her father's career (Los Angeles, March 1, 1949).

Information on the inception of the Los Angeles Aqueduct was gained from the *Report of the Aqueduct Investigating Board*, Los Angeles, August 30, 1912, which contains testimony of Mulholland, W. B. Mathews, J. B. Lippincott, and others (in the Los Angeles Public Library); from "Owens Valley correspondence" in the files of the Los Angeles Department of Water and Power, which was made available through the courtesy of J. Gregg Layne, department historian; from a seven-volume scrapbook of newspaper clippings on the aqueduct, 1905-7, with the Department of Water and Power; from a pamphlet by **Andrae** B. Nordskog, *Communication to the California Legislature relating to the Owens Valley Water Situation* (Sacramento, 1931), which contains quotations from Reclamation Service correspondence, 1904-6; from documents in the Los Angeles County records, including instruments on the Porter Ranch sale (option, October 13, 1903, and deed, January 13, 1905); from files of the Inyo *Register*, 1903-13 (microfilms at the Henry E. Huntington Library, San Marino); Inyo *Independent*, 1904-8 (at Southwest Museum, Pasadena); Los Angeles *Times*, July-September 1905, June and December 1906, April-June 1907; *Examiner*, July-September 1905; *Express*, July-September 1905; *Evening News*, March-April, June 1906, March-June 1907 (all in Los Angeles Public Library); from a letter from J. C. Clausen, engineer in charge of the federal Owens Valley reclamation investigation, 1903-5 (Aromas, California, February 19, 1949); from interviews with Harry J. Lelande, Los Angeles city clerk, 1903-10 (Los Angeles, February 23, 1949); and with Fred Eaton's sons – Harold Eaton (Bishop, August 21, 1948) and Burdick Eaton (Los Angeles, December 3, 1948).

Material on Los Angeles Aqueduct construction was drawn from the following: the Mulholland scrapbook; the *Final Report of Construction of the Los Angeles Aqueduct*, Los Angeles, 1916; Mulholland's Annual Reports to the Aqueduct Advisory Committee, 1907-12 (in the Los Angeles Public Library); Minutes of the Advisory Committee of the Los Angeles Aqueduct, 1906-13 (now with the Board of Public Works); files of the Los Angeles *Times*, May 1910, November-December 1911; Los Angeles *Record*, May 1912; and interviews with H. A. Van Norman, superintendent of the Owens Valley Division and later chief engineer of the Department of Water and Power (Los Angeles, December 31, 1948); D. L. Reaburn, superintendent of the Saugus Division (Los Angeles, May 9, 1949); and George Nordenholt, tunnel foreman at Sand Canyon (Los Angeles, May 5, 1949).

The Owens Valley conflict was largely written from these sources: "Owens Valley correspondence," 1923-26, Department of Water and Power, including the useful "Proposal for Settlement with Owens Valley," submitted with accompanying data to the Los Angeles Clearing House Association, November 19, 1924, by W. W. Watterson, and the "Reply to Proposal," submitted by the Board of Public Service Commissioners, 1924; report of W. F. McClure, state engineer, concerning the Owens Valley-Los Angeles Controversy, Sacramento, 1925 (in Huntington Library); *Story of Inyo*, 2d ed., W. A. Chalfant (Bishop, 1933); compilations of school and voting registration statistics, Inyo County, for which I am grateful to Mrs. Dorothy Craven, superintendent of schools, and Mrs. Fay

Lawrence, county clerk; files of the Owens Valley *Herald*, 1921-27; Inyo *Register*, 1923-28; Big Pine *Citizen*, 1923-27; Mount Whitney *Observer* (Lone Pine), 1924-27, all of which were used through the kindness of Miss Anne Margrave, Inyo County librarian; selected issues of the Los Angeles *Times*, 1923-28; *Examiner*, 1924-27; *Record*, 1924-27; San Fernando *Sun*, 1923-24; and the following interviews: Jerome Watterson, son of W. W. Watterson (Bishop, August 25, 1948); Walter Young, friend and associate of the Watterson brothers (Bishop, August 25, 1948); Charles Collins, Inyo County sheriff in the 1920s (Bishop, August 21, 1948); Ed Shepherd, former Inyo County deputy sheriff (Independence, August 22, 1948); Mrs. Frank Butler (Bishop, August 21, 1948); Ward Parcher (Bishop, May 22, 1949); William D. Dehy, judge of Superior Court, Inyo County, 1909 to present (Independence, May 22, 1949); H. A. Van Norman (Los Angeles, December 13, 1948); S. B. Robinson (Los Angeles, February 24, 1949); Edward F. Leahey, Los Angeles representative in Owens Valley during the 1920s (Los Angeles, July 11, 1948, and February 24, 1949); Alfred Watterson, son of George Watterson (Los Angeles, August 10, 1948); Leicester C. Hall (Glendale, May 29, 1949); George Warren, who also provided a signed statement, dated July 19, 1927, describing the siege of his home a few months before (Los Angeles, May 29, 1949); and Jackson Berger, Associated Press correspondent covering Owens Valley incidents in the 1920s (North Hollywood, June 8, 1949).

Sources on the San Francisquito Dam failure include various engineering reports, particularly the *Report of the Commission appointed by Governor C. C. Young to Investigate Causes Leading to Failure of St. Francis Dam* (Sacramento, 1928) and *San Francisquito Canyon Dam Disaster* – report to Governor G. W. P. Hunt of Arizona by Guy L. Jones (Phoenix, 1928); also the extensive material in the Huntington Library collected by C. C. Teague, head of the Santa Clara Valley Citizens Relief Committee; the Mulholland scrapbook; the article by Lippincott in *Civil Engineering;* and news stories in the Santa Paula *Chronicle* (March 13, 1928), Fillmore *Herald* (March 16, 1928), Fillmore *American* (March 15 and 22, 1928), and Los Angeles *Times* (March 14 and 22, 1928) all in the Los Angeles Public Library.

Details on the settlement of Imperial Valley and the fight to stop the Colorado flood of 1905-7 were mainly gathered from the following: hearings before the House Committee on Irrigation of Arid Lands, March 21, 1904, on a bill for legalizing the appropriation and diversion of water from the Colorado River for irrigation purposes (in the Huntington Library); article by Charles Rockwood in the Calexico *Chronicle*, May 1909 (also in the Huntington Library);

various hearings before the House Judiciary Committee, 1907-11, on a bill for reimbursing the Southern Pacific Railroad for expenditures in stopping the Colorado flood (for the use of this and other material in the very extensive "water" collection at the Claremont Colleges Library, I am indebted to Dr. Willis Kerr); *Life of George Chaffey*, J. A. Alexander (Melbourne, 1928); *Salton Sea*, George Kennan (New York, 1917); *Colorado Conquest*, David O. Woodbury (New York, 1941); selected issues of the Los Angeles *Times*, 1905-7; *Examiner*, November-December 1906; *Express*, November-December 1906; and, most important of all, an interview with Dr. H. T. Cory, engineer in charge of closing the Colorado break, 1906-7 (Los Angeles, June 27, 1949), together with the seven volumes of photographs which he gave to the University of California at Los Angeles Library, and his exhaustive work on the subject, *The Imperial Valley and the Salton Sink* (San Francisco, 1915).

The story of the Colorado Compact and the Boulder Canyon Project was largely pieced together from these sources: correspondence and other material collected by John R. Haynes, former chairman of the Los Angeles Board of Public Service Commissioners, contained in the John R. Haynes Memorial Foundation Library, Los Angeles; a scrapbook on Boulder Canyon Project development in the Department of Water and Power Library; microfilm minutes of the first eighteen meetings of the Colorado River Commission, January-November 1922, obtained from the National Archives, Washington, D.C.; typewritten minutes of the twenty-sixth meeting, at Claremont Colleges Library; an article by Arnold Kruckman in the Los Angeles magazine, *Saturday Night* (November 18, 1922); correspondence, minutes, and publications of the Boulder Dam Association, 1923-28, in the care of Mrs. Burdett Moody, Los Angeles; hearings before the Senate and House Irrigation and Reclamation committees, 1919-28, on protection and development of the lower Colorado River basin, of which the most helpful were those before the House committee, Sixty-eighth Congress, First Session, 1924, and the Senate committee, Sixty-ninth Congress, First Session, 1925-26 (almost complete collections of hearings are in the Department of Water and Power Library and the Claremont Colleges Library); the Congressional Record, February 1927, April-May, December 1928; *Problems of Imperial Valley and Vicinity* (Senate Document 142, U. S. Printing Office, 1922); *Hoover Dam Documents*, Ray Lyman Wilbur and Northcutt Ely (U.S. Printing Office, 1948); *Colorado River Compact*, Reuel L. Olson (Los Angeles, 1926); an extensive file of Los Angeles and Phoenix newspaper clippings of the 1920s, in the Claremont Colleges Library; a scrapbook of Boulder Canyon Project Clippings, 1926-31, at the University of Southern California Library; selected issues of the Los Angeles *Times* and *Examiner*, 1920-22; a letter from Charles P. Squires, joint commissioner from Nevada on the 1922 Colorado River Commission (Las Vegas, April 14, 1950); and finally from interviews with Senator William J. Carr, who was chief counsel for the Boulder Dam Association (Pasadena, September 24, 1949); H. C. Gardett, former Los Angeles Department of Water and Power official (South Pasadena, October 1, 1949); and an especially valuable four-hour talk with Phil D. Swing, co-author of the Boulder Canyon Project Act (San Diego, November 6, 1949).

Construction of the Boulder Canyon Project features is well covered in the *Construction of Hoover Dam*, Ray Lyman Wilbur and Elwood Mead (U. S. Printing Office, 1935); *So Boulder Dam Was Built*, George A. Pettitt (Berkeley, 1935), which was published by Six Companies for political purposes but which is invaluable for detailed episodes; various publications of the Metropolitan Water District, including *History and First Annual Report*, June 30, 1938 (Los Angeles, 1939), *The Colorado Aqueduct* (Los Angeles, 1939), and *The Great Aqueduct* (Los Angeles, 1941); the special Colorado Aqueduct edition of *Engineering News-Record*, November 24, 1938; the scrap-book on Boulder Canyon Project development in the Department of Water and Power Library; and the large file of newspaper clippings on the same subject in the Claremont Colleges Library. Best coverage of the "Arizona Navy" incident is in Chester Hanson's dispatches to the Los Angeles *Times*, March and November 1934.

Information on the Mexican treaty was gained largely from the following: hearings before the Senate Committee on Foreign Relations, Seventy-ninth Congress, First Session (*Water Treaty with Mexico*, 1945); a bound compilation of *Arguments, Memoranda and Information by Opponents and Proponents of Treaty*, Department of Water and Power (Los Angeles 1945); the Congressional Record, April 1945; interviews with S. B. Robinson, former member of the Committee of Sixteen (San Marino, October 1, 1949); and Arvin Shaw, assistant attorney general of California, who also made available the *Proceedings of the Committee of Sixteen* at the crucial meeting in Santa Fe, April 14-16, 1943 (Los Angeles, December 19, 1949).

The California-Arizona controversy may be traced in these congressional hearings: *Reauthorizing the Gila Project*, House Committee on Irrigation and Reclamation, Seventy-ninth Congress, Second Session, 1946; *Bridge Canyon Project*, Senate Subcommittee on Irrigation and Reclamation, Eightieth Congress, First Session, 1947; and others on *Colorado River Water Rights* and the *Central Arizona Project*, 1948-49, which offer an exhaustive treatment of both sides of the dispute and which are available in most university libraries. Other information was gained from a comprehensive letter

271

from Charles A. Carson, chief counsel for the Arizona Interstate Streams Commission (Washington, D.C., February 18, 1950); and from interviews with Don Kinsey, chief of public relations for the Metropolitan Water District; Robert Lee, public relations secretary for the California Colorado River Association; and Gilbert Nelson, attorney for the California Colorado River Board (all in Los Angeles, December 19, 1949).

Lastly I want to thank my wife, Margaret, for invaluable help in research over a two-year period.

FOR FURTHER READING

Bain, Joe Staten. *Northern California's Water Industry*. Baltimore, 1966.

Blake, Nelson Manfred. *Water for the Cities: A History of the Urban Water Supply Problem in the United States*. Syracuse, 1956.

Cooper, Erwin. *Aqueduct Empire. A Guide to Water in California, Its Turbulent History and Its Management Today*. Glendale, Calif., 1968.

Frank, Bernard, and Netboy, Anthony. *Water, Land and People*. New York, 1950.

Harding, Sidney Twichell. *Water in California*. Palo Alto, Calif., 1960.

Mann, Dean E. *The Politics of Water in Arizona*. Tucson, 1963.

Moreell, Ben. *Our Nation's Water Resources, Policies and Politics*. Chicago, 1956.

Moss, Frank E. *The Water Crisis*. New York, 1967.

Nikolaieff, George A., Ed. *The Water Crisis*. New York, 1967.

Ostrom, Vincent. *Water and Politics: a Study of Water Policies and Administration in the Development of Los Angeles*. Los Angeles, 1953.

Seckler, David, Ed. *California Water; a Study in Resource Management*. Berkeley, 1971.

Williams, Albert Nathaniel. *The Water and the Power; Development of the Five Great Rivers of the West*. New York, 1951.

Wollman, Nathaniel, and Bonem, Gilbert W. *The Outlook for Water: Quality, Quantity and National Growth*. Baltimore, 1971.

Wright, James Claud. *The Coming Water Famine*. New York, 1966.

INDEX

273